John Paul II
Poet and Philosopher

For Mum, Dad, Michael and Eamonn
with heartfelt thanks and love.

John Paul II

Poet and Philosopher

JOHN McNERNEY

burns & oates

Burns & Oates

A Continuum imprint

The Tower Building
11 York Road
London SE1 7NX, UK

15 East 26th Street
New York NY 10010
USA

www.continuumbooks.com

Copyright © T&T Clark Ltd, 2003
This Edition Published 2004

British Library Cataloguing-in-Publication Data
A catalogue record for this book is available from the British Library

ISBN 0-86012-386-3

Typeset by Waverley Typesetters, Galashiels
Printed and bound in Great Britain by MPG Books Ltd, Bodmin

Contents

Acknowledgements

First and foremost, I want to thank Dr Brendan Purcell of the Philosophy Department in University College Dublin for his continuous encouragement in the successful completion of this project. The many discussions with him gave me new insights and a more profound understanding of Wojtylan anthropology. My gratitude is also due the Philosophy Department in University College Dublin for their original acceptance of my research project.

Stratford Caldecott, of Platter College, Oxford, was enormously helpful in the text's recommendation to the publishers T&T Clark, Edinburgh. Dr Geoffrey Green, the publishing director, and Philip Hillyer the managing editor with T&T Clark, were most encouraging and kept me up-to-date at the initial stages. At later stages Veronica Miller, the managing editor very ably saw the project through to its completion. I'm deeply indebted to Francesca Murphy of the University of Aberdeen who kindly read the original manuscript and was extremely supportive of its final publication.

I am appreciative of Jerzy Peterkiewicz's co-operation in my use of his translation of Karol Wojtyla's poems. Random House kindly gave permission for the use of the *Collected Poems*.

I would like to express my gratitude to the artist Michel Pochet for the use I made of his painting in the cover design of the book. Luke Gertler, the son of the artist Mark Gertler, kindly gave me permission to include his father's painting entitled 'Merry-Go-Round' in the text. The Tate Gallery, London, was most helpful in its inclusion. I would like to thank Fiona Murphy, editorial manager of T&T Clark, for her help and work on the cover design of the book along with the sales and marketing. I am indebted to Michael O'Kelly for his formatting of the original text: indeed, without his adroit computer wisdom the manuscript would have been all the poorer.

It is a great honour for me that David Walsh of the Catholic University of America could write the foreword to the book and I want to record my sincere gratitude to him for this.

Finally, I would like to acknowledge the original and seminal thought of John Paul II which made this philosophical investigation possible.

Foreword

What is most distinctive about John Paul II is that he speaks first as Karol Wojtyla. We hear the man before we hear the Pope. This accounts for his amazing ability to communicate with human beings all over the world. The advantages of authority, institution, tradition have all been dispensed with as Wojtyla speaks with the voice of our common nature. This may seem an unusual strategy for an actor to step outside of the role he has been assigned. But it can also be seen as the consummate skill of putting oneself so much into the character that we forget the difference. The ideal of the theatre is carried to a new level by a Pope who understands that his role is precisely to identify with suffering broken humanity. He is first a witness to the human reality through which he allows the light of Christ to shine.

It is a personal charism of enormous impact, evidenced by his capacity to address a million people simultaneously as if he were talking to each one. But it would be a great mistake to assign his influence merely to an unusual personal gift, as John McNerney demonstrates so well. The intention of speaking first as one human being to another is precisely that, a deliberately chosen strategy. Personal gifts are of inestimable value but they are not the core of what the Church provides to the world. Only the gifts of faith, hope and love can really change hearts. Wojtyla early understood that to undertake the task of evangelizing a secular world one first had to begin where the secular world is. One must step forward not as a spokesman for institutional Christianity, but for the human being whose lostness Christ came to serve. Where we find the human being we also find Christ. In many ways this is the direction imparted by the Second Vatican Council's reconsideration of its role in the modern world. It is only in the papacy of John Paul II, however, that the intimations have become fully explicit.

His capacity to crystallize the requirements of Christianity in the modern age has much to do with his own personal emergence from the totalitarian convulsion. The need to find a common language with the non-Christian world is undoubtedly one of the factors that drew him toward a philosophical career. For John Paul II is unique among pontiffs in functioning as a professional philosopher, rather than as a theologian, within his pastoral office. John McNerney's study is one of the few that gives full weight to this dimension of Wojtyla's development. Such an approach is indispensable if we are to appreciate the strategy of placing the human encounter first. Philosophy is the common language of humanity. It takes its beginnings in questions rather than texts and is therefore the royal road toward the opening of the soul in search of God. Wojtyla understood the necessity for Christians to strike out into the philosophical jungle of the modern world, confident that they would find there the same truth they already knew through the light of faith. His own philosophical odyssey attests to this possibility and grounds his capacity to bear witness to Christ from within the heart of the modern world.

Footbridge Toward the Other is a moving account of the central line of Wojtyla's philosophical investigation which is centred on man himself. As an essay in philosophical anthropology, Wojtyla's *Acting Person* is a work of large philosophical ambition. It recognizes that philosophy cannot be done piecemeal. Even a study that focuses on a particular segment of reality, the human person, cannot confine its reference within those parameters. It must address the broader challenges of truth and meaning and, in particular, the possibility of metaphysics, of piercing the boundaries of phenomenal reality within space and time. *The Acting Person* is not only an account of the person in the context of ethical responsibility but an opening toward the even deeper questions of what constitutes the person, how we recognize his transcendent finality, and ultimately glimpse the presence of God as the constitutive source of our reality. A 'footbridge toward the other' turns out to be a unique point of openness toward the mystery of the whole in which human beings participate.

McNerney situates Wojtyla's philosophical anthropology within this broader context of modern philosophy. He shows that the personalist reflections of *The Acting Person* and the other writings are no merely Catholic mode of philosophizing. They are continuous with and contributory toward the emerging consensus within contemporary philosophy as such. The representative character of Wojtyla's work is perhaps best demonstrated, McNerney shows, by the parallel unfolding of Emmanuel Levinas's philosophy of the other. Levinas too has identified the openness toward the other as not only a mode of human self-transcendence but as the primary opening toward the mystery of being that has its source in God. The fact that Wojtyla has followed a more or less parallel path to one of the most respected postmodern thinkers attests to his philosophical penetration. Deriving from common sources in phenomenology and existentialism, as well as intersecting revealed traditions, Wojtyla and Levinas point us toward the key experience of responsibility for the other as the priviliged access human beings have to the inner meaning of reality.

Such an insight suggests a different kind of philosophy. Both Wojtyla and Levinas accept the Kantian critique of metaphysics. There is no longer any possibility of elaborating an account of the structure of existence as if it could be contained within propositional form. God and man, meaning and truth, are not given as objects lying around for an observer to describe them. They are dimensions of existence that we can know only from the perspective of our participation within them. Philosophy becomes in this sense something far more serious than an exercise in contemplation. It becomes an invitation to responsibility in which the structure of existence is disclosed only through the enactment of its reality. Our only access to the inexhaustible mystery of the person is through the movement of love that pierces the veil of externality to the point of encountering what lies beyond all finite categories. In recognizing the other who is other than all labels we glimpse the openness of the infinite.

Even today such an unreserved acceptance of the existential mode of philosophizing has hardly been accepted within Catholic circles. Wojtyla is in this sense ahead of most Christian philosophy as well. He understood the need to abandon the security of a scholastic metaphysics that could provide a barrier against the sceptical slide toward relativism, but only at the cost of irrelevance to a world that no longer shared Christian premises. Only a philosophy that was prepared to risk the failure of truth could either adequately ground the movement toward truth or speak meaningfully to those in search of it. Ironically it is faith in the capacity of reason that underpins his more adventurous approach to reason itself. What makes this possible is of course that Wojtyla's philosophical faith is not merely a faith in reason but in the God who is its source. In this sense the philosophical inquiry is continuous with the parallel movement of faith. The demonstration is reached in each case not by presupposing what we set out to find, but by trusting in the order that prompts us to undertake the inquiry in the beginning. Like the adventure of faith, philosophy too cannot demand a surety in advance. There is no access to truth other than the search that eventually discloses the presence whose invitation is the source of the questions themselves. On the footbridge toward the other we realize the Other has been with us every step of the way.

DAVID WALSH
The Catholic University of America
Washington, DC

Preface

In his paper, 'The other as oneself: friendship and love in the thought of St Thomas Aquinas', James McEvoy notes how quickly any historian can discover that 'the other' was regarded by the ancients as a 'school' of learning 'wherein the other virtues [for example, justice, etc.] are perfected'.[1] Nevertheless, with the advent of the modern era in philosophy 'the other' ends up decommissioned because of the emergence of the philosophy of the 'cloistered self'[2] or the 'dislocated self'.[3] Thus within the history of philosophy there occurred an eclipse of the very reality of 'intersubjectivity'[4] itself. In this contracted philosophical milieu, Karol Wojtyla seeks to recapture the full reality of the human person. As we will see, he is unafraid of any human experience or negative phenomenon. Rather he finds there an opportunity and the raw material for a recovery of an adequate philosophy of the person, leading to the foundation of a fruitful 'school' of the 'other'.

Wojtyla launches out into the deep[5] of philosophical inquiry in order to apprehend *'how'* the human being is a 'person' and the corresponding significance of the 'other' in that exploration. *Footbridge Toward the Other* is, therefore, intended as an account of the philosophy of the human person underlying the life and work of Karol Wojtyla/Pope John Paul II. It is essentially an investigation into the philosophical anthropology worked out by him as a philosopher and subsequently applied by him as John Paul II to the different dimensions of human existence. In the poem entitled 'Identities', he speaks of

---

[1] James McEvoy and Michael Dunne (eds.), *Thomas Aquinas: Approaches to Truth: The Aquinas Lectures at Maynooth, 1996–2001* (Dublin: Four Courts Press, 2002), p. 18.
[2] McEvoy and Dunne (eds.), *Thomas Aquinas*, p. 19.
[3] Jeffrey L. Kosky, *Levinas and the Philosophy of Religion* (Bloomington: Indiana University Press, 2001), p. xvii.
[4] Kosky, *Levinas*, p. 19.
[5] See Pope John Paul II, *Novo Millennio Ineunte*, Apostolic Letter § 1.

himself as being on a pilgrimage 'to a view', a view of what he calls 'the bay of sight'.[6] This is perhaps suggestive of his quest for philosophical insight into the nature of the 'person'. He describes how 'man is the land' he journeys across and that he is 'on a pilgrimage of identity'.[7]

So in his key philosophical work *The Acting Person*, he sought to work out this identity and to lead his readers to an adequate understanding of the human person. Wojtyla felt, however, that he had insufficiently investigated in that study the fact that we exist together with others. Contemporary philosophy refers to this reality by the use of terms like 'alterity' or 'intersubjectivity'. In Wojtyla's work, it is under the heading of 'Participation' that he explores this reality and it is here he introduces a novel philosophical approach, taking into account the fullness of human experience in terms of the reality of our acting together-with-others. Into his methodology Wojtyla introduces the concept of the 'neighbour' and scrutinizes who he or she is.

What emerges in the Wojtylan explorations is that the lawyer's question posed in the famous text in Luke 10:29, 'who is my neighbour?' is not merely of philanthropic significance. It is of considerable philosophical relevance. *Footbridge Toward the Other* presents and develops Wojtyla's philosophical response to this question. We can see that his analysis of who the 'other' is does not describe the other in 'an otherworldly and divine'[8] way. The 'neighbour', in fact, reveals *how* I am a person, for he or she is another *I*. It was Emmanuel Levinas who wrote that the encounter with the face of the 'other' 'calls me into question'.[9] In similar vein, and making use of a Levinasian-type language of the 'face'[10] we can say that it is Wojtyla's contention that the 'face' of the 'other' reveals and confirms the true being of the 'person' as another *I*. This particular study of his philosophy, in fact, enriched by his poetry and life experiences attests to the fact that he sees in the face of the other an epiphany of the

[6]   Karol Wojtyla, *Collected Poems*, tr. Jerzy Peterkiewicz (London: Hutchinson, 1982), p. 126.
[7]   Ibid.
[8]   McEvoy and Dunne (eds.), *Thomas Aquinas*, p. 34.
[9]   Emmanuel Levinas, *Totality and Infinity: An Essay on Exteriority*, tr. Alphonso Lingis (Pittsburg: Duquesne University Press, 1969), p. 171.
[10] Levinas defines the 'face' as being 'the way in which the other presents himself' in *Totality and Infinity*, p. 50.

reality of what it means to be a human person. We shall see that the faces he encounters in his life-history are many – the faces of the orphan, student worker, stranger, actor, priest and neighbour.

Therefore, the reality of the 'other' is not primarily an epistemological problem, nor is its analysis on a purely sociological level wholly sufficient. There is a need to develop the ontological underpinnings attached to the common human experience of participation with the 'other'. It is in writings subsequent to *The Acting Person* that Wojtyla seeks to articulate such foundations. The 'other' we act with is for him another *I*; he/she is not accidental to my being but constitutive of who I am as a person. There are also onto-ethical implications to this philosophical insight. Wojtyla presents the norm of the new commandment of love, 'love your neighbour as yourself', as the application and safeguarding of the truth of being a 'person'. Unfolded in the living out of the commandment is the very rule of my being. Love alone is the way of the human person.[11]

After an investigation of some these elements in Wojtyla's thought, *Footbridge Toward the Other* proceeds to apply the Wojtylan insight about *how* I am a person to the various dimensions of human existence, surveying the person in his or her ethical, interpersonal, aesthetic and economic dimensions, as these are developed in the second Wojtylan period under the authorship of Pope John Paul II. Already in the preface to *The Acting Person* Wojtyla states that his intention was not to produce a theory about a theory of the human person but a 'personal effort'[12] by him of philosophical clarification with regard to the human person. In similar terms, this study of Wojtylan philosophical personalism is, it is hoped, not simply another book about a book but an invitation to the reader to embark upon the Wojtylan adventure of understanding who the 'Other' is.

JOHN MCNERNEY
University College Dublin

---

[11] Cf. Hans Urs von Balthasar's book, *Love Alone: The Way of Revelation* (London: Burns & Oates, 1968). There is a close parallel between the work of Wojtyla and von Balthasar in that the latter conceives of being as intelligible only as love.

[12] Karol Wojtyla, *The Acting Person*, tr. Andrzej Potocki (Dordrecht and Boston: Reidel, 1979), p. vii.

To the Heart of the Drama[1]

Introduction

My overall theme is to examine philosophically the concept of the human person in the writings of Karol Wojtyla. In this exploration I will make special reference to the paradigm of the 'neighbour' as a key to interpreting *how* we are 'persons'. This will be further elaborated and developed in chapter 2 of this book. Wojtyla seeks in his philosophical studies to map out the landscape[2] of the human person. On that map there are, he believes, some definite contours and characteristics that help bring into relief all that is philosophically necessary in approaching a comprehensive understanding of personhood. To begin with then, it is important if we are to be successful in our philosophical orienteering, to be clear headed about the direction in which we seek to go. Thus, this opening chapter seeks to assist us in orienteering the anthropological landscape of the human person.

The question

As a first step in guiding ourselves on this philosophical journey, let me set out as clearly as I can the fundamental philosophical question at the heart of Wojtyla's work. Secondly, taking up that fundamental question, I will endeavour to give a brief précis of his *magnum opus, The Acting Person*. Bergson once made a statement 'that great philosophers have only one word to say and spend their whole life saying it'.[3] Wojtyla's word is 'person'. His focus is on *how* a human being is a person, 'in which way *the person reveals himself*

---

[1] This title is inspired by the poem written by Wojtyla entitled 'I reach the heart of the drama', in Karol Wojtyla, *Collected Poems*, tr. Jerzy Peterkiewicz (London: Hutchinson, 1982), p. 152.

[2] Cf. Kenneth Schmitz, 'The Geography of the Human Person', *Communio* 13 (Spring, 1986).

[3] Cf. Mary Shivanandan, *Crossing the Threshold of Love: A New Vision of Marriage in the Light of John Paul II's Anthropology* (Washington, DC: Catholic University of America Press, 1999), p. xvii.

in action'.[4] The Wojtylan emphasis is not on the fact *that* a human being is a person; it is rather, to understand in what way the individual is revealed as a 'person'. It is his assertion that action is the prism through which human experience can be refracted or exfoliated[5] in order to give us insight into the essence of what it is to be a person. Instead of beginning with any abstract notion of person, Wojtyla starts with the concrete person who manifests himself or herself in action.

> [Action] *reveals* the person, and we look at the person through his action . . . Action gives us the best insight into the inherent essence of the person and allows us to understand the person most fully. We experience man as a person, and we are convinced of it because he performs actions.[6]

Wojtyla tells us: 'in this study our first and chief concern is to educe from the experience of action (that is, of "man-acts") that evidence which shows man to be a person or "brings the person into view"'.[7] His philosophical approach seeks the avoidance of the circuitous modern tendency 'in which to "philosophize" often means to reflect upon theories about theories'.[8] It is in light of this that we can say that he is not in any sense an intellectual archaeologist merely seeking to go over the remains of an outdated philosophical debate. Moreover, his project 'proposes a hermeneutic of human existence which requires confirmation through the experience of each reader'.[9] He states that it has not been his

> intention to produce a historical or even comprehensive, systematic study of the subject. It is merely his own individual endeavour to understand the object of his concern . . . the understanding of the human person for the sake of the person himself.[10]

[4]   Rocco Buttiglione, *Karol Wojtyla, The Thought of the Man Who Became Pope John Paul II*, tr. Paolo Guietti and Francesca Murphy (Grand Rapids: Eerdmans, 1997), p. 125.
[5]   Karol Wojtyla, *The Acting Person*, tr. Andrzej Potocki (Dordrecht and Boston: Reidel, 1979), p. 10. There are well-known difficulties with the English translation of Wojtyla's text. In the writing of this book I have consulted the German and Italian editions since they are regarded as more faithful to the original.
[6]   Wojtyla, *Acting Person*, p. 11.
[7]   Wojtyla, *Acting Person*, p. 20.
[8]   Wojtyla, *Acting Person,* p. vii.
[9]   Buttiglione, *Karol Wojtyla*, p. 118.
[10] Wojtyla, *Acting Person*, p. 22.

Central to his objective is an adequate philosophy of the human person. 'Since Descartes', Wojtyla explains,

> knowledge about man and his world has been identified with the cognitive function . . . And yet, in reality, does man reveal himself in thinking or, rather, in the actual enacting of existence – observing, interpreting, speculating, or reasoning . . . or in the confrontation itself when he has to take an active stand upon issues, requiring vital decisions and having vital consequences and repercussions? In fact, it is in reversing the post-Cartesian attitude toward man that we undertake our study: by approaching him through action.[11]

There is a certain philosophical correlation between Wojtyla's emphasis on the analysis of action as revelatory of the human person and Bernard Lonergan's exploration into human 'Insight' as activity. Lonergan discloses that in his study, *Insight*,

> we are concerned not with the existence of knowledge but with its nature, not with what is known but with the structure of the knowing, not with the abstract properties of cognitional process but with a personal appropriation of one's own dynamic and recurrently operative structure of cognitional activity.[12]

As I have said, Wojtyla is uninterested in the person in abstraction; rather his philosophical focus is upon man in the concrete.

In the attempt to arrive at the irreducible kernel of the human person Wojtyla is philosophically unafraid of the analysis of any human experience. In a letter written to Henri de Lubac on completing the first draft of *The Acting Person*, he described how this study is

> a work that is close to my heart and devoted to the metaphysical sense and mystery of the PERSON. It seems to me that the debate today is being played out on that level. The evil of our times consists in the first place in a kind of degradation, indeed in a pulverization, of the fundamental uniqueness of each human person . . . To this disintegration planned at time by atheistic ideologies, we must oppose, rather than sterile polemics, a kind of 'recapitulation' of the inviolable mystery of the person.[13]

---

[11] Wojtyla, *Acting Person*, p. vii.
[12] Bernard Lonergan, *Insight: A Study of Human Understanding* (London: Longman, 1958), p. xxiii.
[13] Cited in George Weigel, *Witness to Hope: The Biography of John Paul II* (New York: HarperCollins, 1999), p. 174.

Philosophical reflections unfolded

Unfortunately, one could survey Wojtyla's philosophical work in vain for practical, worked-out examples of what he means in terms of the thematization of the human person. There are reasons for this and I will give a possible explanation later. If we keep the fundamental question of his project in mind, that is, *how* the human being is a person, we can complement his arid philosophical style with examples. It is only in subsequent writings that he alludes to historical examples of what he actually means, as for example, in the case of negative verifications of personalization.[14] This in itself can lead understandably to a reader's frustration and to some rather obscure interpretations of his intentions. This is where a careful reading of Wojtyla's poems and plays can help us understand the philosophical question he discusses. Indeed, Wojtyla's 'first initiation to phenomenology came about indirectly and outside orthodox philosophy, through the theory of theatre and, above all, the existential experience of being an actor'.[15]

Throughout his poetic and philosophical works, Wojtyla seeks to unmask the hidden face of the human person. Such a philosophical odyssey pushes words to their limits in trying to express human thought. His poem, 'Thought's resistance to words', communicates this tension. He writes:

> Sometimes it happens in conversation: we stand
> facing truth and lack the words,
> have no gesture, no sign;
> and yet – we feel – no word, no gesture
> or sign would convey the whole image
> that we must enter alone and face, like Jacob.
> This isn't mere wrestling with images;
> carried in our thoughts;
> we fight with the likeness of all things
> that inwardly constitute man.
> But when we act can our deeds surrender
> the ultimate truths we presume to ponder?[16]

---

[14] He refers to the experience of dehumanization in concentration camps in the paper he sent to the Fourth International Phenomenological Conference in Fribourg, Switzerland, 1975, entitled, 'Participation or Alienation?' in *Person and Community, Selected Essays*, tr. Theresa Sandok (New York: Peter Lang, 1993), pp. 197–207.

[15] Buttiglione, *Karol Wojtyla*, p. 21.

[16] Wojtyla, *Collected Poems*, p. 70.

Wojtyla's poetic and dramatic writings as a phenomenological manifesto

It is of course Wojtyla's philosophical belief that we can reach the ultimate truth about the human person if we pause and reflect upon human action. He seeks to press the pause button, so to speak, in our lived experience in order to discover *how* the human person is unique and unrepeatable. His plays and poems are in fact 'the medium *par excellence* for capturing and revealing'[17] in his thought the experience of the human person. Wojtyla's poetic gifts have made 'him more sensitive to the richness and complexity of the interiority of the human person'.[18] Indeed, one can detect in his literary work a kind of 'phenomenological manifesto'.[19] He speaks of this pausing and making space in the poem entitled 'Space necessary for the drops of spring rain'. He writes:

> Rest your eyes for a moment
> on the drops of fresh rain:
> the greenness of spring leaves in this bright focus,
> weighing the drops down, not enough space for leaves –
> and though your eyes are full of wonder
> you can't, you cannot open your thought any farther.
>
> You try in vain calming it like a child
> woken from sleep: Don't move away, dear thought,
> from this bright focus of things,
> remain in wonder!
>
> Useless words, you feel. It is thought
> that places you deep in the luminosity of things,
> and you have to seek for them the ever-deepening space in
> yourself.[20]

In an introduction to an edition of Wojtyla's play *The Jeweller's Shop*, Boleslaw Taborski explains how, due to the Nazi occupation of Poland, 'Karol Wojtyla and his colleagues had to perform in secret to small audiences of some twenty people, in private flats'.[21]

---

[17] Shivanandan, *Crossing the Threshold of Love*, p. 5.
[18] Jaroslaw Kupczak, *Destined for Liberty: The Human Person in the Philosophy of Karol Wojtyla/John Paul II* (Washington, DC: Catholic University of America Press, 2000), p. 58.
[19] Kupczak, *Destined for Liberty*, p. 59.
[20] Wojtyla, *Collected Poems*, p. 74.
[21] Karol Wojtyla, *The Jeweller's Shop*, tr. Boleslaw Taborski (San Francisco: Ignatius Press, 1992), p. 15.

Hence, his plays are not of external action 'but drama[s] of moral attitudes, of chances taken or lost'.[22] The jeweller's speech quoted by Andrew[23] in the same drama gives an example of the rich philo-sophical parameters of the Wojtylan project. Andrew recalls the jeweller saying:

> Ah, the proper weight of man!
> This rift, this tangle, this ultimate depth –
> this clinging, when it is so hard
> to unstick heart and thought.
> And in all this – freedom,
> a freedom, and sometimes frenzy,
> the frenzy of freedom trapped in this tangle.
> And in all this – love,
> which springs from freedom,
> as water springs from an oblique rift in the earth.
> This is man! He is not transparent,
> not monumental,
> not simple,
> in fact he is poor.[24]

Wojtyla's writing here is 'compact, often turning into [the] semi-philosophical' and 'laden with symbols relating to the central theme . . . as to the nature of man'.[25] It is 5 October 1962, during the Second Vatican Council, that Wojtyla has his first contact with Africans and this encounter is an inspiration for him. In the margins of the official working documents he scribbles the poem, 'The Negro'. He writes:

> My dear brother, it's you, an immense land I feel
> where rivers dry up suddenly – and the sun
> burns the body as the foundry burns ore.
> I feel your thoughts like mine;
> if they diverge the balance is the same:
> in the scales truth and error.
> There is joy in weighing thoughts on the same scales,
> thoughts that differently flicker in your eyes and mine
> though their substance is the same.[26]

---

[22] Ibid.
[23] Andrew is the young man in Act 1 of Wojtyla's play, who is happily married to Teresa but soon killed in the war.
[24] Wojtyla, *Jeweller's Shop*, p. 38.
[25] Cf. Boleslaw Taborski's introduction to Wojtyla, *Jeweller's Shop*, p. 14.
[26] Wojtyla, *Collected Poems*, p. 116.

As I have said about this author, his poetic works illuminate his philosophical reflections. In this poem we begin to catch a glimpse of the nature of his philosophical project. In his 'dear brother', the Negro, he discovers in the neighbour an 'immense land' waiting to be discovered. He hints at the incommunicability, the uniqueness of the human person, but whatever their differences there is a communion because 'their substance is the same'. There is a resonance between this poetic insight and his philosophical analysis of the *other*. He observes in a philosophical essay that 'although I cannot experientially transfer what constitutes my own *I* beyond myself, this does not mean that I cannot understand that the *other* is constituted in a similar fashion – that the *other* is also an *I*'.[27] In fact, this one verse composition is fertile ground enough for delving deeply into our theme of the special reference to the 'neighbour' in the Wojtylan project. There emerges here the insight into perceiving the neighbour, the *other* as a paradigm for understanding the human person within the context of a relationship of communion. Another important characteristic that I will examine in the next chapter is that of 'participation' but there is already an anticipation of this in the poem. We can see the theme alluded to when Wojtyla says of the *other*, 'I feel your thoughts as mine . . . There is joy in weighing thoughts on the same scales'. The *Other*, the Negro in this case, is my neighbour, not so much because we share the same humanity, but because he is another *I*.[28] Wojtyla writes that

> to participate in the humanity of another human being means to be vitally related to the other as a particular human being, and not just related to what makes the other (*in abstracto*) a human being. This is ultimately the basis for the whole distinctive character of the evangelical concept of *neighbor*.[29]

Indeed, in essays written subsequent to *The Acting Person* he asserts that he wants to define 'participation' even more precisely because 'the consciousness that the *other* is another *I* stands at the basis'[30] of what he was speaking about in his seminal work. To use a neologism, Wojtyla sees in the 'other' a 'personscape', to which the philosophical observer must advert and take cognizance.

[27] Wojtyla, 'Participation or Alienation?', in *Person and Community*, p. 200.
[28] Wojtyla, 'The Person: Subject and Community', in *Person and Community*, p. 237.
[29] Ibid.
[30] Ibid.

In another poem entitled 'The Crypt', he indicates the way in which we can explore the reality of the 'other'. He writes:

> We must go below the marble floor,
> with its generations of footsteps,
> and drill through the rock to find the man
> trampled by hooves of sheep.
> They knew not whom they trampled – a passing man?
> the Man who never will pass?
> The crypt speaks: I am bound to the world and besieged;
> the world is an army of exhausted soldiers
> who will not pull back.[31]

Reading between these lines we can perhaps make an inference to his use of the tools of phenomenology and his philosophical determination at experiencing '*in which way man is a person*'.[32] He wants to get to the reality of things-as-they-are. Adverting to Wojtyla's time as a young man working in the mines, Weigel comments that he had 'to go back to quarrying, but now of an intellectual sort'.[33] The rock face for this philosophical excavation is the lived experience of the human person.

Quid est homo?

A common experience is that of the depersonalizing treatment of human beings and it is often 'in [the] right and wrong ways of dealing with human beings [that] we encounter them precisely as persons'.[34] In other words, it is often in cases of depersonalization that we can gain an insight into a more comprehensive understanding of the human person. John F. Crosby observes:

> '[I]t is a well known psychological fact that a thing often shows itself with particular clarity when we are deprived of it, or when we see the thing being violated or ignored where it should be noticed'.[35]

Crosby recalls a moving passage in *The Brothers Karamazov*

---

[31] Wojtyla, *Collected Poems*, p. 117.
[32] Buttiglione, *Karol Wojtyla*, p. 356.
[33] George Weigel, *Witness to Hope*, p. 128.
[34] John F. Crosby, *The Selfhood of the Human Person* (Washington, DC: Catholic University of America Press, 1996), p. 9.
[35] Ibid.

in which Zosima strikes his servant in the face: as he is later tormented
by the humiliated, bloody face of the boy, he is overwhelmed with a
sense of the dignity, the preciousness of the boy as a human being, this
sense is so strong that it is the beginning of his conversion.[36]

Dostoevsky describes how Zosima used 'to look upon the soldiers
who waited on us at school as cattle'.[37] After beating his servant
Afanasy, Zosima then realizes 'it was a crime and the realization was
like a long, sharp piercing needle piercing my heart. So I stood there
like a lost soul while the sun shone'.[38] Vital to Wojtyla's approach is
the avoidance of 'the temptation of falling into the rut of habit',[39] of
analysing the human person as purely ordinary and commonplace.

Karol Wojtyla's own life story and that of his contemporaries is
testament enough to the need for a balanced conception of the person.
It is after all, in the shadows of the negativity of two totalitarian systems
of Nazism and communism that he speaks of knowing about depersonalization from within, 'so it is easy to understand [his] deep
concern for the dignity of every human person'.[40] Wojtyla, as I will
mention in subsequent chapters, is not unique in this regard. Thinkers
like Adorno, Buber, Levinas and Ricoeur all reflect on the experience
of the Second World War and its consequences for the human person.
Levinas who was interned during the war describes how

> the other men, the ones we called free, who passed by or gave us work,
> or orders or even a smile – and the children and women who also passed
> by and occasionally looked at us – they stripped us of our humanity
> . . . With the strength and misery of the persecuted, a small voice, in
> spite of it all, recalled our fundamental essence as thinking human
> beings. But we were no longer part of the world.[41]

Stefan Swiezawski, Wojtyla's former colleague at the University of
Lublin points out that although 'the war and occupation was a time of
terrible devastation of life and culture . . . it was also a time of great

[36] Crosby, *Selfhood*, pp. 9–10.
[37] Fyodor Dostoevsky, *The Brothers Karamazov*, tr. Andrew R. MacAndrew (New
     York: Bantam, 1981), pp. 355–6.
[38] Dostoevsky, *Karamazov*, p. 358.
[39] Wojtyla, *Acting Person*, p. 22.
[40] Cf. Maciej Zieba, *The Surprising Pope: Understanding the Thought of John
     Paul II* (New York: Lexington Books, 2000), p. 52.
[41] Emmanuel Levinas, *Difficult Freedom: Essays on Judaism*, tr. Sean Hand
     (Baltimore, Johns Hopkins University Press, 1990), p. 178.

efforts to deepen and enrich our understanding of reality'.[42] He observes how

> we knew with vivid clarity that all the evil that had assailed us in a dreadfully pure form, as well as all the good, which included incredible acts of heroism and sacrifice, had been the work of human beings. What then is the human being? What in the deepest sense constitutes the human person? What causes people on the one time to resemble evil incarnate and to engage in acts of satanic brutality, and at another to exhibit super powers of love and devotion? *Quid est homo?*[43]

Wojtyla and the Lublin School of Philosophy

KUL canons of philosophy

The negative experiences to which Swiezawski adverts became for Wojtyla and the other KUL philosophers[44] 'a critical gauge for assessing the philosophical and ideological' weight of certain approaches to the question of the human person. The Lublin School of Philosophy's four main canons of doing philosophy were firstly, the primacy of realistic metaphysics. 'If our thinking and choosing lacks a tether to reality, the KUL philosophers believed, raw force takes over the world and truth becomes a function of power, not an expression of things-as-they-are.'[45] For 'human beings can only be free in the truth, and the measure of truth is reality'.[46] Second, is the central role of philosophical anthropology. The starting point for any adequate philosophical inquiry begins 'with a disciplined reflection on human experience rather than with cosmology (a general theory of the universe), as ancient and medieval philosophy and the neo-scholasticism Wojtyla had been taught at the Angelicum had done'.[47] The KUL philosophers saw that 'if philosophy could get to the truth of things-as-they-are through an analysis of human experience, then . . . modernity would be free from the dungeon of solipsism . . .'[48]

---

[42] Cited in Wojtyla, *Person and Community*, p. ix.
[43] Cited in Wojtyla, *Person and Community*, p. x.
[44] The term KUL stands for Katolicki Uniwersytet Lubelski, Catholic University of Lublin. The philosophers on the faculty included Kalinowski, Krapiec, Swiezawski and Wojtyla.
[45] Weigel, *Witness to Hope*, p. 133.
[46] Ibid.
[47] Ibid.
[48] Ibid.

The third norm for Wojtyla and his colleagues was 'the affirmation of a rational approach to philosophy'.[49] For the Lublin philosophers 'the experiences of the war, in their overwhelming realism, were too horrible to allow [them] still seriously to maintain a subjective or idealistic philosophy'.[50] At the same time there was 'a determination that they would not get caught in the endless cycle that the Polish philosopher Wojciech Chudy would later call the "trap of reflection". Rather their thought would illuminate what good men and women *ought* to do'.[51]

The fourth canon for these philosophers was that the history of philosophy has insights relevant to the contemporary philosophical investigation of the human person. Indeed, the whole

> history of the twentieth century's various torments, proved that defective understandings of the human person, human community, and human destiny were responsible for the mountains of corpses and oceans of blood. If they could help the world get a firmer purchase on the truth of the human condition, in a way distinctively modern *and* grounded in the great philosophical tradition of the West, the future might be different.[52]

In light of this, the reductive[53] depersonalization experiences on the historical level can help us unravel anew[54] a coherent philosophy of the person on the individual and social levels.

The foregoing account has sought to present the subject matter of Wojtyla's philosophical inquiry. The various literary sources used attempt to put flesh on the philosophic bones given to us by Wojtyla in the Preface and Introduction to *The Acting Person*. In answer to the question, *how* is a human being a person, Wojtyla works out an answer within the framework of the KUL canons. In this context one can discern the effects of Thomism upon the KUL philosophers. George Huntston Williams describes that 'beneath the ice on which Wojtyla, like a figure skater, displays his phenomenological configurations, lie

---

49 Wojtyla, *Person and Community*, p. xiii.
50 Wojtyla, *Person and Community*, p. ix.
51 Weigel, *Witness to Hope*, p. 134.
52 Ibid.
53 Wojtyla, *Acting Person*. The editor writes 'the book counteracts the deviant, reductive tendencies . . . so prevalent in contemporary philosophy and culture' (p. xxi).
54 Wojtyla, *Acting Person*, p. 21.

the deep waters of Thomism'.[55] The Polish writer Jaroslaw Kupczak describes four main influences of the Thomistic tradition upon Wojtyla. They actually coincide with the canons I have just outlined. They are, firstly, that Wojtyla's understanding that '*philosophia prima*' consists in realistic ontology; secondly, his trusting of 'human experience and human intellect in striving toward truth about reality'; thirdly, his respect for tradition and openness to contemporary philosophical questions; finally, how Thomism helps Wojtyla to see the human person 'in all its complexity and richness'.[56]

Encounter with Phenomenology

Many authors have written about Wojtyla's encounter with phenomenology, in fact, 'the complex interdependence of these two elements [Thomism and Phenomenology] in [his] philosophical synthesis is still a matter of lively debate'.[57] I do not intend to get involved in the debate because it strays from my primary intention.[58] Wojtyla is constantly at

---

55 George Huntston Williams, *The Mind of John Paul II: Origins of his Thought and Action* (New York: Seabury Press, 1981), p. 188.
56 Kupczak, *Destined for Liberty*, p. 56.
57 Wojtyla, *Person and Community*, p. xiv.
58 On 26 November 1978, in the *New York Times*, an article appeared entitled 'Phenomenology Has a New Star'. This provoked great controversy as is evidenced in a letter written by Prof. Alfred Block, the authorized translator of *The Acting Person*. He wrote on 24 December 1978, in response to the original article written by Lynda Rosen Obst that 'Professor Tymieniecka, [interviewed in the article] claims that [the book written by Wojtyla] places him in the ranks of phenomenologists . . . I cannot let this incredible misreading and misinterpretation of his philosophical work be left unchallenged . . . The use of the concept phenomenology does not make its user a phenomenologist.' The problems with the actual English translation by Anna-Teresa Tymieniecka are well documented. Subsequent to the actual English version there was consensus among most commentators that Tymieniecka's version does show signs of philosophical kidnapping of the phenomenological kind. George Weigel in *Witness to Hope*, gives a succinct account of the whole controversy. There is no doubt that Tymieniecka's publishing of several of Wojtyla's articles in *Analecta Husserliana* brought him to the notice of other philosophers. Andrzej Potocki translated a revised Polish text into English. This was sent to Tymieniecka in the United States. It is here that things began to go wrong. She 'significantly changed the Potocki translation, confusing its technical language and bending the text toward her own philosophical concerns [phenomenology]' (Weigel *Witness to Hope*, pp. 174–5). Kupczak, for example speaks of 'the creativeness of Dr. Tymieniecka's translation' (cf. Jaroslaw Kupczak, 'The Human Person as an Efficient cause in the Christian Anthropology of Karol Wojtyla' [Ph.D. diss., John Paul II Institute, Washington, DC, 1996], p. 122, note 9). He goes on to give an example of this. She 'never uses the Latin word "suppositum" which appears

pains to avoid reductionism whether of the Cartesian, Kantian, Schelerian, phenomenalist or empiricist[59] kind in any understanding of human experience. The starting point already determines the final outcome of any philosopher's investigations, that is, in their theories of human experience. Wojtyla writes: 'our prime concern in this study is *to allow experience to speak for itself as best it can right to the end*'.[60] To carry out this project in terms of the human person, Wojtyla devises a method in which he seeks, firstly, to describe the analysed human phenomenon, that is, grasping the essential elements of the phenomena and important relations between them. The focus of his attention is obviously as outlined by us, that is, to discover *how* a human being is a person. Pure description is not enough. There is, therefore, secondly, the need to interpret, that is, to understand the essence of the phenomenon by seeing it in the context of the whole person and of interpersonal relations.

Methodological considerations

In the context of this study, the description and analysis involved concerns the human being. However, as I have said, pure description of itself cannot arrive at the reality of the human person. There is also a need for interpretation, and 'only metaphysics is able to provide some notions and categories that can adequately interpret

---

frequently in the text of *Osoba I czyn*', instead there is a paraphrasing of scholastic Latin terms for more modern terms like 'ontological basis of action' and 'ultimate ontological foundation' (cf. Kenneth Schmitz, *At the Center of the Human Drama: The Philosophical Anthropology of Karol Wojtyla/Pope John Paul II* [Washington, DC: Catholic University of America Press, 1993, p. 60]). The effect of this is 'to reduce the importance of the *hypokeimenon* or of the *suppositum*, which is the metaphysical subject to which all attributions regarding the person refer' (cf. Buttiglione, *Karol Wojtyla*, p. 117). In light of these difficulties, I had private access to an unpublished corrected version of the 1979 edition of *The Acting Person*. In this book as I mentioned earlier, the Italian edition, *Persona e atto* (Rusconi, 1999), and the German text, *Person und Tat* (Herder, 1981), have been consulted since they are considered more faithful to the original Polish edition.

[59] For Wojtyla, most empiricists are not thoroughgoing enough. There is a correlation between Wojtyla's approach to most modern concepts of empiricism and that of Jacques Maritain. Maritain asserts that prudence requires one 'not [to be] a mere empiricist, but [to be in fact] a good deal of an empiricist'. in *From an Abundant Spring*, ed. by staff of *The Thomist* (New York: Kennedy & Sons, 1952), p. 451. Kapzcak in *Destined for Liberty* (p. 70) notes this similarity in their critique of empiricism between Wojtyla and Maritain.

[60] Wojtyla, *Acting Person*, p. 133.

the content of human experience'.[61] Hence, we can understand Wojtyla's methodology as aiming 'not to replace metaphysics with phenomenology but to supplement metaphysical reflection with phenomenological description as a way of gaining access'[62] to an adequate philosophy of the human person. He understands that 'the method of phenomenological analysis allows us to pause at lived experience as the irreducible' but that the method itself 'is not just a descriptive cataloguing of individual phenomena (in the Kantian sense, i.e. phenomena as sense-perceptible contents)'. For 'when we pause at the lived experience of the irreducible, we attempt to permeate cognitively the whole essence of this experience'. This is phenomenology's contribution to the search for the whole picture of the human person. In this way he believes we can understand 'both the essentially subjective structure of lived experience and its structural relation to the subjectivity of the human being'.[63]

Exactness as a fake

Just as Wojtyla notes the limitations in traditional philosophy, phenomenology too is not some new antiseptic method of approach in philosophy. Joseph Pieper picks up this point in his lecture entitled 'The Condition of Philosophy Today', and quotes Alfred North Whitehead's dictum, 'exactness is a fake'.[64] This is an enlightening philosophical comment following Whitehead's extensive career devoted to his 'method of extensive abstraction'. Pieper concludes from this 'that not the *modus* of perceiving is decisive but the rank of *what* you perceive'.[65] In light of this we can infer that Wojtyla can be considered as a philosophical pluralist when it comes to method, for he understands the need for complementarity and collaboration. Imperative to him is not the way we arrive at a coherent philosophy but *that we* undertake the enterprise in the first place.

He perceives the restrictions inherent in any system of philosophy and when speaking of phenomenology he affirms that

[61] Kapczak, *Destined for Liberty*, pp.101–2.
[62] Wojtyla, *Person and Community*, p. xiv.
[63] Wojtyla, 'Subjectivity and the Irreducible in the Human Being', in *Person and Community*, pp. 215–16.
[64] Josef Pieper, 'The Condition of Philosophy Today', in *The Future of Thomism*, eds. Deal W. Hudson and Dennis Wm. Moran (Notre Dame, IN: University of Notre Dame Press, 1992), p. 31.
[65] Ibid.

when it is said that the essence of a thing is manifested in immediate experience, this should not be understood to mean the essence in the metaphysical sense. What interests phenomenologists is not what a thing is in itself, but how something manifests itself to us in immediate experience.[66]

There is undoubtedly a need to describe indiscriminately the whole content of the human experience. On this level phenomenology is descriptive in its recounting the basic categories of our experience. However, Wojtyla is of the view that 'the phenomenological method can be used well beyond the limits set by Scheler's paradigms . . . in order to reconstruct an original human experience and build an adequate theory of the acting person'.[67] In collaboration with a realistic ontology and metaphysical analysis, phenomenology can move beyond the descriptive and become explanatory in its efforts to reveal the essential nature of the human person.

In a paper sent to an international philosophical conference in Paris in June of 1975, there is a sentence that reveals some of the implications of Wojtyla's encounter with phenomenology. Wojytla asserts, 'Phenomenological analysis thus contributes to transphenomenol understanding'.[68] This is a clear case in point, where the meaning behind such a condensed sentence should be explicated since, as I have mentioned before, there is a constant need to quarry out the meaning in Wojtylan texts. Herbert Spiegelberg, in dealing with the phenomenology of Jean-Paul Sartre explains that one of Sartre's 'main concerns was to make room for what he called the transphenomenol or, more generally, the ontological'.[69] The Wojtylan cavernous sentence about 'transphenomenol understanding' is, in fact, a terse summary of his evaluation of phenomenology.

Phenomenology can end up limiting itself solely to description, and when it comes to searching for something in order adequately to explain the person outside of the present experience and not just in consciousness, it is unable in principle to do this. The methodology of phenomenology does not allow for causal explanation. Wojtyla

---

[66] Wojtyla, 'The Separation of Experience from the Act in Ethics', in *Person and Community*, p. 33.
[67] Kapczak, *Destined for Liberty*, p. 70.
[68] Wojtyla, 'Subjectivity and the Irreducible', in *Person and Community*, p. 216.
[69] Herbert Spiegelberg, *The Phenomenological Movement: A Historical Introduction* (Dordrecht: Kluwer, 1994), p. 509.

observes this particularly with regard to the phenomenology of Max Scheler.[70] He states that

> we are standing here in the presence of the phenomenologist's fatal mistake. Scheler fails to perceive a most elementary and basic truth, namely, that the only value that can be called ethical value is a value that has the acting person as its efficient cause . . . What is primary is the fact that this value comes from the person as its efficient cause. Because Scheler did not manage to objectify this basic fact in his phenomenological interpretation of ethical experience, his whole interpretation deals only with secondary elements, which he tries – at times rather artificially – to elevate to the primary level.[71]

In brief, Scheler in his philosophical analysis mistakes the part for the whole and in so doing he does not explain the universal human experience of being the cause of one's own actions. Therefore, he is unable to present the full reality of the human person. In fact, Wojtyla believes if we use phenomenological analysis to its optimum it leads inevitably to the 'transphenomenol', the 'ontological'. Only in this way can we arrive at an adequate philosophy of the human person. Hence,

> for Wojtyla it is not a question of demonstrating phenomenologically that man is a person, but seeing with the aid of phenomenology *in which way man is a person*, in which way the metaphysical structures proper to his being are reflected in consciousness.[72]

Wojtyla's use of phenomenology has been contentious. It has provoked differing reactions within the schools of Thomism[73] and

---

[70] The book Wojtyla had in mind when he was writing *The Acting Person* was Max Scheler's *Formalism in Ethics and Non-Formal Ethics of Values: A New Attempt toward the Foundation of an Ethical Personalism*, tr. Manfred S. Frings and Roger L. Funk (Evanston: Northwestern University Press, 1973). Frings, in fact, refers to Wojtyla's work on Scheler in his later translation of Scheler's work, given the title of *Person and Self-Value: Three Essays* (The Hague: Martinus Nijhoff, 1987). He notes: 'In his many writings and prior to his becoming Pope John Paul II, Karol Wojtyla has, like others, argued that the human will in Scheler's ethical writings is somewhat underestimated . . .' (p. xiv, n.1).

[71] Wojytla, 'The Separation of Experience from the Act in Ethics', in *Person and Community*, p. 38.

[72] Buttiglione, *Karol Wojtyla*, p. 356.

[73] I already mentioned the various reactions of the Lublin Thomists to Wojtyla's philosophical endeavours. Cf. Wojtyla's *Person and Community*, pp. ix–xvi.

phenomenology alike. Indeed, both Levinas and Wojtyla's use of phenomenology has produced much debate within French philosophical circles. Apart from the actual methodological questions involved, it is interesting to note that contemporary discussion takes cognizance of their contributions. When Wojtyla originally wrote *The Acting Person* the only noteworthy reactions came from Marxist philosophers like Jozeph Keller.[74] In a comparable fashion the modern French philosopher Dominique Janicaud reacts negatively to the Wojtylan methodology. Commenting specifically on the 1998 encyclical letter *Fides et Ratio*, he claims

> in violation of both the letter and the spirit of the phenomenological method, they [that is, Karol Wojtyla, Emmanuel Levinas, Jean-Luc Marion, Jean-Louis Chrétien, and Michel Henry, who are also called the 'new phenomenologists'] have committed '[s]trict treason of the reduction that handed over the transcendental I to its nudity'.[75]

Janicaud, Jacques Derrida and others perceive a 'theological hostage-taking'[76] of phenomenology has occurred in these so-called 'new phenomenologists'. Jeffrey Kosky's recent book, *Levinas and the Philosophy of Religion* is a further contribution to the growing discussion on the issue. But Kosky argues on the contrary, that some of the traditional phenomenologists and their modern-day disciples are in actual fact not radical enough in their application of phenomenology. He observes that the charge of 'theological hijacking' is 'a reading [that] fails to appreciate the sense in which the discovery of the subject's religiosity happens through a phenomenology of the subject as such, a subject we all are (even if each says I alone am responsible)'.[77] I bring this debate to the reader's attention because it illustrates my viewpoint that the whole Wojtylan project cannot be understood as being merely on the margins of philosophical debate. Indeed, in Wojtyla's dialogue with phenomenology, which some see as occupying 'a central place in the philosophical trajectory of modernity'[78] he has

---

[74] Cf. page 121 of this book.
[75] Dominique Janicaud *et al.*, *Phenomenology and the 'Theological Turn': The French Debate*, tr. Bernard G. Prusak (New York: Fordham University Press, 2000), p. 5.
[76] Janicaud *et al. Phenomenology*, p. 43.
[77] Jeffrey L. Kosky, *Levinas and the Philosophy of Religion* (Bloomington, Indiana University Press, 2001), p. xx.
[78] Colin Davis, *Levinas: An Introduction* (Notre Dame, IN: University of Notre Dame Press, 1996), p. 8.

perhaps penetrated into the marrow of the bone of contemporary argument.

Between Scylla and Charybdis

Wojtyla sets out in *The Acting Person* to navigate the seas of philosophical enquiry and to steer a course between the Scylla of a metaphysical tradition of the person that has left the relational dimension undeveloped, and the Charybdis of a phenomenological tradition that has highly developed the relational aspect but lost its metaphysical grounding. A problem emerges in the philosophy of the human person, when one aspect is hypostatized to the exclusion of other. Phenomenology can aid the recovery of objectivity in cognitive acts. This is when consciousness is seen 'to be consciousness of something transcendent to consciousness in the sense of the intended and intentional object of acts of knowing awareness'. Wojtyla is interested in a similar recovery of 'the suppositum of the philosophy being [a retrieval of the human person as "suppositum"] within the philosophy of consciousness'.[79] A balanced description and interpretation of consciousness within lived human experience can be the window of opportunity to arrive at an adequate philosophy of the person. In discussing the task of philosophy, Wojtyla comments

> the problem of the subjectivity of the person, and especially this problem in relation to the human community, imposes itself today as one of the central questions concerning the world outlook. This is at the basis of the human praxis and morality and at the basis of culture, civilization and politics.[80]

Norris Clarke gives credit to Wojtyla and others for perceiving the need to remedy any lacunas in the traditional philosophy of the person and contributing towards a creative retrieval 'wherein relationality would become an equally primordial aspect of the person as substantiality'.[81]

---

[79] Peter Simpson, *On Karol Wojtyla* (New York: Wadsworth Press, 2001), p. 18
[80] Karol Wojtyla, 'The Task of Christian Philosophy Today', *Proceedings of the ACPA*, 52, 1979, p. 3.
[81] W. Norris Clarke, *The Aquinas Lecture: Person and Being* (Milwaukee: Marquette University Press, 1993), p. 2.

The 'traditional Aristotelian anthropology was based . . . on the definition . . . *homo est animale rationale*'.[82] This definition does not allow us to gain insight into 'the question of that which is original and essentially human, that which accounts for the human being's complete uniqueness in the world'.[83] Wojtyla calls it a type of cosmological understanding that implies 'a belief in the reducibility of the human being to the world'.[84] As such the definition is not sufficiently comprehensive and differentiated.

Aristotle's abstract definition of man as 'rational animal' is unquestionably useful, along with the subsequent Boethian formulation: *persona est rationalis naturae individua substantia*,[85] 'individual substance of a rational nature'. Both are on the level of substance and clearly differentiate the human being from the whole world of objective entities. Hence, this tradition offers the 'metaphysical terrain' for mapping out an adequate theory of the person but

> we should pause in the process of reduction, which leads us in the direction of understanding the human being in the world (a *cosmological* type of understanding), in order to understand the human being inwardly. This latter type of understanding may be called *personalistic*.[86]

Wojtyla does not see these as antinomies but as complementing each other. He notes that

> the experience of the human being cannot be derived by way of cosmological reduction; we must pause at the irreducible, at that which is unique and unrepeatable in each human being, by virtue of which he or she is not just *a particular human being* – an individual of a certain species – but *a personal* subject.[87]

He admonishes that 'only then can we get a true and complete picture of the human being'.[88]

---

[82] Wojtyla, 'Subjectivity and the Irreducible in the Human Being', in *Person and Community*, p. 210.
[83] Ibid.
[84] Wojtyla, 'Subjectivity', p. 211.
[85] Cited in Wojtyla, *Person and Community*, p. 167.
[86] Wojtyla, *Person and Community*, p. 213.
[87] Wojtyla, *Person and Community*, p. 214.
[88] Ibid.

We can detect here Wojtyla's openness to dialogue with the contemporary philosophy of the subject because it 'seems to be telling the traditional philosophy of the object' that 'we cannot come to know and understand the human being in a reductive way alone'.[89] He looks upon this as a challenging perspective in which to understand *how* a human being is a person. Wojtyla's perspicacity is in discerning in both 'the metaphysical realism of Aristotle and Thomas Aquinas and the sensitivity to human experience of Max Scheler's phenomenology'[90] a way to formulate an adequate philosophy of the person.

In writing *The Acting Person* and some of his earlier works there were in all probability the writings of Aquinas, Ingarden, Scheler and Maritain among others on his desk. Nevertheless, his project on the human person was more importantly written in the shadows of the chimneys of Auschwitz, in the dimness of experiences when ideologies treated human beings as numbers and objects instead of as persons, and any such 'lived experience', he says, 'essentially defies' any such 'reduction'[91] of it. Wojtyla seizes the opportunity provided to him and to others in order to adequately lay out the geography of the human person. He sees it positively as the 'means of arresting further disintegration'[92] on the individual, societal and historical levels of the unfolding philosophical drama of the human person.

From under the rubble

An adequate philosophical differentiation of the reality of the human person should, according to Wojtyla, be capable of dealing with 'the major issues . . . concerning life . . . directly as they present themselves to man in his struggle to survive while maintaining the dignity of the human being'.[93] Wojtyla is a critical realist in this regard. His own personal history, that of the society in which he grew up, and examples taken from history are all smudged with the mark of aberrations in people when it comes to the understanding and treatment of others. Since a consistent theory of the human person had become lost in the theoretical and ideological fog of concepts, Wojtyla and others saw

[89] Wojtyla, *Person and Community*, p. 215.
[90] Weigel, *Witness to Hope*, p. 128.
[91] Ibid.
[92] David Walsh, 'Are Freedom and Dignity Enough?: A Reflection on Liberal Abbreviations' (Unpublished essay: Catholic University of America, 2001), p. 3.
[93] Wojtyla, *Acting Person*, p. vii.

the need for a philosophical procedure to recapture the reality of the person. The cultural and philosophical milieu he found himself in following the cataclysmic experience of the Second World War and the subsequent experiences of totalitarianism was, as I already observed, cathartic and therapeutic in itself. In one sense, there is no alternative after such experiences but to take up Adorno's interrogative about the possibility of philosophy after Auschwitz and to do philosophy. The philosophical 'personscape' had been reduced to the bareness of mere 'immediacy'. A recovery of meaning was needed in a world where, as depicted in literature like Solzhenitsyn's *One Day in the Life of Ivan Denisovich*, 'the camp lights [symbols of the prevailing ideology in the Gulags] [had] drive[n] away the stars',[94] a recovery that requires the injection of understanding and judgment, in order that 'winter twilight [as in the concentration camp ideology whereby the person is treated as specimen] cannot be mistaken for the summer noonday sun'[95] of the human person.

Wojtyla was familiar with the writings of Camus, Dostoevsky and Solzhenitsyn.[96] He had the insight that what separates these writers 'even from the many others who have undergone the same kind of cathartic regeneration is precisely [the] elaboration of the larger philosophical significance of their experience'.[97]

Wojtyla observes 'that in the concentration camps there were people who managed to relate to others as other *I*'s, as *neighbours* – often to a heroic degree'.[98] He wants to elaborate the philosophical significance of these cathartic human experiences, which are representative of the kernel of the human person and illustrate how, for example, people treated as numbers in the concentration camps could become persons. Viktor Frankl, the psychiatrist, investigated the same matter from his own professional perspective. He commented:

> we who lived in concentration camps can remember the men who walked through the huts comforting others, giving away their last piece of bread. They may have been few in number, but they offer sufficient proof that everything can be taken from a man but one thing: the last

---

[94] Alexander Solzhenitsyn, *One Day in the Life of Ivan Denisovich*, tr. Ralph Parker (London: Penguin Books, 1963), p. 18.
[95] Lonergan, *Insight* (London: Longman, 1958), p. xix.
[96] Cf. Weigel, *Witness To Hope*, pp. 117, 279, 325, 569.
[97] David Walsh, *After Ideology: Recovering the Spiritual Foundations of Freedom* (New York: HarperCollins, 1990), p. 3.
[98] Wojtyla, 'Participation or Alienation?', in *Person and Community*, p. 206.

of human freedoms – to choose one's attitude in any given circumstances, to choose one's way.[99]

Solzhenitsyn on his release from the gulag prisons showed how he had gained wisdom in the midst of the human suffering when he claimed 'I nourished my soul there, and say without hesitation: "Bless you, prison, for having been in my life!"'[100] Philosophers like Paul Ricoeur and Emmanuel Levinas had similar experiences during the war. Ricoeur remarks that:

> the period of captivity spent in different camps in Pomerania was the time of extraordinary human experiences . . . I am indebted to Karl Jaspers for having placed my admiration for German thinking outside the reach of all the negative aspects of our surroundings and of the 'terror of history'.[101]

Levinas too had to deal with the experiences of war and peace. The fundamental alienation of war, he observes, is that it estranges the human person from their proper self.[102] Eric Matthews notes that it is following these experiences that Levinas 'was able to return to philosophical activity' and resembling Wojtyla's proposal in the preface to *The Acting Person*, he too begins 'to develop a philosophy of his own, as opposed to commenting on the thought of others'.[103]

The important point for Wojtyla and others is to have the question that emerges from beneath the rubble of a system where man has lost 'his proper place in the world that he has shaped himself'.[104] After all 'question and answer are held together, and related to one another, by the event of the search . . . The answer will not help the man who has lost the question; and the predicament of the present age is characterized by loss of the question rather than of the answer'.[105] Wojtyla invites

99   Viktor Frankl, *Man's Search for Meaning: An Introduction to Logotherapy*, tr. Ilse Lasch (New York: Simon & Schuster, 1962), p. 65.
100 Alexander Solzhenitsyn, *The Gulag Archipelago* [2], tr. Thomas P. Whitney (London: Collins Harvill Press, 1975), p. 617.
101 *The Philosophy of Paul Ricoeur: The Library of Living Philosophers*, Vol. XXII, ed. Lewis Edwin Hahn (Chicago, IL.: Open Court, 1995), p. 9.
102 Emmanuel Levinas, *Totality and Infinity: An Essay on Exteriority*, tr. Alphonso Lingis (Pittsburgh: Duquesne University Press, 1969), p. 21.
103 Eric Matthews, *Twentieth-Century French Philosophy* (Oxford: Oxford University Press, 1996), p. 159.
104 Wojtyla, *Acting Person*, p. 22.
105 Eric Voegelin, 'Gospel and Culture', in *The Collected Works of Eric Voegelin: Published Essays 1966–1985*, vol. 12 (Baton Rouge: Louisiana State University Press, 1990), pp. 172–212.

his readers to struggle themselves with the question and acknowledges that his work 'may lead either [to the reader's] victories or to his defeats'.[106]

The Acting Person

The primary sources used in this book are the writings of Karol Wojtyla. In this regard it is proper to make a distinction between his early and later writings. We can entitle this as 'Wojtyla I' and 'Wojtyla II' respectively. The main works I will refer to from the early writings ('Wojtyla I') are as follows: *Love and Responsibility*, *The Acting Person*, and the collection of essays contained in *Person and Community*. His later writings ('Wojtyla II') refer to his writings as John Paul II and include his papal Encyclicals and his books *Sources of Renewal*, and *Crossing the Threshold of Hope*. The reader might well object to a philosophical use of the writings of the 'Wojtyla II' period because they are not exclusively philosophical, or indeed, because of a hermeneutical problem in terms of knowing the true authorship of some of the writings in this phase of Wojtyla's life. There is none the less a philosophical precedent for proceeding with our enquiry using these later writings. Alasdair MacIntyre considers the encyclical *Veritatis Splendor*, for example, as 'a striking contribution by the Polish phenomenological and Thomistic philosopher Karol Wojtyla to ongoing philosophical enquiry'. As regards the hermeneutical problem of exact authorship, MacIntyre stresses that 'any reader of Karol Wojtyla's major philosophical writings, from his doctoral dissertation onward, will recognize, both in the style of arguments and in the nuances with which particular arguments are developed, a single namable authorial presence in this text'.[107]

An outline of The Acting Person

To facilitate our philosophical investigation into the concept of the human person in the Wojtylan writings, let me now conclude this chapter with a brief outline of his main philosophical study on the person, as contained in *The Acting Person*. The Polish edition, *Osoba i Czyn*, appeared in 1969. The English version was published in 1979.

[106] Wojtyla, *Acting Person*, p. vii.
[107] Alasdair MacIntyre, 'How Can We learn What *Veritatis Splendor* Has To Teach', in J. A. DiNola and Romanus Cessario (eds.), *Veritatis Splendor: and the Renewal of Moral Theology* (New Jersey: Scepter Publishers, 1999), p. 73.

It opens with the author's Preface and then twenty pages of introduction and in it he seeks to explore the whole concept of human experience. As I will observe later, a retrieval of an adequate theory of experience is fundamental to a coherent philosophy of the person.

There are four parts to *The Acting Person*, with seven chapters in all. Part One is on consciousness and efficacy, with chapter 1 looking at the acting person in relation to efficacy. In fact, a cursory glance at the first chapter heading, that is, 'The acting Person in the Aspect of Consciousness', gives us the plot of this first part. It is intended to correct idealism's propensity to absolutize human consciousness. In reality the human person is not simply a consciousness; in truth, he or she is more than this. The Cartesian and Kantian identification of the person with their consciousness 'as though the consciousness might be the principal object of inner experience, of introspection',[108] should to be avoided. In short: 'Wojtyla is willing to grant that consciousness conditions experience'[109] but it does not constitute it.

Wojtyla distinguishes between the interior and exterior experiences of man. The first chapter deals with the interior experience of man in consciousness, while chapter 2 explores the exterior experience of 'action'. 'Action' contains the philosophical anthropological key for unlocking the secrets of the person. Action and not consciousness reveals the irreducible of man. Schmitz says: 'from the beginning, Wojtyla has insisted that consciousness is not, as idealism would have it, an autonomous subject and the source of action. On the contrary, it is man, the human person, who acts in the full concrete sense, and not consciousness'. Schmitz also makes a useful reference in a footnote to the Aristotelian insistence in *De Anima* 'that it is not the eye that sees nor the mind that knows, but rather the man who sees with his eyes and knows with his mind'.[110] Wojtyla takes up this differentiation when he distinguishes between 'Man-acts' and 'something which happens in man'. Here there is described the difference between acting and happening in man. In acting we have the experience that we are the actor, that is, of being a cause. 'Man-acts' are what distinguishes the human person. Man is the efficient cause of his own action. Such actions require the person's freedom and ability to relate them to the truth. 'Man-acts' occurs with the context of 'the total dynamism that

---

[108] George Huntston Williams, *The Mind of John Paul II*, p. 195.
[109] Ibid.
[110] Schmitz, *At the Center of the Human* Drama, p. 69, n. 23.

is present in the complete experience of man',[111] and Wojtyla wants to 'rely upon the total experience of man and not merely on the evidence which might be supplied by our consciousness'.[112]

Part Two of *The Acting Person* is titled: 'The Transcendence of the Person in Action'. Through the analysis of the personal structure of self-determination it shows that the person is the efficient cause of the action because he is self-determining. Hence, chapter 3 is called 'The Personal Structure of Self-Determination'. Chapter 4 looks at how performing an action brings about personal fulfilment. The person does not simply reflect internal and external conditioning but can decide by conforming their choice to the truth, which they know about the good. It is in virtue of self-determination that an action penetrates into the *ego*.[113] Thus the person is brought to their proper fulfilment.[114] This fulfilment is the implementation of self-governance.[115] Wojtyla writes:

> To fulfill oneself means to actualize, and in a way bring to the proper fullness, that structure in man which is characteristic for him because of his personality and also because of his being somebody and not merely something; it is the structure of *self-governance* and *self-possession*.[116]

Evident here is the philosophical development by Wojtyla of a theory of the *person* who is not caught in a web of genetic, environmental and economic determinism. The human person is not 'like a fly caught up in a spider-web of economic, political, and techno-medialogical determinants which effectively render him or her a pawn of impersonal structures and mechanisms'.[117]

Part Three concerns the integration of the person in the action. Chapter 5 outlines such integration in terms of the body with chapter 6 exploring it in terms of the psyche. Wojtyla discusses the outerness and innerness of the human body. He observes that 'the outwardly discernible entirety, however, by no means accounts for all the reality constituting the human body, just as it does not in the case of the

---

[111] Wojtyla, *Acting Person*, p. 60.
[112] Wojtyla, *Acting Person*, p. 61.
[113] Wojtyla, *Acting Person*, p. 150.
[114] Wojtyla, *Acting Person*, p. 151.
[115] Wojtyla, *Acting Person*, p. 152.
[116] Wojtyla, *Acting Person*, p. 151.
[117] Maciej Zieba, *Surprising Pope*, p. 24.

animal body or of plants. The body has, in fact, simultaneously its own particular inwardness'.[118] The body does not constitute a separate subject distinguished from the man-person, but there is a specific autonomy of the somatic dynamism.[119] The person realizes their own self-mastery not by concealing the natural dynamisms of the body and psyche but by regulating them and integrating them in action which is expressed in the unity of the person. The human person not only moves beyond the body and the psyche by transcending them but also integrates them in action. Action is the element that belongs neither to one's transcendent spiritual faculties nor to one's psychic or bodily dynamisms but to the personal unity, which integrates all these bodily aspects.

Part Four has the title, 'Participation', that is, the acting of the person together with others. Linked to transcendence and integration it is one of the fundamental dimensions of the person. It is this part of Wojtyla's work that is of particular interest and the focus of my particular study. Acting-together-with-others should be organized in such a way that the person can realize himself or herself through participation.[120] Individualism leads to a denial of participation 'since it isolates the person from others by conceiving him solely as an individual who concentrates on himself and his own good'.[121] Totalism, which sees the individual as the chief enemy, is a form of 'reversed individualism'.[122] Wojtyla tells the reader how 'numerous historical examples'[123] confirm the anti-individualism intrinsic to totalism. The focal point of Wojtyla's analysis in this final part of his major philosophical work is still on the structure of the person in the phenomenon 'I act'. But it is here that he begins to thematize the human person in terms of the 'other', and more specifically in relation to the paradigm of the 'neighbour'. In the next chapter I will examine his particular treatment of the theme of the 'neighbour'.

Obscure style

Let me add here that the average reader might find Wojtyla's language unduly opaque. Authors like Williams find the Wojtylan use of

---

[118] Wojtyla, *Acting Person*, p. 201.
[119] Wojtyla, *Acting Person*, pp. 211–12.
[120] Wojtyla, *Acting Person*, p. 271.
[121] Wojtyla, *Acting Person*, pp. 273–4.
[122] Wojtyla, *Acting Person*, p. 274.
[123] Wojtyla, *Acting Person*, p. 275.

terminology frustrating in the extreme. He believes Wojtyla 'has chosen to write in such a technical vocabulary, and with such care for etymology and definition, that in the end his meaning is obfuscated'.[124] He also indicates that a far better contextual reading can be achieved by discovering what we can call skeletons hiding in Wojtyla's philosophic cupboard. According to Williams, they are of two types, Wojtyla's philosophical opponents (e.g. idealists) and his social opponents (e.g. Marxists). Parts One, Two and Three of the book deal with the main philosophical-anthropological analysis of the person, and are therefore directed against his philosophical adversaries, while Part Four concerns man's place in society, and so is addressed to the totalitarian systems of his day. I agree with Williams, that 'totalism', 'individualism' and other such terms are code words that have to be deciphered.[125]

Although Williams's historical contextual interpretation of the *Sitz im Leben* behind the work has merit, his philosophical judgment is somewhat lacking in that it occludes the fundamental goal of the Wojtylian project.[126] Lack of examples[127] and no direct reference to other authors can be explained by the sensitive political environment in which the author lived and also because he wanted the 'experiencer' (the reader) to experience the experience itself. As we have seen, Wojtyla affirms that 'our prime concern in this study is to allow experience to speak for itself as best it can right to the end'.[128] Most commentators attest to the fact that a common characteristic of Wojtyla's philosophical approach is openness and dialogue. Weigel confirms this when he concludes: 'Wojtyla didn't lock himself into intellectual combat'[129] with others. He simply 'absorbed what was enduring'[130] and believed 'that philosophy could get to the truth of-things-as-they-are'.[131] For example, Dermot Moran, in his recent study, *Introduction to Phenomenology*, describes the phenomenological

---

[124] Williams, *Mind of John Paul II*, p. 202.
[125] Williams, *Mind of John Paul II*, p. 204.
[126] Rocco Buttiglione praises Williams for his rich analysis of the origins of Wojtyla's thought, but adds, '[his] philosophical judgments are not always reliable', in *Karol Wojtyla*, p. 126.
[127] Williams writes: 'but this work is almost devoid of *exempla gratiae*, examples for the sake of grace (relief)', *Mind of John Paul II*, p. 202.
[128] Wojtyla, *Acting Person*, p. 133.
[129] Weigel, *Witness to Hope*, p. 128.
[130] Ibid.
[131] Ibid.

approach in philosophy as wanting to get at the truth of matters, and as describing human experience 'to the experiencer'.[132] Similarly, Wojtyla sees the reader as being in the role of that 'experiencer', therefore, he does not want to usurp him or her from the experience.

---

[132] Dermot Moran, *Introduction to Phenomenology* (London: Routledge: 2000), p. 4.

2

The Neighbour as Paradigm:
Toward an Adequate Philosophy
of the Human Person

The Acting Person: the new element

Wojtyla's study *Love and Responsibility* precedes *The Acting Person* chronologically but not logically. Simpson observes that *The Acting Person* deals 'with the fundamental anthropology that Wojtyla had developed while *Love and Responsibility* deals with that anthropology's ethical application and development'.[1] In this chapter I will explore the specific reference to the reality of the 'neighbour' that emerges in Part Four, chapter 7 of *The Acting Person*. The whole section in that book is entitled: 'Intersubjectivity by Participation'.[2]

Wojtyla points out that this last chapter in his study now adds 'one more element to the previously constructed and outlined whole' and that this new element has not 'received the attention it deserves and must be examined more thoroughly'.[3] The new factor is the reality that we act together with others. In the language of Edmund Husserl and other phenomenologists we are concerned here with the question of 'intersubjectivity'. However, Wojtyla employs the term 'participation' more frequently. He uses it deliberately because he wants to avoid a purely cognitive treatment of the human experience of acting 'together with others'.[4] I will deal with the notion of 'participation' later in this chapter, but it is vital to say a little more about the *Fremdserfahrung* (the experience of the other) question in Husserl. In Husserl the experience of the 'other' is approached from the point of view of consciousness. His question is 'how is the other *constituted* for me? How does the other enter into my consciousness?'[5] Dermot Moran speaks about the way in which Husserl struggled with the reality

---

[1] Peter Simpson, *On Karol Wojtyla* (New York: Wadsworth, 2001), p. 5.
[2] Karol Wojtyla, *The Acting Person*, tr. Andrzej Potocki (Dordrecht and Boston: Reidel, 1979), p. 261.
[3] Ibid.
[4] Wojtyla, *Acting Person*, p. 315.
[5] Dermot Moran, *Introduction to Phenomenology* (London: Routledge, 2000), p. 176.

of 'communication and communion between persons', but that the nature of this actually 'eluded him'.[6] It may have escaped him because he conceived of consciousness not as an aspect of the human person but as his totality. Hence, as I have just remarked, we can notice the preponderance of the term 'participation' in the Wojtylan writings. For Wojtyla the encounter with the other is not just a question for consciousness but it in fact 'discloses a new dimension [of man as a] person'.[7]

Dramatic-poetic insights into the significance of the 'neighbour'

In 1956 Wojtyla wrote a philosophical poem called 'The Quarry'.[8] In it he initially 'probes into man's emotions that are born from man's struggle with matter'.[9] The first part of the poem is called 'Material', the second, 'Inspiration', the third, 'Participation', and it concludes with an elegy 'In memory of a fellow-worker'. His language moves from descriptive detail to 'thought reflecting thought'.[10] We are invited firstly, to:

> Listen: the even knocking of hammers,
> so much their own,
> I project on to people
> to test the strength of each blow.
> Listen now: electric current
> cuts through a river of rock.
> And a thought grows in me day after day:
> the greatness of work is inside man.

Then we are led on to discover the all-important element of efficacy in human action, when Wojtyla notes:

> Work starts within, outside it takes such space
> that it soon seizes hands, then the limits of breath.
> Look – your will strikes a deep bell in stone,
> thought strikes certainty, a peak
> both for heart and for hand.

---

6   Moran, *Introduction to Phenomenology*, p. 178.
7   Wojtyla, *Acting Person*, p. 315.
8   Karol Wojtyla, *Collected Poems*, tr. Jerzy Peterkiewicz (London: Hutchinson, 1982), pp. 80–8.
9   Cf. Introduction to *Easter Vigil and Other Poems*, tr. Jerzy Peterkiewicz (London: Hutchinson, 1979), p. 11.
10 Ibid.

In the third section of the poem he speaks of 'participation'. He refers to the inter-relationship between 'heart, stone, and tree' and the role of the worker (the human person) in the unfolding drama of life. He recalls:

> How splendid these men, no airs, no graces;
> I know you, look into your hearts,
> no pretence between us.
> Some hands are for toil, some for the cross.
>
> The fence over your heads, pickaxes scattered on the tracks.

A fellow-worker is then killed in a mishap. We can discern in Wojtyla's description of how his co-workers treat him that they perceive him as a person, who possesses a substance uniquely his own. Yet, their respect for him betrays a participation in their fellow-worker's irreducible distinctiveness. Wojtyla describes how:

> They took his body, and walked in a silent line.
> Who will lift up that stone, unfurl his thoughts again
> under the cracked temples? So plaster cracks on the wall.
> They laid him down, his back on a sheet of gravel.
> His wife came, worn out with worry; his son returned from school.
> Should his anger now flow into the anger of others?
> It was maturing in him through its own truth and love.
> Should he be used by those who come after,
> deprived of substance, unique and deeply his own?
> The stones on the move again: a wagon bruising the flowers.
> Again, the electric current cuts deep into walls.
> But the man has taken with him the world's inner structure,
> where the greater the anger, the higher the explosion of love.

One can readily notice from this and other poems that the category of 'neighbour' as person is a fruitful concept in the poems and dramas of Karol Wojtyla. Let us briefly examine his play, *Radiation of Fatherhood. A Mystery*.[11] In it the young girl, Monica, asks her adoptive father, Adam:

> When will be spoken of what is contained in you and me, what lies in the depth of consciousness and must wait for words? Being together, shall we find one day the moments for such words that bring to the surface what is really deep down?

---

[11] Karol Wojtyla, *The Collected Plays and Writings on Theater*, tr. Boleslaw Tabroski (Berkeley: University of California Press, 1987), p. 346.

Those very words of Monica, that is, 'what is contained in *you* and *me*' introduces the whole theme of the 'other' and its philosophical significance. In the same play Adam gives a very insightful analysis of loneliness, when he remarks

> I am afraid of the word 'mine', though at the same time I cherish its meaning. I am afraid because this word always puts me face to face with You. An analysis of the word 'mine' always leads me to You. And I would rather give up using it than find its ultimate sense in You. For I want to have everything through myself, not through You.[12]

Thus, the word 'mine' in itself suggests relationality; albeit in the negative sense, that is, 'not yours'. When it is applied not just externally in terms of property but 'inwardly to the relation between persons' then the 'very word cancels loneliness, because it cannot exclude from its meaning a reference to what is not mine, to what is "yours" '.[13]

According to Józef Tischner, the hermeneutical key to this drama is

> the idea of the creative interaction of persons. This idea can be expressed as follows: Thanks to you I become myself, and thanks to me you become yourself. The experience of creative interaction is mysterious. I know that alone I am myself. I know that alone you are yourself. Each of us lived for himself even before we met. Yet we could not be ourselves without each other. Fatherhood and motherhood are good examples here. The father has a right to say, I am father. And the mother has the right to say, I am mother. But the mother becomes a mother thanks to the father; they give birth to each other. How deep a part of us is our mutual birth giving? Who knows how much of our interaction is creative? We know only that every human 'I' bears the mark of a 'You' . . . In the creative interaction of persons is the nucleus of a drama. One could argue that all dramas in the world describe the course of interaction – the creative one and the destructive one.[14]

Tischner finds the paradigms of fatherhood and motherhood in Wojtyla's play to be good examples of the interactive drama between persons. My analysis in this second chapter will focus on the paradigm of the neighbour. The 'other' will be disclosed in the investigation as not just accidental to my being but constitutive of it. As we have seen

---

[12] Wojtyla, *Collected Plays*, p. 337.
[13] Kenneth Schmitz, *At The Center of The Human Drama: The Philosophical Anthropology of Karol Wojtyla/Pope John Paul II* (Washington, DC: Catholic University of America Press, 1993), p. 23.
[14] Cited in Wojtyla, *Collected Plays*, p. 327.

already in the Wojtylan poetic–dramatic literature, the 'other', as in 'The Negro',[15] the 'fellow-worker'[16] is ever-present. Hence, it is my task here to present Wojtyla's philosophical analysis of the 'other', of the 'neighbour', as being revelatory of *how* we are persons in the first place. In other words, we can discover in the encounter with the 'other' what it is, that is the irreducible kernel of human personhood.

Wojtylan philosophical awakenings to the paradigm of the 'neighbour'

Schmitz affirms that it is in the final chapter of *The Acting Person* that Wojtyla takes up 'the topic of interpersonal relations and of participation in community with others'.[17] Numerous commentators notice that it is here that Wojtyla begins to develop and extend 'the meaning of the term and reality of the neighbour'.[18] In an article written in 1979, entitled: 'Community of persons in the thought of K. Wojtyla', Alfred Wilder notes 'a new emphasis on the notion of personal community' in what he calls Wojtyla's 'most recent major philosophical work, *Person and Act*'.[19]

As mentioned already in chapter 1, the early writings of the 'Wojtyla I' period include *Collected Poems*, *The Collected Plays and Writings on Theater*, *Love and Responsibility*,[20] *The Acting Person* and the collection of essays contained in *Person and Community*.[21] Wilder considers the essays 'Person: Subject and Community', published in 1976, and 'Participation or Alienation', in 1977, that are contained in *Person and Community*, as a development of what is already to be found in *The Acting Person*. In *The Acting Person* Wojtyla writes:

> the notion of *neighbor* forces us not only to recognize but also appreciate . . . in him something that is far more absolute. The notion of neighbor is strictly related to man as such and to the value itself of the person regardless of any of his relations to one or another community or to society.[22]

---

[15]   Wojtyla, *Collected Poems*, p. 116.
[16]   Wojtyla, *Easter Vigil*, p. 32.
[17]   Schmitz, *Center of the Human Drama*, p. 86.
[18]   Schmitz, *Center of the Human Drama*, p. 88.
[19]   Alfred Wilder, OP, 'Community of persons in the thought of Karol Wojtyla', *Angelicum*, 56 (1979), pp. 211–12.
[20]   Karol Wojtyla, *Love and Responsibility*, tr. H. T. Willets (London: Collins, 1981).
[21]   Karol Wojtyla, *Person and Community*, *Selected Essays*, tr. Theresa Sandok (New York: Lang, 1993).
[22]   Wojtyla, *Acting Person*F5Yp. 349–50.

Hence, a philosophical exploration of the significance of the *neighbour/other* can actually help us specify and unfold a more adequate philosophy of the human person.

The German philosopher, Hans-Georg Gadamer, in a conference on the future of Europe, gave some hermeneutical advice, relevant to the present theme. He advised: 'we have to learn to stop before the other as other . . . we have to understand the other and others as the other of ourselves, in order to participate one with the other.'[23]

Gadamer's recommendation is that the '*other*' be taken account of not just as *other than me* but also as the *other of me*.[24] The fundamental task of man whether it is on the micro or macro levels, he sees as 'Living with the other, as other of other . . . How we learn to live as one with the other, as we develop and enter into life, is so to speak, valid also for the great associations of humanity, for peoples and for states.'[25]

Wojtyla has analogous concerns when he speaks of 'acting together with others'. He underlines the importance of

> coordinating acting and being 'together with others' so as to protect the fundamental and privileged position of the 'neighbor' . . . our concern must be to make the system of reference to the neighbor the ultimate criterion in the development of the coexistence and cooperation of men in the communities and societies.[26]

We can, I would argue, discern a correlation between Wojtyla's analysis of human action as revelatory of the person and the concept of the 'neighbour' as a paradigm disclosing the philosophical reality of the person.

The philosophy of the other

There is undoubtedly an affinity between the Wojtylan concern for the 'neighbour' and the new insights apparently discovered by the so-called philosophers of the 'other'.[27] In a Levinasian sense the various

---

[23]   Cited in Gennaro Cicchese, *I Percorsi dell'Altro: Anthropologia e Storia* (Rome: Città Nuova, 1999), p. 21.

[24]   Cicchese, *I Percorsi dell'Altro*, p. 21.

[25]   Cicchese, *I Percorsi dell'Altro*, pp. 21–2.

[26]   Wojtyla, *Acting Person*, p. 298.

[27]   There is a rich literature on the philosophy of the 'Other'. We could classify Buber, Marcel, Mounier, Levinas and Wojtyla as philosophers of the 'other'. Hans Urs von Balthasar's thought develops along similar lines. He gives a phenomenological analysis of the mother–child relationship. He writes: 'man exists only in dialogue

philosophies of nihilism, personalism, deconstructionism, and of otherness can be seen as clearing the site for an adequate philosophy of the human person. In *Otherwise Than Being,* Levinas[28] contends that 'modern antihumanism, which denies the primacy that the human person [has for itself] . . . clears the place for subjectivity positing itself in abnegation, in sacrifice, in a substitution which precedes the will'.[29] Thus there are within anti-humanism seeds of veracity. One such truth consists in the claim that the subject can no longer support itself by denying its need of others. In Levinasian language, 'the imperialism of the ego'[30] is over. Reminiscent of various Wojtylan insights on the neighbour, Levinas writes: 'the fact that the other, my neighbour, is also a third party with respect to another, who is also neighbour, is the birth of thought, consciousness, justice and philo-sophy'.[31] In short, the other is other because they are totally other. Moreover, for Wojtyla the notion of neighbour contains the capability of the person 'participating in the *very humanity of others*'.[32] Humanity here understood by Wojtyla is not a generalization or abstraction 'but possesses the specific gravity of the personal being in each man'.[33] Wojtyla clearly acknowledges the need for attention to the 'new element' of the 'other' and sees the presentation given in *The Acting Person* as incomplete.[34] To this end he develops the concept in further writings and this I will examine in due course.

---

with his neighbour . . . The "I" is always indebted to a "we".' Cited in *Hans Urs von Balthasar: His Life and Work*, ed. David L. Schindler (San Francisco: Ignatius Press, 1991), pp. 3, 239.

[28] As Pope John Paul II, Karol Wojtyla started in August 1983 a biennial series of summer humanities conferences at Castel Gandolfo. In 1983 the participants included philosophers like Hans-Georg Gadamer, Charles Taylor and Emmanuel Levinas. Weigel notes: 'John Paul had known Emmanuel Levinas, the French Jewish philosopher of dialogue and intellectual heir of Martin Buber, prior to being elected Pope, and had a great respect for his work.' George Weigel, *Witness to Hope: The Biography of Pope John Paul II* (New York: HarperCollins, 1999), p. 467.

[29] Emmanuel Levinas, *Otherwise than Being, or Beyond Essence*, tr. Alphonso Lingis (Pittsburg: Duquesne University Press, 1999), pp. 127–8.

[30] Levinas, *Otherwise than Being*, p. 128.

[31] Ibid.

[32] Wojtyla, *Acting Person*, p. 294. The English text uses the word 'humanness' but in the Italian text the word is 'umanità' which translates as 'humanity'. Cf. *Persona e atto*, p. 683.

[33] Karol Wojtyla, 'The Person: Subject and Community', in *Person and Community*, p. 237.

[34] Wojtyla, 'The Person', p. 236.

A more detailed reading of the Wojtylan thematization of the human person

It is somewhat frustrating that Wojtyla does not preface chapter 7 of *The Acting Person* with a synopsis for the reader of the philosophical analysis of the person that has taken place earlier in the work. Hence, I think it useful here to summarize briefly what Wojtyla is speaking about when he speaks of adding 'one more element to the previously constructed and outlined whole'.[35] What is it that he has already outlined? All the previous chapters in *The Acting Person* have sought to lead to a retrieval of the human person as *suppositum*, that is, to the real individual substance that each human being is. The emphasis in this earlier part of his study is upon the individual human person, thus, the 'other' is not as yet the focus of the enquiry.

To the question '*How* do I know that a human being is a person?' Wojtyla would answer that if we describe the lived experience of the human being, and seek then to interpret it in terms of a metaphysics of the real, we can reach through to the core of the person. The difficulty of course, is to avoid all the philosophical culs-de-sac along the way, like for example, 'hypostatizing consciousness and making it into a subject all by itself without grounding it in anything further'.[36] Wojtyla claims that the right method and analysis can, as observed earlier in this book, retrieve what is unique in man.

Phenomenological x-ray

Wojtyla says of the traditional Boethian[37] definition of the human being as a person, as in, '*rationalis naturae individua substantia*', that it articulated the individuality of the human being as a substantial being with a rational nature, rather than the distinctiveness of the subjectivity indispensable to the human being as a person. This traditional perspective, therefore, marks 'out the "metaphysical terrain" – the dimension of being – in which personal human subjectivity is realized, creating, in a sense, a condition for "building upon" this terrain on the basis of experience'.[38] The 'metaphysical site' Wojtyla refers to, is the abstraction of the definition 'rational animal', or 'individual

[35] Wojtyla, 'The Person', p. 261.
[36] Simpson, *Karol Wojtyla*, p. 10.
[37] Boethius, a Roman philosopher and theologian (*c.* 475/480–524).
[38] Wojtyla, *Person and Community*, p. 212.

substance of a rational nature'. He sees this as useful and indispensable, but incomplete as noetically unrealistic. This is where he sees
the place for the incorporation of phenomenology into the philosophical
methodology.

If we phenomenologically x-ray lived human experience, we can
in fact successfully come up with a coherent philosophy of the person.
When we do this, Wojtyla observes, the self that comes to the surface
'is neither substance nor accident but the two fused together . . . in a
single experience of self-possession'.[39] Wojtyla holds that we must
pause at the irreducible, that is, 'at the unique presence of the self to
itself in lived experience'.[40] The human person as *suppositum* is in
fact, directly given 'in our experience of ourselves; it is taken up into
that experience and becomes part of it'.[41] Kant and Scheler correctly
diagnosed the importance of consciousness, for an adequate account
of the human person. However, although identifying the role of consciousness, they fail 'to locate [it] in the real human suppositum, the
real human person, who exists alongside other real supposita'.[42]

Self-determination

Wojtyla's emphasis for most of *The Acting Person* is upon 'I act'.
This is, he carefully points out, 'without obscuring the intersubjectivity
that is needed for the understanding and interpretation of human
acting'.[43] His lengthy analysis and description of 'I act' leads him to
observe that the 'I' that acts in the human person is fundamentally
free and self-determining. 'Self-determination' is the relation in which
the 'I will' is seen as essential to the person. In this experience 'the
will manifests itself as an essential of the person, whose ability to
perform actions derives directly from the possession of this essential
rather than from some inherent feature of the action performed by the
person'.[44] It is the person 'who manifests himself in the will and not
that the will is manifested in or by the person'.[45] We can discern here
Wojtyla's personalistic realism in not wanting to detach or hypostatize
the 'I will' from the reality of the person. It is this self-becoming of

[39] Wojtyla, *Person and Community*, p. 15.
[40] Wojtyla, *Person and Community*, p. 16.
[41] Ibid.
[42] Wojtyla, *Person and Community*, p. 21.
[43] Wojtyla, *Acting Person*, p. 60.
[44] Wojtyla, *Acting Person*, p. 105.
[45] Ibid.

the person that Wojtyla asserts can be 'disclosed in a phenomenological way'.[46]

Wojtyla proceeds to analyse the self's free self-determination in the 'I act'.[47] It is an exploration of 'how an I can be an I'.[48] Self-determination reveals the structure of self-governance and self-possession as essential to the human person.[49] Self-possession and self-governance are two co-essential principles of the person. We cannot determine what we do not possess or what is not within our control to decide.

Exempla gratiae

I think we could profit here from the use of an example taken from world literature. The writings of Alexander Solzhenitsyn go far beyond a mere analysis of the Russian tragedy, as they are 'also an effort to explore through the medium of literature fundamental historical and philosophical questions'.[50] He gives us a historical reminder of the dangers for society at large of an unbalanced philosophy of the person that does not comprehend the importance of the principle of 'self-determination', the responsibility of decision in human experience. In *August 1914* we see the Russian leaders trying to climb from underneath the rubble of their own *hubris* and failure. However, among the officers Solzhenitsyn describes the staff Colonel George Vorotyntsev as having 'never suffered from an exaggerated respect of persons, and never less than now. He spoke of corps commanders as though they were inefficient platoon leaders whom he could remove.'[51]

The Battle of Tannenberg had been disastrous for Russia. The regime needed a scapegoat to blame for the collapse at the hands of the Germans. That person was found in General A. V. Samsonov.[52] As Solzhenitsyn describes, the officers gathered together in the 'Quarter-master-General's department' argued that the debacle 'was

---

[46]   Ibid.
[47]   Cf. 'The Personal Structure of Self-Determination', in *Acting Person*, ch. 3, pp. 105–48.
[48]   Simpson, *Karol Wojtyla*, p. 25.
[49]   Wojtyla, *Acting Person*, p. 106.
[50]   Daniel J. Mahoney, *Aleksandr Solzhenitsyn: The Ascent from Ideology* (New York: Rowman & Littlefield Publishers, 2001), p. 66.
[51]   Alexander Solzhenitsyn, *August 1914*, tr. H. T. Willetts (New York: Farrar & Giroux, 1989), p. 774.
[52]   See chapter 82 of *August 1914*, pp. 784–95.

entirely the fault of General Samsonov'.[53] In reaction to General Zhilinsky's further castigation of Samsonov, Vorotyntsev writhes and fumes and can take no more. Contained within Vorotyntsev's attempts at unmasking the lies behind the generals is the insight that the breakdown in Russian society in terms of 'self-determination' reaches, in fact, from the lower levels right up to the Tsar. General Zhilinsky is described by Vorotyntsev as 'this Living Corpse',[54] in other words, he is even less than a person, in that he refuses to take responsibility for 'I act' with respect to the military catastrophe. Vorotyntsev seeks to expose the deception being perpetrated with regard to personal responsibility and efficacy. In the scene before the officers and the Grand Duke, Solzhenitsyn describes how 'Vorotyntsev . . . lost his patience, retorted in a voice full of hatred: "Under the convention Russia promised to give 'resolute aid', not to commit suicide! It was you who signed Russia's suicide note, Your Excellency!"'[55]

It is interesting to note that General Vorotyntsev is actually a fictional hero in Solzhenitsyn's writings. But the reality of disintegration with regard to 'self-determination' in Russia is, according to Solzhenitsyn, historical and real. Vorotyntsev's character is perhaps fictive because the characteristic of 'self-determination' on the personal and social levels had been anesthetized within the Russian experience. Thus, the hero Vorotyntsev can be seen as a paradigm of what it means to re-awaken to the reality of the 'I act', the 'I will' of the human person.

In *August 1914*, when the Tsar learns of the military calamity endured by the Russian army, he sends a telegram to the Grand Duke, and in it we can discern a certain state of mind, a kind of 'pietistic fatalism'[56] when he comments: 'we must submit to the will of God [the destruction of the Russian army]'.[57] There is clearly no sense of personal efficacy even at the highest levels. The dialogue between Vorotyntsev and general Svechin reveals how the disintegration in respect to 'self-determination' permeates the Russian military command. Svechin argues that in apportioning blame it should be remembered that

[53] Solzhenitsyn, *August 1914*, pp. 784–5.
[54] Solzhenitsyn, *August 1914*, p. 785.
[55] Solzhenitsyn, *August 1914*, p. 794.
[56] Mahoney, *Aleksandr Solzhenitsyn*, p. 94 n. 6.
[57] Solzhenitsyn, *August 1914*, p. 776.

'Yes, but it was the Grand Duke, if you remember, who gave the order
to cross the frontier on 14th August . . . Zhilinsky actually asked for a
postponement. He himself thought that the offensive was doomed.'
Vorotyntsev's light grey eyes flashed fire. 'So he shouldn't have carried
out the order! He should have had the courage to speak his mind!
And refuse!' 'Now you're asking rather a lot', said Svechin, almost
laughing.[58]

The whole tragedy that unfolds in Solzhenitsyn's writing is that
this failure on the personal level sets off a systemic breakdown that is
evidenced on the societal level. Edward Ericson, observes that 'the
primacy of the person underlies the very structure of Solzhenitsyn's
novels'.[59] Man's 'self-determination' can be effectual, that is, it matters
to himself as a person but also to others. In other words 'individuals
can change history, they are not pawns swept along by huge historical
forces outside their control. Persons can make a difference'.[60] Brendan
Purcell, in his work *The Drama of Humanity: Towards a Philosophy
of Humanity in History*,[61] adverts to the importance of personal efficacy
in Solzhenitsyn's works and that the drama of humanity occurs on the
personal, social and historical levels. He writes:

> It's not surprising, then, that he [Solzhenitsyn] can consider the whole
> of Russia as being confronted by the kind of tragic decision on which
> a people's fate will turn, like King Pelasgos' reflection in the *Suppliant
> Maidens*, of whether 'to act or not to act'.[62]

Lonergan describes how Aeschylus the Greek dramatist depicts just
one thing in *The Suppliants*, and that is 'a decision'. In the play the
daughters of Danaus are fleeing from the Egyptian youths. They seek
asylum on an island where Pelasgos is King. Lonergan observes:

> [T]he whole play is the decision of the king to risk war with the
> Egyptians by giving asylum to the maidens. In other words, the play
> consists in objectifying, in setting before one's eyes as a spectacle, the
> inner process of deciding, of making a choice. Free will is a property
> of man, but it is one thing to have a free will, and it is another to be

[58] Solzhenitsyn, *August 1914*, pp. 778–9.
[59] Edward E. Ericson, *Solzhenitsyn and the Modern World* (Washington, DC: Regnery
      Gateway, 1993), p. 33.
[60] Ericson, *Solzhenitsyn*, p. 35.
[61] (Peter Lang: Frankfurt am Main, 1996).
[62] Purcell, *Drama of Humanity*, p. 193.

able to think about one's own free will as one does about any other object. To take that step was an achievement of Greek tragedy.[63]

It is a mistake to judge earlier writings by later insights but we can discern throughout history outbreaks of the search for the truth of reality, and this can be seen also in the differentiations of insight leading towards an adequate philosophy of the human person. What Wojtyla seeks to explore is the structure of self-determination, and firstly on the personal level. Indeed, Simpson regards Wojtyla's analysis of self-determination as 'the most pregnant of his phenomenological elaborations'.[64] While Wojtyla gives us a philosophical thematization of this theme in terms of the individual, it is only in chapter 7 of *The Acting Person* that he comes to the philosophical significance of the reality of working out 'self-determination' in terms of acting together-with-others. An ample philosophical account must be inclusive of the fact that man lives 'together with other men', and indeed we may even go so far as to say that he exists together with other men.[65]

The Jeweller's Shop: A dramatic-philosophic articulation of the 'new element'

In his dramas, Wojtyla gives us further *exempla gratiae* in regard to the theme of the 'other'. In *The Jeweller's Shop*, Teresa and Andrew, the first couple in the play, know that their decision to become lifelong companions penetrates their existence 'like a weaver's shuttle, to catch the weft that determines a fabric's pattern'.[66] Even the noun used here, 'weft', is suggestive of the notion of participation. The Concise Oxford Dictionary defines it as 'cross-threads woven into warp to make a web'. The web here in this drama is, of course, the web of interpersonal relationships. Andrew speaks about his deep reflection upon one's 'other self' when he says:

> I thought much at the time about the 'alter ego'.
> Teresa was a whole world, just as distant as any other man, as any other woman
> – and yet there was something that allowed one to think of throwing a bridge.

[63] Bernard Lonergan, *Collected Works of Bernard Lonergan: Philosophical and Theological Papers 1958–1964*, Vol. 6 (London: University of Toronto Press, 1996), p. 246.
[64] Simpson, *Karol Wojtyla*, p. 27.
[65] Wojtyla, *Acting Person*, p. 262.
[66] Wojtyla, *The Jeweller's Shop*, in *Collected Plays*, p. 280.

I let that thought run on, and even develop within me.
It was not an assent independent of an act of will.
I simply resisted sensation and the appeal of the senses,
For I knew that otherwise I would never really leave my 'ego'
and reach the other person – but that meant an effort.[67]

Wojtyla seeks, of course, to make a similar effort to reach the heart of
the significance of the 'other' in his subsequent philosophical works.
Andrew also endeavours to do this when he describes how he:

decided then to seek a woman who would be indeed
my real 'alter ego' so that the bridge between us
would not be a shaky footbridge among water lilies and reeds.[68]

The 'shaky footbridge' between the 'I' and the 'Other' occurs when
there is a failure to articulate an adequate philosophy of the person
that takes into account the full reality of participation. Otherwise, as
Wojtyla clearly outlines in *The Acting Person* there is the danger of
'totalism' and or 'individualism'. Andrew in the play adverts to the
same problematic in the unfolding drama of life, that is, of deciding to
stay locked up in his own solipsistic self or making the choice to throw
a bridge to the 'other'. If not, he would run the risk of never really
leaving his own ego.[69] Buttiglione speaks of how Andrew's discovery
of the 'other'

lifts this man [Andrew] out of his existential solitude and allows him
to picture the bridge which will join his own unfathomable personal
depth with that of the other. The other becomes like the road toward
his own destiny, which allows his true self to emerge and to become
self-aware. In the encounter with the other, the experience of love
liberates the man, releasing what was implicit and unknown to him
and manifesting it to all. Whoever does not live this encounter dies
without coming out of himself, that is, without his original grandeur
ever having the power to manifest and to realize itself.[70]

Nevertheless, Wojtyla remarks that 'in acting together with others'
human actions can be limited in two ways. There may firstly 'be a
lack of participation caused by the person as the subject-agent of

[67] Wojtyla, *Collected Plays*, p. 280.
[68] Wojtyla, *Collected Plays*, p. 281.
[69] Ibid.
[70] Rocco Buttiglione, *Karol Wojtyla, The Thought of the Man who became Pope John Paul II*, tr. Paolo Giuetti and Francesca Murphy (Grand Rapids: Eerdmans, 1997), p. 253.

acting', that is, 'individualism', secondly, 'participation may become impossible for reasons external to the person and resulting from defects in the system according to which the entire community of acting operates'.[71] The latter system Wojtyla terms 'totalism' or 'anti-individualism'.[72] He comments that

> each of the two systems or trends – whether it be individualism or objective totalism – tends in different ways to limit participation either directly, as a possibility or an ability to be actualized in acting 'together with others', or indirectly, as that feature which is of the essence of the person and which corresponds to his existing 'together with others', his living in a community.[73]

Individualism is in his words a denial of participation 'since it isolates the person from others by conceiving him solely as an individual who concentrates on himself and on his own good'.[74] This is evidently the notion at the root of the Hobbesian analysis of the person. Eric Voegelin in his exploration of the Hobbesian project outlines the inherent dangers in the anthropological principle that states 'society is man written in large letters'.[75] He notes:

> Hobbes insisted that any order would do if it secured the existence of society. In order to make his conception valid he had to create his *new idea of man* [own emphasis]. Human nature would have to find fulfillment in existence itself; a purpose beyond existence [transcendence] would have to be denied.[76]

Hobbes was then faced with the difficulty 'of constructing an order of society out of isolated individuals who are not oriented towards a common purpose but only motivated by their individual passions'.[77]

Wojtyla adjudges that the conception of the human being under-lying 'totalism' and 'individualism' to be '"impersonalistic" or "anti-personalistic", inasmuch as the distinctive personalistic approach is the conviction that to be a person means to be capable of

[71] Wojtyla, *Acting Person*, p. 272.
[72] Wojtyla, *Acting Person*, p. 273.
[73] Ibid.
[74] Wojtyla, *Acting Person*, pp. 273–4.
[75] Eric Voegelin, *Order and History*, Vol. 3, *Plato and Aristotle* (Baton Rouge: Louisiana State University Press, 1985), p. 69.
[76] Eric Voegelin, *The New Science of Politics* (Chicago: University of Chicago Press, 1952), p. 179.
[77] Voegelin, *New Science of Politics*, p. 180.

participation'.[78] He himself had experienced in his own lifetime how different ideologies can deny and distort the true meaning of 'participation'. Simpson notes how Poland

> like many another unfortunate country of eastern Europe, was crushed by two brutal tyrannies one after the other, Nazism and Communism. In both cases the capacity of man to sink to the level of a beast or rise to that of an angel must have been a matter of all too present observation . . . they were also ideologies. They were built on and enforced, as a matter of policy, a distinctive view of man. To oppose these tyrannies, if only in one's desires and thoughts, was to oppose a philosophy of man. It was perforce, therefore, to have or at least to want another and different philosophy of man.[79]

In 1976 Wojtyla wrote:

> The need for such understandings and justifications always accompanies humankind in its sojourn on earth . . . the present age is such a moment. It is a time of great controversy, controversy about the very meaning of existence, and thus the nature and significance of the human being . . . This aptly describes the situation in Poland today with respect to the whole political reality that has arisen out of Marxism, out of dialectical materialism, and strives to win minds over to this ideology . . . The truth about the human being, in turn, has a distinctly privileged place in this whole process, it has become clear that at the centre of this debate is not cosmology or philosophy of nature but philosophical anthropology and ethics: the great and fundamental controversy about the human being.[80]

The bridegroom Andrew in *The Jeweller's Shop* recalls the deep thoughts of the jeweller on the concept of participation on the inter-personal level. The jeweller remarks:

> 'The weight of these golden rings',
> he said, 'is not the weight of metal,
> but the proper weight of man,
> each of you separately
> and both together.
> Ah, man's own weight,
> the proper weight of man!'[81]

[78] Wojtyla, *Acting Person*, p. 275.
[79] Simpson, *Karol Wojtyla*, p. 8.
[80] Wojtyla, *Person and Community*, p. 220.
[81] Wojtyla, *Collected Plays*, p. 289.

Wojtyla uses the golden rings in the drama as a literary device and a symbol of the human reality and necessity of participation. In Act II we see Anna, whose marriage to Stefan is close to breakdown, attempting to make contact with other men and trying to sell her ring. The jeweller rejects this, protesting:

> 'This ring does not weigh anything,
> the needle does not move from zero
> and I cannot make it show
> even a milligram.
> Your husband must be alive –
> in which case neither of your rings, taken separately,
> will weigh anything – only both together register.
> My jeweller's scales
> have this peculiarity
> that they weigh not the metal
> but man's entire being and fate'.
> Ashamed, I [Anna] took the ring back
> and left the shop without a word
> I think, though, that he followed me with his eyes.[82]

The scales

As I have already observed, Wojtyla uses the methods of Thomism and phenomenology in order to balance the scales so that he weighs 'man's entire being and fate'. He thus attempts to navigate a clear course between the Scylla of a Boethian tradition that emphasizes the notion of person as an 'individual substance of a rational nature', and the Charybdis of a more phenomenological tradition that seeks only to develop the relational aspect.[83] Wojtyla is not unique in wanting to retain such a balance.

Norris Clarke in *The Aquinas Lecture* 1993 accepts Wojtyla's point in support of the need to develop a philosophical 'dynamic and relational notion of the person within the classical framework of the metaphysical'.[84] He asserts that the lack of equilibrium in the philosophy of the person is caused by a rejection among contemporary thinkers of 'substance' in favour of 'relation'. But this is because they

---

[82] Wojtyla, *Collected Plays*, pp. 297–8.
[83] Cf. Chapter 1.
[84] W. Norris Clarke, *The Aquinas Lecture: Person and Being* (Milwaukee: Marquette University Press, 1993), p. 3.

have a distorted notion of substance, that is, they have either the Cartesian, Lockean or Humean concepts of substance. These major distortions of the classical idea of substance break up 'the dynamic polarity between substance and action – plus – relations' and get submerged 'and almost forgotten in the post-medieval period from Descartes on'.[85] When this is applied to a thematization of the human person, that is, as the specific instantiation of being that is intellectually conscious being, the person runs the risk of being reduced 'to nothing but a relation or set of relations'.[86] The problem subsequently emerges that if

> the substance, or *in-itself,* pole of being is dropped out, the unique interiority and privacy of the person are wiped out also and the person turns out to be an entirely extraverted bundle of relations, with no inner self to share with others.[87]

The dilemma is, according to Clarke, to work out a 'creative integration' of the older metaphysical tradition of the person that has left the relational dimension underdeveloped and, on the other, with a more recent phenomenological tradition that has highly developed the relational aspect but lost its metaphysical grounding.[88]

Wojtyla's philosophical contribution is, I would argue, to work towards such a 'creative integration' of the two approaches so that what is disclosed is a 'complementarity of substantiality, the *in-itself* dimension' of the human person, and 'relationality, the *towards-others* aspect'.[89]

Participation defined: the ontological underpinning

Let us now examine the Wojtylan attempt at that 'creative integration' in which he attempts to give an ontological foundation to the lived human experience of the need for the 'other'. As I have remarked previously, Wojtyla understood that phenomenological description was not enough in the articulation of a comprehensive philosophy of the person. Thus, the next step in the process is an adequate interpretation of the phenomenological data concerning human action taking place

---

[85] Clarke, *Person and Being*, p. 18.
[86] Clarke, *Person and Being*, p. 19.
[87] Ibid.
[88] Clarke, *Person and Being*, p. 5.
[89] Ibid.

THE NEIGHBOUR AS PARADIGM

together-with-others. Among the canons of the KUL philosophers was the principle of the primacy of a realistic metaphysics of reality.[90] Scheler's phenomenology had definitely contributed positively towards the analysis of human experience, but at the same time he was unable 'to interpret the whole content of human experience because he rejects metaphysics as a legitimate method of interpretation. It is only through realistic ontology, Wojtyla writes, that the whole content of human experience can be properly understood'.[91]

Kupczak tells us that according to Wojtyla's analysis any phenomenological anthropology is:

> in need of a synthesis, or integration, since it divides the human person into many irreducible parts . . . this integration can be obtained only through metaphysical analysis, which is able to describe the ultimate roots of all phenomenological aspects of the human phenomenon.[92]

Thus, the Wojtylan presentation of the underlining ontological reality of participation is not a societal exploration based upon the fact that man is a social animal. If Aristotle's classic definition of man as a rational animal ran the risk perhaps, of being reductionist and cosmological, Wojtyla would equally regard a purely sociological analysis of man's 'acting together with others' as being insufficient. He writes that, 'our purpose here is not to investigate the nature of society'.[93] He wants, in fact, to keep the primary focus on confining himself 'to the acting person'. He is not interested in all the sociological implications of the person's 'acting together with others'.[94] If action is revelatory of the human person, as Wojtyla argues, then acting 'together with others' equally discloses the irreducible of the human person.[95] Being with others is, therefore, not just of sociological but also of ontological significance. This fact of universal lived human experience is not just accidental but constitutive of the human person. Acting together with others is 'not only frequent and usual, but indeed of universal occurrence'.[96] Wojtyla does not apologize for his initial starting point, that is, 'Man–acts, I act', because

---

[90] Cf. Chapter 1.
[91] Jaroslaw Kupczak, *Destined for Liberty* (Washington, DC: Catholic University of America Press, 2000), p. 62.
[92] Kupczak, *Destined for Liberty*, p. 108.
[93] Ibid.
[94] Wojtyla, *Acting Person*, p. 263.
[95] Wojtyla, *Acting Person*, p. 262.
[96] Ibid.

actions, which man performs in all different social involvements and as a member of different social groups or communities, are essentially the actions of the person. Their social or communal nature is rooted in the nature of the person and not vice versa.[97]

The Wojtylan philosophical analysis of person as a participant in community aims, therefore, 'at discovering the necessary conditions for this relation, given in an eidetic experience, and is not to be confused with the phenomenological description of man's particular living situations as presented in existential philosophy'.[98]

To be is to be substance-in-relation

An important point to clarify in the Wojtylan investigation is that our need for the 'other' derives not from any 'poverty' or 'lack' in terms of the human person but from the self-communicative 'abundance' found therein. Clarke comments that there is clearly

> an acquisitive side to our going out to others, because we are poor and seeking self-fulfilment. That is all too obvious on the human scene. But in St. Thomas's metaphysics of existential being there is also a more generous drive toward self-communication of one's own being because it is positively rich.[99]

Wojtyla is similarly at pains to stress that the person's social or communal nature is rooted, in the first place, in the metaphysical reality of the person. Underlying this is a dynamic rather than a static notion of substance, that is, to be is to be substance-in-relation. When this is applied to the human person, Wojtyla and others do not see why 'there is a need to play down the substance pole of being in order to safeguard the relational', because 'the substance itself is the active source from which flow the relations as its own self-expression'. The danger exists of seeking to absorb 'the person entirely into its relations, into its "towards-others" [and this] is to empty it of anything truly belonging to it that is worth expressing to others. There is no merit in giving oneself totally to others unless one has something to give'.[100]

[97] Wojtyla, *Acting Person*, p. 263.
[98] Elzbieta Wolicka, 'Participation in community: Wojtyla's social anthropology', *Communio*, Summer, 1981, p. 109.
[99] Clarke, *Person and Being*, p. 75.
[100] W. Norris Clarke, *Explorations in Metaphysics: Being – God – Person* (Notre Dame, IN: University of Notre Dame Press, 1994), p. 117.

This points to the essential characteristic of 'self-possession' as outlined by Wojtyla in *The Acting Person*.[101] Modern phenomenology risks running aground when it fails to explore the metaphysical roots of what it describes in 'relationality'. That is why Wojtyla and others speak of the necessity of the metaphysical interpretation of 'relationality'. Wojtyla writes:

> what interests phenomenologists is not what a thing is in itself, but how something manifests itself to us in immediate experience. Phenomenologists do not have the kind of cognitive ambitions that Aristotelians and Thomists have – they do not give priority to the philosophy of being.[102]

In the modern treatment of the person Wojtyla discerns that the 'I' loses its metaphysical footing because it becomes 'absolutized' and 'subjectivitized'. In this view 'the person is not a substance, an objective being with its own proper subsistence – subsistence in a rational nature'. This is, he remarks,

> a completely different treatment from the one we find in St. Thomas ... [He] gives us an excellent view of the objective existence and activity of the person, but [and here Wojtyla shows his critical realist credentials] it would be difficult to speak in his view of the lived experience of the person.[103]

The 'missing-link' in the modern treatment of the person is the failure to erect a bridge between the '*how*' (phenomenological) and the '*what*' (metaphysical) of the human person. Wojtyla's introduction and analysis of the paradigm of the 'neighbour' is an attempt to bridge the chasm between the two, the phenomenological and metaphysical traditions in terms of the human person. The fact that I have to address the 'other' and his or her philosophical significance opens up an opportunity for further reflection on the problematic. In fact, what emerges from the Wojtylan investigation

> is that by probing the selfhood of the person we attain to a vastly deeper level ... for we attain to the level at which the person has dignity, ontological nobility, and even to the level at which we find that

---

[101] Wojtyla, *Acting Person*, pp. 106–7.
[102] Wojtyla, *Person and Community*, p. 33.
[103] Wojtyla, *Acting Person*, pp. 170–1.

preciousness in a person that can awaken the love of another [that is, the interpersonal matrix of such an experience].[104]

As we can see in *The Jeweller's Shop* Wojtyla dramatizes this for us in the characters of the engaged couple Teresa and Andrew.

Norris Clarke's elaboration

I would maintain that Norris Clarke unpacks to some extent the compact argumentation offered by Wojtyla in *The Acting Person* concerning the ontological reality of participation of the human person with others. Wojtyla, as already outlined, affirms that the communal nature of human actions relates to the reality of the person as such and not because of any sociological context. There is a correlation, I would maintain, between the Wojtylan shift in his final chapter of *The Acting Person* towards an exploration of the 'neighbour' as a paradigm for understanding the human person, and Norris Clarke's investigation in his work of the person as 'self-communicative' and relational.[105] He writes:

> A person, like every other real being, is a living synthesis of substantiality and relationality, and the relational side is equally important as the substantial side, because it is through the former that the self as substance can actualize its potentiality and fulfil its destiny. This is especially true of the human person.[106]

Not unlike Wojtyla, he speaks of how the

> sensitive phenomenological descriptions have made it clear just *how* [own emphasis] we come to the awareness of ourselves as 'I' through the reaching out of another to us who is already an 'I' and appeals to us to respond as another self, 'Thou', not merely as the stimulus-response of an impersonal thing but as another personal 'I' self-consciously and freely open to the other. Unless someone else treats me as a 'Thou' I can never wake up to myself as an 'I', as a person.[107]

Wojtyla has similarly sought in *The Acting Person* to employ a phenomenological x-ray to the human person so as to articulate and

---

[104] John F. Crosby, *The Selfhood of the Human Person* (Washington, DC: Catholic University of America Press, 1996), p. 71.

[105] Clarke, *Person and Being*, chapter 2, section 4, pp. 64ff.

[106] Clarke, *Person and Being*, p. 64.

[107] Clarke, *Person and Being*, p. 66.

contribute comprehensively to the ontological underpinning of the 'other'. Through this philosophical exploration the person's description that emerges is with the characteristics of 'self-determination', 'self-possession' and 'self-governance'. In 'acting-together-with others', that is, in 'participation', we have the actualizing of one's own 'self-determination'. The reality of 'acting-together-with-others' is the personalistc terrain in which this 'self-actualization' of the human *suppositum* occurs.

Our lived human experience brings to the fore that we act in concert with others. The philosophical question posed by this factor is: what is the correlation between this acting (that is, together-with-others) and the structure of self-determination (that is, 'I act')? Is the 'I' lost in acting with others? If it is to be authentic action it must fit in with what Wojtyla has analysed to be characteristic of human action. Acting together-with-others should not negate the actualization of one's own self-determination; on the contrary it should lead to its fulfilment. Wojtyla observes:

> To be capable of participation thus indicates that man, when he acts together with other men, retains in this acting the personalistic value of his own action and at the same time shares in the realization and the results of communal acting. Owing to this share, man, when he acts together with others, retains everything that results from the communal acting and simultaneously brings about – *in this very manner* – the personalistic value of his own action.[108]

Personalistic value involved in human action

Central to Wojtyla's thematizing of the human person is that the action of the person has a 'personalistic value'. This means that in completing an action the person simultaneously realizes himself/herself. The person carries out an action according to the requirements of 'self-determination' and realizes transcendence and integration in their many stages. This can be described as Wojtyla's general axiological principle of the human person's participation in community. It necessitates 'openness in truth' and it is what shows forth the worth of the person. Schmitz gives a concise and insightful summary of Wojtyla's analysis of this topic when he writes:

---

[108] Wojtyla, *Acting Person*, p. 269.

The personalistic value of human action is constituted by the following factors: (1) performance by the person, (2) in a manner appropriate to his or her nature, and so (3) according to self-determination through capacity for reflection, reflexivity, practical reason, and the decisive will. In authentic action the person realizes (4) the transcendence uniquely and properly his or hers, while at the same time (5) advancing integration of both *soma* and *psyche*, (6) in an efficacious way that satisfies the requirement of both the subjective and objective sides of that being which in its entirety is at once human and personal.[109]

Thus, for Wojtyla the value of the person is more fundamental than the action. In man's 'acting-together-with-others', a man should be able to act freely and at the same time experience himself in relationship with others. To quote Wojtyla again on this, the necessary condition of participation is that 'when he acts together with other men, [he must retain] in this acting the personalistic value of his own action and at the same time [participate] in the realization and the results of communal acting'.[110]

The 'Neighbour' as revelatory of the full significance of participation

Wojtyla states clearly in *The Acting Person* that 'the notion of "neighbour" brings out at last the full significance of that specific reality which from the beginning of this chapter [that is, chapter 7] we have been referring to as "participation"'.[111] As various commentators[112] have stated, this part[113] in Wojtyla's *opus* is perhaps his most novel, and yet the least worked out of his philosophical elaborations with respect to the human person. Schmitz comments on how Wojtyla begins to develop and extend 'the meaning of the term and reality of the neighbour'.[114] Williams explains that in 1976 when Wojtyla was 'revising *The Acting* Person . . . he was also developing further the thoughts expressed in chapter seven'.[115] This development appears in

---

[109] Schmitz, *Center of the Human Drama*, p. 88.
[110] Wojtyla, *Acting Person*, p. 269.
[111] Wojtyla, *Acting Person*, p. 294.
[112] Cf. Alfred Wilder, 'Community of Persons in the thought of Karol Wojtyla', *Angelicum*, 56 (1979), pp. 213ff.
[113] Wojtyla, *Acting Person*, pp. 292ff.
[114] Schmitz, *Center of the Human Drama*, p. 88.
[115] George Huntston Williams, *The Mind of John Paul II: Origins of his Thought and Action* (New York: Seabury Press, 1981), p. 216.

the essay 'The Person: Subject and Community'.[116] Williams comments that this essay 'might well serve as an introduction to the core of the author's [Wojtyla] philosophical thought, as he rehearses the main ideas of his whole book in part one of the article before proceeding to expand on its last chapter'.[117] Andrzej Szostek affirms that

> The analysis of participation, arising from the entire perspective of the vision of man which is sketched out in *The Acting Person*, shows how the reference to others as neighbours and not as rivals has an essentially personalistic meaning ... We must constantly and diligently purify the way we see man in such a way as to be able to perceive to what extent man is a person and fulfils himself as a person, along with the entire structure of self-determination which is proper to him. This can be done only through the 'reference system of the neighbour'.[118]

I will now concentrate on the 'neighbour' in *The Acting Person* and in Wojtyla's subsequent essays.[119]

Fellow member and neighbour

Wojtyla affirms that participation can be considered in relation to two complementary systems of reference. One system is related to the concept of membership in a community and the other to that of neighbour. Wojtyla writes:

> neighbor and member of a community are two different notions each representing different forms and different reference systems, because to be and to 'act together with others' places man within the range of diverse relations. The terms 'neighbor' and 'member of a community' (society) may help to bring order into these relations or reference systems and thereby lead to a better and more accurate understanding of the idea of participation. Indeed, 'participation' itself means one thing when it refers to a member of a community and something else when it refers to a neighbor.[120]

---

[116] Wojtyla, 'The Person: Subject and Community', in *Person and Community*, pp. 219–61.

[117] Ibid.

[118] Andrzej Szostek, 'Karol Wojtyla's View of the Human Person in the Light of the Experience of Morality', *Proceedings of the American Philosophical Association*, 60 (1986), p. 61.

[119] Cf. the following essays, written by Wojtyla subsequent to the publication of *The Acting Person*: 'Participation or Alienation?', 'Subjectivity and the Irreducible in the Human Being', and 'The Person: Subject and Community', contained in *Person and Community*.

[120] Wojtyla, *Acting Person*, p. 293.

For Wojtyla the notion of neighbour is more fundamental than that of 'member of a community'. In fact 'membership of any community presupposes that men are neighbours'.[121] But membership of a community, as such, does not constitute nor abolish the fact of being a neighbour. Wojtyla describes how 'People are or become members of different communities; in these communities they either establish close relations or they remain strangers – the latter reflects a lack of the communal spirit – but they are all neighbours and never cease to be neighbours.'[122] Thus, he adjudges the primary system of reference to be the 'neighbour'. The deepest root of participation is not the ability to take part in this or that particular community but the capacity to share, as man, the humanity of other human beings. Wojtyla contends that 'the ability to share in the humanity itself of every man is the very core of all participation and the condition of the personalistic value of all acting and existing "together with others"'.[123] He argues that it is not enough to be a member of one or more communities because we are also called upon to be 'neighbours'. In other words to be a neighbour is also a task. He is careful in his analysis not to reduce the terms 'neighbour' and 'member of a community' to the reality of 'interhuman relations' and 'social relations' respectively. He writes:

> we are not to assume, moreover, that the system of reference denoted by the term 'neighbor' is the basis of all interhuman relations or that 'member of a community' refers to the basis of social relations. Such an interpretation would be superficial and insufficient. The two systems of reference do not overlap and interpenetrate only in the objective order, which shows every neighbor as belonging to a community and every member of a community as a neighbor, but also in the subjective order of participation. We have presented in this respect participation as a dynamic enactment of the person. Enactment, which is the person's essential feature, is manifested in that performance of actions 'together with others', in that cooperation and coexistence which simultaneously serves the fulfilment of the person. Participation is closely associated with both the community and the personalistic value. This is precisely why it cannot be manifested solely by membership in some community but through membership must reach to the humanity of every man. Only because of the share in humanity itself, which is indicated in the

[121] Ibid.
[122] Ibid.
[123] Wojtyla, *Acting Person*, p. 295.

notion of neighbor, does the dynamic property of participation attain
its personal depth as well as universal dimension.[124]

The ethical expansion of participation: the commandment of love

Having examined the phenomenological analysis of the person and
its ontological underpinnings we can now expand the theory of
participation onto the ethical level. I intend by the ethical not merely
an abstract idea but 'an existential reality of the person who creates
himself'.[125] The ethical is about the 'becoming' of the whole human
person and cannot be sidelined purely into an aspect of consciousness.
Hence, any adequate account of participation will necessarily entail
an ethical expansion of the notion. If Wojtyla has sought to interpret
philosophically *how* a human being is a person, then the real, lived
human experience of *how* I can actualize that in acting together-with-
others is equally as important in order to achieve a comprehensive
philosophical understanding of personhood. Wojtyla attempts to
recapture the reality of the human act and its metaphysical significance
for the human person. He observes that by

> 'becoming' – the Latin *fieri*– we mean that aspect of human dynamism
> – whether it is the aspect of man's acting[126] or the aspect of what happens
> in him – which is centered on man himself, the subject of this dynamism,
> insofar as it introduces or carries on a process of change. In point of
> fact, in all dynamizations the subject does not remain indifferent: not
> only does it participate in them, as demonstrated to some extent above,
> but it is itself in one way or another formed or transformed by them.
> (At this point we touch upon the inner structure of the life-process
> itself.)[127]

Wojtyla deems that when the 'human being acts' in a self-conscious
way (*agere*), 'then each of his or her conscious acts is an ethical

[124] Wojtyla, *Acting Person*, pp. 294–5.
[125] Kupczak, *Destined for Liberty*, p. 111.
[126] Wojtyla makes an important distinction in regard to 'happening' in the human person.
There are two aspects, 'man-acts' (*agere*) and 'something-happens-in-man' (*pati*).
Cf. *Acting Person*, p. 80. Apply this important distinction to human love and you
can understand that 'true love does not just happen [*pati*] in the person but involves
an experience of being an efficient cause of the act of love' (cf. Kupczak, *Destined
for Liberty*, p. 46).
[127] Wojtyla, *Acting Person*, p. 96.

experience'.[128] To describe phenomenologically the lived experience of such human acts is one thing, and this focuses 'only on what happens in the person while performing an action [*pati*]'.[129] We must, however, also explore 'what happens to the person through the act that person consciously performs'.[130] Wojtyla concludes:

> [W]hat happens to the person is that the person himself or herself *becomes* good or bad depending on the act performed. And the becoming good or bad of the person through the performance of a conscious action is what constitutes the essential core of ethical experience. This becoming of the person also belongs to the totality of experience: the person *experiences* his or her ethical becoming.

Any realistic ontology will therefore, take into account the fact that 'I act' together-with-others. 'I act' together-with-others who are 'neighbours'. Here I anticipate the next section in this book; the neighbour is another 'I'. If the 'other' is 'neighbour' it means they are also 'person'. This is the totality of human becoming and any explanation must seek to arrive at an understanding of participation that is inclusive of my 'sharing in the humanness of every man'.[131] It is here and in answer to the question '*How* can I become a fully realized person and participate with others?' that Wojtyla introduces the concept of 'the evangelical commandment of love',[132] that is, 'Love your neighbour as yourself' (Matt. 19:19). The argumentation here is in no way religious. It is strictly philosophical. Of course, for the religious believer it gives a unique reading of the evangelical commandment, but that is not Wojtyla's primary intention. His philosophical development of the theme affords the opportunity for believer and non-believer alike to enter into the dynamic. He stresses that the exclusive object of his reflections are to 'emphasize the confirmation [that the commandment of love] contains for our claim that the reference system centred on "thy neighbour" has crucial significance in any acting and existing "together with others" '.[133]

Simpson gives an insightful commentary in relation to this final section of *The Acting Person*. He notes how

---

[128] Wojtyla, *Person and Community*, p. 19.
[129] Ibid.
[130] Wojtyla, *Person and Community*, p. 20.
[131] Wojtyla, *Acting Person*, p. 295.
[132] Ibid.
[133] Wojtyla, *Acting Person*, p. 295.

we must recognize that the idea of love of neighbor has a philosophical and phenomenological foundation too. It is something that can be recognized from within our experience of the personhood of ourselves and others. It expresses a special attitude of regard that we should have towards every person simply because of the fact of their personhood. Every person should be treated as a person and not as a means for furthering one's own interests. Love of neighbor is in fact the necessary basis for any community that is to be human, and for any relation to a member of a particular community. Without it there arises the phenomenon of what Wojtyla calls alienation . . . The fundamental source of alienation is disregard of the command to love one's neighbors, one's fellow human beings, in all their fullness.[134]

As I have proposed, Wojtyla is unafraid of the philosophical analysis of any human experience. There is ample proof of this attitude in his various literary texts. The fundamental universal human experience is that of love. Adam in Wojtyla's play, *The Jeweller's Shop* analyses human love with great insight, saying:

This is just what compels me to think about human love. There is no other matter embedded more strongly in the surface of human life, and there is no matter more unknown and mysterious. The divergence between what lies on the surface and the mystery of love constitutes precisely the source of drama. It is one of the greatest dramas of human existence. The surface of love has its current – swift, flickering, changeable. A kaleidoscope of waves and situations full of attraction. This current is sometimes so stunning that it carries people away – women and men. They get carried away by the thought that they have absorbed the whole secret of love, but in fact they have not yet even touched it. They are happy for a while, thinking they have reached the limits of existence and wrested all its secrets from it, so that nothing remains. That's how it is: on the other side of that rapture nothing remains, there is nothing left behind it. But there can't be nothing, there can't! Listen to me, there can't. Man is a *continuum*, a totality and a continuity – so it cannot be that nothing remains.[135]

In a somewhat similar vein, Shakespeare's *King Lear* can be interpreted as an exploration into the nature of filial love. Lear encourages his favourite daughter Cordelia, to speak up and make the choice for him in the love-test he sets for her and her sisters, Goneril and Reagan. Cordelia responds by protesting:

[134] Simpson, *Karol Wojtyla*, pp. 44–5.
[135] Wojtyla, *Collected Plays*, pp. 301–3.

> Now must my Love, in Words, fall short of theirs
> As much as it exceeds in Truth – Nothing, my Lord.

Lear chides Cordelia and retorts:

> Nothing can come of Nothing, speak agen [again].[136]

So too, Adam's final speech, in *The Jeweller*'s *Shop*, centres on the choice open to all in terms of human love. He observes:

> [S]ometimes human existence seems too short for love. At other times it is, however, the other way around: human love seems too short in relation to existence – or rather, too trivial. At any rate, every person has at his disposal an existence and a Love. The problem is: How to build a sensible structure from it?

But this structure must never be inward-looking. It must be open in such a way that on the one hand it embraces other people, while on the other, it always reflects the absolute Existence and Love; it must always, *in some way*, reflect them.[137]

Wojtyla discerns that in the command: 'Love your neighbour as yourself', we find a way to build that 'sensible structure'[138] Adam speaks of, because the command itself 'entails the juxtaposition of my neighbor with my own ego'.[139] This stems from the discovery that the 'other', the 'neighbour' is another 'I'. As we have examined, Wojtyla has, in the preceding chapters of *The Acting Person*, sought first to work out what it means to be an 'I'. Being a philosophical realist, he knows that we act 'together with others'. Thus, he cannot fail to explore the philosophical significance of the 'other' in the encounter with my 'I'.

He is not alone in this analysis of the importance of the need for love in the encounter with the neighbour. There are interesting parallels, for instance, in the work of Mikhail Bakhtin. Aleksandr Pigalev, writing on Bakhtin, notes how he

> discusses the role of the 'absolute need of love' as a force for salvation and regeneration. He [Bakhtin] says that the Other is the intermediary power that overcomes my blindness . . . This Other is like a mirror,

---

[136] Cited in *Icon Critical Guides*: *King Lear*, ed. Susan Bruce (Cambridge: Icon Books, 1997), p. 19.

[137] Wojtyla, *Collected Plays*, p. 321.

[138] Ibid.

[139] Wojtyla, *Acting Person*, p. 295.

since, according to the paradigm of monologue, while I see the Other as my opponent, I do not see myself. Only within the framework of dialogue can one see both oneself and one's opponent, who immediately becomes an *interlocutor* [neighbour in the Wojtylan sense]. Bakhtin insists that 'I feel an absolute need for love that only the other is capable of internally actualizing from his own unique place *outside* of me'. Within the frame of dialogue, the Other gains self-sufficiency as the result of its recognition, since to recognize means to love, and to love means to overcome death as the power of 'objectification'.[140]

Pigalev points out that in Bakhtin's discussion of the philosophy of the act, he characterizes the love directed towards the Other as the power which can 'encompass and retain the concrete manifoldness of Being, without impoverishing and schematizing it', and as the possibility to 'linger intently over an object'.[141]

In writings subsequent to *The Acting Person* Wojtyla outlines and further develops 'the ethical significance of love',[142] but this is not his main concern at this stage of the investigation. Wojtyla's aim is, rather, to show as I have noted how the paradigm of the 'neighbour' is co-essential to understanding who I am as a person and this has obvious implications in terms of 'any acting and existing "together with others"'.[143] As we have seen in the discussion of 'participation', our life entails acting with 'others', that is to say, 'the sovereign person is not "an impermeable monad"'.[144] Any adequate philosophy of the person must factor-in the 'neighbour' as another 'I' to the equation, in order to safeguard authentic participation and avoid what John Crosby 'calls a heteropathic identification with others', where the 'I' becomes 'a mere doormat or mirror'[145] for the 'other'. But we must also circumvent:

an idiopathic identification of others with oneself, which is what we find in those people who seem to experience only themselves and who in countering others can do no better than to project something of their inner lives into the others.[146]

[140] Carol Adlam, Rachel Falconer, Vitalii Makhlin and Alastair Renfrew (eds.), *Face-to-Face: Bakhtin in Russia and the West* (Sheffield: Sheffield Academic Press, 1997), p. 124.
[141] Ibid.
[142] Wojtyla, *Acting Person*, p. 295.
[143] Wojtyla, *Acting Person*, p.295.
[144] Williams, *Mind of John Paul II*, p. 216.
[145] Cited in Clarke, *Person and Being*, p. 58.
[146] Cited in Crosby, *Selfhood of the Human Person*, p. 115.

Wojtyla had himself at first hand experienced the risks involved in 'heteropathic and idiopathic identifications', and witnessed it in the dehumanization of the human person wrought by the ideologies of Nazism and Communism. However, as I have remarked before, he also speaks of how 'in the concentration camps there were people who managed to relate to others as other I's, as *neighbors* – often to a heroic degree'.[147]

Who is the neighbour?

Succinctly stated, the 'neighbour' is another 'I'. Already in *Magna Moralia*, Aristotle had classified the 'other' as 'a second self' and discerned that it is not possible to know ourselves without the other; he observes:

> when we wish to see our own face, we do so by looking into the mirror, in the same way when we wish to know ourselves we can obtain that knowledge by looking at our friend. For the friend is, as we assert, a second self.[148]

In his *Politics*, Aristotle speaks of man's communal nature, as follows:

> The man who is isolated, who is unable to share in the benefits of political association, or has no need to share because he is already self-sufficient, is no part of the city, and must therefore be either beast or god.[149]

Nevertheless, Aristotle's insight was limited and does not open up to the horizon of the 'neighbour'. The 'other' in the Aristotelian theory on friendship does include the '*other of me*' but not '*the other as other*'. A relationship to the other as friend is only possible with those who are similar, that is, in Aristotle's case with the Greek citizens of the *polis*. There is, in other words, a vanishing point in the Stagirite's theory. Gennaro Cicchese observes that in Aristotle, 'friendship decreases in the measure in which the difference between the other and me increases, right up to vanishing if the other is a barbarian or a slave'.[150]

---

[147] Wojtyla, 'Participation or Alienation?, in *Person and Community*, p. 206.
[148] Aristotle, *Magna Moralia*, II, 15, 1213a 20–26. Cf. *The Works of Aristotle*, Vol. IX, tr. David Ross (Oxford: Oxford University Press, 1966).
[149] Aristotle, *The Politics*, I, 2, 1253a. Cf. tr. T. A. Sinclair (London: Penguin Books, 1992).
[150] Cited in Cicchese, *I Percorsi dell'Altro*, p. 64.

It is Thomas Aquinas who takes Aristotle's theory of friendship and develops it into a theory of love. James McEvoy argues that Aquinas's theory of love 'goes through and beyond the noble Aristotelian idea of the friend as *alter ipse*, another self, to rejoin the love of "neighbour as oneself" . . . he developed a rich notion of truly loving the other person'.[151]

It is against this backdrop that Wojtyla opens up the whole horizon in terms of the paradigm of the neighbour. We can get an insight into who the neighbour is when he discusses its negative verification, that is, in the 'stranger' and the experience of alienation. He writes:

> alienation as the antithesis of participation denotes . . . the limitation or annihilation of all by which man is for man another 'I'. Then, this experience of the truth of humanity, the essential value of the person in the human 'Thou', is shaken. The 'I' will remain cut off and without contact, and by the same token will remain undiscovered in full for himself. Then, also, in interhuman relations the 'neighbour' disappears and there remains instead the 'other', the 'stranger', or even the 'enemy'.[152]

To be related to another as a neighbour is to be related to that individual in his or her very being precisely as a person. The 'neighbour' is another 'person', one like oneself. Hence, the special reference in this study to the neighbour as a paradigm for understanding *how* a human being is a person. Wojtyla considers that

> the man-person is capable not only of partaking in the life of a community, to be and to act together with others; he is also capable of participating in the very humanity of others. It is this ability to participate in the humanity of every human being that all types of participation in a community are rooted, and it is there that it receives its personal meaning. This is what is ultimately contained in the notion of 'neighbor'.[153]

With greater clarity, admittedly somewhat lacking in the cursory treatment given in *The Acting Person*, Wojtyla in the paper entitled 'Participation or Alienation?' sums up his views as follows:

---

[151] James McEvoy and Michael Dunne (eds.), *Thomas Aquinas: Approaches to Truth* (Dublin: Four Courts Press, 2002), p. 28.
[152] Cited in Szostek, '*Karol Wojtyla's View of the Human Person*', p. 61.
[153] Wojtyla, *Acting Person*, p. 294.

as human beings, we are capable of participating in the very humanity
of other people, and because of this every human being can be our
neighbor. This is the point at which what I said in the book [*The
Acting Person*] converges with my reflections here concerning the *other*.
'The *other*' does not just signify that the being existing next to me or
even acting in common with me in some system of activities is the
same kind of being as I am. Within the context of this real situation,
'the *other*' also signifies my no less real – though primarily subjective
– participation in that being's humanity, a participation arising from
my awareness that this being is another *I*, which means 'also an *I*'.[154]

The paradigm of Prisoner Number 16670

Theodore Adorno, the German sociologist and political thinker, asks
whether, following the greatest pulverization of the human person in
history at Auschwitz, it is still possible to write poetry or philosophy.
The question is not just on the cultural level. It is fundamentally
anthropological, and 'there is no getting out of [it] . . . no more than
out of the electrified barbed wire around the camps'.[155] After Auschwitz
philosophy and poetry might be possible though 'the less cultural
question' can surely be raised, that is, if 'after Auschwitz you can go
on living'.[156] Adorno asserts that 'after Auschwitz, our feelings resist
any claim of the positivity of existence as sanctimonious, as wronging
the victims . . . In the concentration camps it was no longer an
individual who died, but a specimen.'[157]

Andre Frossard describes the alienation involved when he describes
inmate number 16670 (St Maximilian Kolbe) of Auschwitz as like 'a
former human being, led from reduction to reduction to the linear state
of a sketch of a skeleton'.[158] He elucidates how the Nazi ideology
clearly understood the enemy within to be 'the person, the promise of
eternity in eternity in man, that had to be destroyed'.[159] The pertinence
of Adorno's question is mirrored repeatedly in human history.
Nadezhda Mandelstam, the wife of Osip Mandelstam, tells of a
conversation between Stalin and Boris Pasternak about the fate of her
husband:

---

[154] Wojtyla, *Person and Community*, p. 200.
[155] Brian O'Connor (ed.), *The Adorno Reader* (Blackwell: Oxford, 2000), pp. 84–8.
[156] Ibid.
[157] O'Connor (ed.), *Adorno Reader*, p. 86.
[158] Andre Frossard, *Forget Not to Love: The Passion of Maximilian Kolbe* (San
Francisco: Ignatius Press, 1991), p. 181.
[159] Frossard, *Forget Not to Love*, p. 183.

'[H]e's [Stalin said of Mandelstam] a genius, he's a genius isn't he?'
... Pasternak replied: 'But that's not the point.' 'What is it then?'
Stalin asked. Pasternak then said that he would like to meet him and
have a talk. 'About what?' 'About life and death', Pasternak replied.
Stalin hung up.[160]

Wojtyla has lived, as we know, under the shadow of the depersonalization wrought by the Nazi and Communist regimes, and it
is for this reason, I would contend, that his work can be understood as
a response to Adorno's question. On a visit to Auschwitz in 1979, on
the square of Brzezinka we hear Wojtyla (then John Paul II) implicitly
accepting Adorno's judgment of the meaning of Auschwitz, but he
suggests it is overturned in the figure of Maximilian Kolbe, the one
who offered to substitute himself (that is, he put the neighbour before
his own ego)[161] in the death chamber for another prisoner [the
neighbour]. Wojtyla says of Auschwitz that it was constructed

> *to trample underfoot radically*, not only love, but all the signs of human
> dignity, of humanity ... In this place of terrible massacre ... Fr
> Maximilian, by offering himself voluntarily to death in the bunker of
> hunger for one of his brothers [a neighbour], carried back a spiritual
> victory.[162]

The triumph involved is seen by Wojtyla in terms of the drama we
have been investigating, that of the 'I' and the 'other'. In the aftermath
of the Second World War Wojtyla perceives man to be 'like a nomad
looking for an oasis – a new dwelling',[163] and in the heroic action of
Kolbe he sees laid bare an island of humanity in the midst of the desert
of depersonalization.

Kolbe's action is a paradigm of what it means to be a human person;
in the words of Buttiglione, he 'shows the essence of human great-
ness'.[164] His jailers also perceived this when they remarked: 'That is a
man.'[165] His example of being a neighbour for the other prisoner
'contains the answer to the fundamental philosophical question:

---

[160] Cited in Purcell, *The Drama of Humanity*, p. 118.
[161] Cf. Wojtyla, *Acting Person*, p. 295.
[162] 'Omelia del 7 giugno 1979 a Oswiecim–Brezezinska', in CSEO *Documentazione*,
p. 305.
[163] Stanislaus Mutajwaha, 'Some Recent Insights in the Philosophy of the Other',
Dissertatio ad doctoratum, Rome 1992, p. 20.
[164] Buttiglione, *Karol Wojtyla*, p. 13.
[165] Frossard, *Forget Not to Love*, p. 198.

whether, and how, it is possible to be human after the horror of war',[166] that is, the answer to Adorno's question. Wojtyla remarks that 'what conquers, through Kolbe, is not the Christian faith but man, man through faith has arrived at the full possession of his own humanity'.[167]

In other words, in Kolbe's action towards the neighbour there is revealed the fullness of what it means to be a human person. Kolbe substitutes his own 'I' for his 'neighbour', and in making such a choice reveals the characteristics essential to an adequate philosophy of personhood, that is, self-determination, self-possession and self-governance. Thus, it is by living and relating to the 'other' as 'neighbour', as another 'I', that we can achieve our own 'self-actualization'. The 'I' and 'neighbour' are, in fact, two co-essential principles required for a comprehensive understanding of the human person.

The neighbour as the fundamental system of reference

Wojtyla asserts that the neighbour is the 'ultimate point of reference'[168] for any adequate philosophy of the human person. He remarks:

> the former [the neighbor] is essentially superior to the latter [membership in a community]. Such is the correct hierarchy of values because the system of reference to the neighbor shows the mutual relation and subordination of all men according to the principle of their common humanity itself while the system based on membership in a community is insufficient to reveal this relation and this subordination. We may also speak of a sort of transcendence of being a 'neighbor' with regard to being a 'member of a community'. All this is indirectly contained in the evangelical commandment of love.[169]

If we ask the question about the primacy of the 'I' or 'You' in the writings of Wojtyla, the emphasis is on the 'I'. But there is a coessential primacy allotted to the 'neighbour' and being a 'member of a community'. The 'neighbour' is also fundamental. But still, Wojtyla sees the danger of an approach that would fail to do justice 'to the substantiality pole of the person'.[170] We can, I believe, see this thinking evidenced in Wojtyla's analysis of the 'neighbour'. He is careful not to end up with a substantiality of the person that is constituted 'by

---

[166] Buttiglione, *Karol Wojtyla*, p. 12.
[167] Buttiglione, *Karol Wojtyla*, p. 14.
[168] Wojtyla, *Acting Person*, p. 296.
[169] Ibid.
[170] Clarke, *Person and Being*, p. 58.

one's relations to others'.[171] In the words of Norris Clarke, this will metaphysically not work, because 'we cannot literally bring into being another person that was not there before simply by relating to the thing that is there with attentive love'.[172] Clarke comments:

> to be a *human person* is to be on a journey from potential self-possession to actual. It is quite true that in the order of time and actuality con-sciously operative self-possession as a person appears only sub-sequently to initiatives taken from without, i.e. to incoming relations. But it does not follow at all that these incoming relations actually *constitute* in being the very nature of that to which they relate. The person is awakened to actual exercise of its personhood by the initiatives of others, but is not constituted in being as person by them.[173]

This points to the incommunicable nature of the human person. McEvoy puts it succinctly when he says

> the friend is indeed another self, *alter ipse* . . . [but] the '*alter*' in '*alter ipse*' retains his self-identity over against me, as the *ipse* he is in and for himself, a free and personal being, and therefore ontologically incommunicable – meaning by that the fundamental truth that individual personhood cannot in its very individuality be replicated.[174]

The commandment of love discloses for Wojtyla what is indispens-able 'for a community to be truly human'.[175] It also reveals the 'true dimension of participation'.[176] I have already noted that according to Wojtyla, authentic participation entails the actualization of one's own self-determination in acting together-with-others. Hence, the command-ment 'Love your neighbour as yourself' unfolds the depth of partici-pation that is entailed in the encounter with the 'other' as 'neighbour'.

Wojtyla does not enter into the epistemological problems connected with the knowing of the other 'I'. His focus is rather on the anthro-pological and ethical significance of the commandment of love.[177] I would suggest that perhaps the most philosophically significant word

---

[171] Ibid.
[172] Ibid.
[173] Clarke, *Person and Being*, p. 59.
[174] McEvoy and Dunne (eds.), *Thomas Aquinas*, p. 36.
[175] Wojtyla, *Acting Person*, p. 296.
[176] Ibid.
[177] The reference here is to Matthew 19:19. Wojtyla argues that 'love is the proper form of relating to persons: it is the form of behavior for which we should strive when our behavior has a person as its object, since this form is demanded by that person's essence, or nature' (*Person and Community*, p. 289).

in the commandment is '*as*'. To treat 'the other as oneself'[178] entails the revelation that the 'Thou' is a 'second I' that carries with him/her their own transcendence and tendency towards self-fulfilment. In other words, I attach to the 'other' all the elements that go into my constitution as a person, as an *I*, that have been already analysed by Wojtyla in the previous chapters of *The Acting Person*. There is therefore, a certain reciprocity between 'I' and the 'neigbour'. The 'neighbour' is another 'I' who seeks to carry out his/her actions according to the requirements of self-determination and realizes transcendence and integration in their many stages.

The commandment of love as a task

Wojtyla asserts, 'the commandment of love is simply the call to experience another human being as another I'.[179] The substitution involved in treating the other as oneself 'takes place by my experiencing that other *I* as a person'.[180] Nonetheless, the actualization of this 'in relation to every other human being arises before us as a task'.[181]

If we are to actualize our participation in relation to other human beings there is a need, according to Wojtyla, for an exterior and interior impulse. The rule of love requires 'that each of us must continually set ourselves the task of actually participating in the humanity of others, of experiencing the other as an *I*, as a person'.[182]

How do I experience the command of love from within me? Wojtyla asserts, 'the impulse that the commandment expresses from without must in each instance arise from within'.[183] Then he makes reference to Max Scheler, when he asks: 'Is this inner impulse purely emotional, as Max Scheler seems to suggest? And does it have an exclusively spontaneous character?'[184]

Time does not permit me to delve into Wojtyla's indebtedness to Max Scheler. Wojtyla was attracted to Scheler's 'emphasis upon love and its importance for the human person'.[185] He judges that

---

[178] McEvoy develops the aspect of 'self-love' suggested by the phrase 'love your neighbour as oneself' (*Thomas Aquinas*, p. 34).
[179] Wojtyla, *Person and Community*, p. 203.
[180] Wojtyla, *Person and Community*, p. 202.
[181] Wojtyla, *Person and Community*, p. 203.
[182] Ibid.
[183] Ibid.
[184] Ibid.
[185] Schmitz, *Center of the Human Drama*, p. 37.

it would be difficult to deny the significance of human spontaneity and emotions in the development of interpersonal relationships. Certainly such factors are enormous resources, variously distributed among people and also variously influencing the development of *I – other* relationships. Scheler's analysis also provides an additional argument for maintaining that people have some sort of basic, innate disposition to participate in humanity as a value, to spontaneously open up to others. This seems to contradict Sartre, whose analysis of consciousness leads him to conclude that the subject is closed in relation to others.[186]

Nonetheless, Wojtyla finds that Scheler 'gravely diminishes man's subjectivity by denying the efficacy of the will'.[187] Thus, he sees the need to develop an adequate philosophy of the person and love that does justice to the 'I act' of *The Acting Person*. According to Scheler's system:

> the person as causal originator (*Urheber*) finds no place in the framework of phenomenological intuition . . . The whole dynamic character of the being of the person is lost . . . The person remains only the subject of experiences, and is strictly a passive subject. On the contrary, the person is not the originator of action, he does nothing.[188]

The fundamental point for Wojtyla is not just that we experience 'self-fulfilment' in loving but that we, in fact, realize it. It is set before us in the *other* 'as a specific *task*'. Wojtyla writes: 'experiencing another human being, one of the others, as another *I* always involves a discreet choice'.[189] The emotions are, of course, involved in the task,[190] but it is fundamentally a question of the will and the choice to accept another individual as a person, as another *I*. Wojtyla explains:

> I thus in a sense *choose this person in myself* – in my own *I* – for I have no other access to another human being as an *I* except through my own *I* . . . The constitution of the *I* of another in my consciousness and will is not the result of choosing among people, among others; it is a matter, as I said, of choosing who is *hic et nunc* given to me and assigned to me. This is also why I do not experience this choice as a choice. Rather, it is a matter of simply identifying one of the others as another *I*, which

---

[186] Wojtyla, *Person and Community*, p. 203.
[187] Mary Shivanandan, *Crossing the Threshold of Love: A New Vision of Marriage* (Washington, DC: Catholic University of America Press, 1999), p. 31.
[188] Schmitz, *Center of the Human Drama*, p. 44.
[189] Wojtyla, *Person and Community*, p. 203.
[190] Ibid.

does not require a more prolonged process of the will – assent or conflict of motives etc.[191]

In *The Jeweller's Shop* we hear Christopher dramatically describe the struggles involved in the choice to love. He says:

> We have to accept the fact that love weaves itself into our fate. If
> fate does not split the love, people win their victory
> but nothing else besides – and nothing above, either.
> These are the limits of man.
> I sometimes wake at night – and at once my consciousness
> is with you. I ask myself if I could
> take your freezing hands, warm them with my hands –
> a unity will emerge, a vision of new existence,
> which will embrace both of us. Will it not die later, though?
> I struggle for hours, unable to sleep till morning,
> tempted to escape somewhere – but I can't anymore.
> We must go together from now on, Monica; we must go
> together,
> even though I were to go away from you as early as my father left
> Mother.
> All that we must leave behind and make our fate from scratch.
> Love is a constant challenge, thrown to us by God,
> thrown, I think, so that we should challenge fate.[192]

The commandment of love as the rule of being

In conclusion to chapter 7 of *The Acting Person* Wojtyla speaks of the 'personalistic implications of the evangelical commandment'. Once again, he is at pains to point out that 'any human community that allows this system of reference [the neigbour] to become defective condemns itself to becoming unfavourable for participation and throws open an unbridgeable gulf between the person and the community'.[193] He continues: 'The commandment of love is also the measure of the tasks and demands that have to be faced by all men – all persons and all communities – if the whole good contained in the acting and being "together with others" is to become a reality.'[194]

[191] Wojtyla, *Person and Community*, p. 204.
[192] Wojtyla, *Collected Plays*, p. 312.
[193] Wojtyla, *Acting Person*, p. 298.
[194] Wojtyla, *Acting Person*, pp. 298–9.

I spoke earlier about the 'personalistic value' in Wojtyla's exploration of the human person, that is, how the action of the person has a
personalistic value in itself. In his earlier work *Love and Responsibility*,
Wojtyla observes a similarity between the commandment of love
and the personalistic norm. Wojtyla proposes the 'personalistic norm'
or rule in counterdistinction to the 'utilitarian principle'. Wojtyla
adjudges the utilitarian principle as always standing 'in the way of
love' because it treats 'a person as a means to an end'.[195]

The commandment of love is not just regulative, in terms of the
human person, but normative. Wojtyla observes:

> strictly speaking the commandment says: 'Love persons', and the
> personalistic norm says: 'A person is an entity of a sort to which the
> only proper and adequate way to relate is love.' The personalistic norm
> does, as we have seen, provide a justification for the New Testament
> commandment. And so, if we take the commandment together with
> this justification, we can say that it is the same as the personalistic
> norm.[196]

The commandment of love is normative because in acting 'together
with others' in this way, the human person will act 'towards the
other person as a person'.[197] In other words, the only adequate way
to treat persons is with love. Simpson concisely states it as follows:
'Love treats the person as an independent being with his own
self-determination and his own self-chosen ends.'[198]

We can say that Wojtyla's careful critical reading of Scheler helps
him create 'a synthetic vision that would serve as the cornerstone of
his philosophy for the next four decades'.[199] Buttiglione notes that
Scheler's 'identification of the faculty of empathy and of sympathy
(also studied by Edith Stein) breaks with a rooted tradition in modern
thought which imprisons the person in a subjectivity, making him a
monad separated from living communication with other subjects'.[200]
He continues:

> Scheler made a unique attempt to break away from the prison of
> solipsism which, in diverse ways, weighs down the whole of modern

---

[195] Karol Wojtyla, *Love and Responsibility* (London: Collins, 1981), p. 40.
[196] Wojtyla, *Love and Responsibility*, p. 41.
[197] Wojtyla, *Love and Responsibility*, p. 43.
[198] Simpson, *Karol Wojtyla*, p. 50.
[199] Kupczak, *Destined for Liberty*, p. 21.
[200] Buttiglione, *Karol Wojtyla*, p. 56.

philosophy . . . Scheler's marked virtue is that he retrieved the
possibility of knowing the other *as the other*, the possibility of sharing
the experience of the other as other, and the possibility of receiving,
through this intersubjectivity, an objective reality which is implied in
the relationship between subjects . . . This person is precisely the human
'I' – when one does not abstract from its concrete cognitive and
emotional contents – and it is that which characterizes its unrepeatable
individuality, an individuality which is nonetheless open to reality,
through sympathy.[201]

However, for Scheler, love is an emotion which has nothing in
common with human acts of willing. In Scheler's perspective 'it is
absolutely impossible to command somebody to love'. His view is
that: 'Love is a spontaneous act, purely internal and emotional. Therefore, it is useless to try to impose it from the outside. The love originates
spontaneously in an encounter with a value.'[202] Wojtyla, on the other
hand, perceives that 'an external command leads to the subject's
recognition of the suggested value and to the experience of an internal
obligation. This internal obligation moves the human will and makes
the person the cause of his own actions.'[203]

In the context of our present debate this would mean that following
out the obligation of the commandment of love 'I' become who I am
as a person. I love, therefore, I am. Wojtyla understands the commandment of love to be the rule of being and of the reality of participation,
that is, of acting 'together-with-others'.[204] It is the rule of being because
of the dynamic self-communicative nature of being itself. As Clarke
notes, when this 'intrinsic dynamism toward self-communication is
realized on the level of personal being as such it turns into self-
conscious, free self-communication. In a word, it turns into love in
some form.'[205]

Notwithstanding our imperfect human nature, Wojtyla would
equally see it as 'connatural for a human person to be a lover, to go
out towards others we love, sharing what we have and wishing them
the good they need for their own flourishing, for they too are good by
a participation in being similar to our own'.[206] A human person is like

---

[201] Buttiglione, *Karol Wojtyla*, p. 57.
[202] Kupczak, *Destined for Liberty*, p. 20.
[203] Ibid.
[204] Wojtyla, *Acting Person*, p. 298.
[205] Clarke, *Person and Being*, p. 76.
[206] Ibid.

any other real being and this necessarily implies that, as such, they are a living synthesis of substantiality and relationality. There is a mutual priority between the relational side and the substantial side, since it is by means of the relational that the self as substance can actualize its potentiality and fulfil its destiny.[207]

Norris Clarke's writings, as I have mentioned, are useful in complementing and clarifying some of Wojtyla's viewpoints with regard to the significance of the commandment of love as a rule of being. Clarke states:

> a personalized being must obey [that is, the Wojtylan notion of obliga-
> tion] the basic dyadic[208] ontological structure of all being, that is,
> *presence in itself* and *presence to others*. But the outgoing, self-
> expressive, self-communicative, relational aspect must be an equally
> intrinsic and primordial aspect of every person as is its interiority and
> self-possession.[209]

A metaphysics of love, as suggested by Wojtyla, seeks adequately to account for the understanding that 'to be a person is to be intrinsically expansive, ordered toward self-manifestation and self-communication'.[210] Wojtyla, I would suggest, concurs with Clarke's assessment, that this philosophical position is:

> [a] decisive advance over the Aristotelian substance, which was indeed,
> as nature, ordered toward action and reception, but, as form, was
> oriented primarily toward self-realization, the fulfillment of its own
> perfection as form, rather than sharing with others.[211]

---

[207] Clarke, *Person and Being*, p. 64.
[208] An interesting debate has opened up between Clarke and David Schindler (cf. *Communio* 20 (Fall 1993), pp. 580–620). Clarke comments: 'He [Schindler] thinks my "dyadic notion of the person as existing *in-itself* and *toward-itself*" [as] too limited in perspective.' But another primordial relation, pointed out by Schindler, is that of receptivity which is also constitutive of being. In the light of this, Clarke acknowledges, 'we should describe every created being as possessing its own existence *from another, in itself*, and oriented *toward others* – a triadic rather than just dyadic structure'. Cited in W. Norris Clarke, *Explorations in Metaphysics: Being – God – Person* (Notre Dame, IN: University of Notre Dame Press, 1994), p. 119. See also David L. Schindler, *Heart of the World, Center of the Church: Communio Ecclesiology, Liberalism, and Liberation* (Grand Rapids: Eerdmans, 1996), pp. 275–309, for a most insightful discussion and development of the philosophical questions involved.
[209] Clarke, *Person and Being*, p. 71.
[210] Ibid.
[211] Ibid.

For Wojtyla, to be an actualized human person, means to 'live a life of inter-personal self-giving and receiving',[212] that is, to be an exemplar of the commandment of love. In *Love and Responsibility*, he attempts to trace this out with particular reference to 'betrothed love'. He observes:

> in the metaphysical analysis of love it was stated that its true nature is most fully revealed in the gift of the self by the person who loves to the beloved person . . . The value of a person, as was said above, is inseparable from the essential being of that person. By its nature, because it is what it is, the person is its own master (*sui juris*), and cannot be ceded to another or supplanted by another in another in any context where it must exercise its will or make commitment affecting its freedom. (It is *alteri incommunicabilis*.) But love forcibly detaches the person, so to speak, from its natural inviolability and inalienability. It makes the person want to do just that – surrender itself to another, to the one it loves. The person no longer wishes to be its own exclusive property, but instead to become the property of the other. This means the renunciation of its autonomy and its inalienability. Love proceeds by renunciation, guided by the profound conviction that it does not diminish and impoverish, but quite the contrary, enlarges and enriches the existence of the person. What might be called the law of *ekstasis* seems to operate here: the lover 'goes outside' the self to find a fuller existence in another. In no other form of love does this law operate so conspicuously as it does in betrothed love.[213]

The commandment of love can as Wojtyla suggests be considered as 'the personalistic norm',[214] for contained within is the axiological truth of the 'other/neighbour' as 'person'. Its living out is equivalent to saying: 'I am myself, not when I close myself off from the other, but when I give myself, when out of love I am lost in the other'[215] and this is what Wojtyla has already identified as, 'the law of *exstasis*'.[216]

It is important to add in conclusion that the 'I act', explored extensively in *The Acting Person* is still fundamental to Wojtyla's analysis. The responsibility to love is an act of the human will. It is only when, as Jacques Maritain describes, a person has been

[212] Clarke, *Person and Being*, p. 76.
[213] Wojtyla, *Love and Responsibility*, pp.125–6.
[214] Wojtyla, *Love and Responsibility*, p. 41.
[215] Chiara Lubich, *Communio* 25 (Winter 1998), p. 753.
[216] McEvoy interestingly notes that it is Aquinas's insistence on the ecstatic nature of love that breaks 'the circularity of centripetal desire'. Cf. *Thomas Aquinas*, p. 30.

really awakened to the sense of being or existence, and grasps intuitively the obscure, living depth of the Self and subjectivity, [that he/she] discovers by the same token the basic generosity of existence and realizes, by virtue of the inner dynamism of this intuition, that love is not a passing pleasure or emotion, but the very meaning of being alive.[217]

The continued importance given to personal efficacy is clear. Wojtyla notes: 'Self-giving can have its full value only when it involves and is the work of the will. For it is free will that makes the person its own master (*sui juris*), an inalienable and untransferable "some-one" (*alteri incommunicabilis*).'[218]

Scheler, as I have commented before, was unable in his analysis to account for the universal human experience of being the cause of one's own actions. This is because he had a methodological reservation against causality that arose from certain presuppositions. For example, he

presupposed that causality is transcendent and therefore outside the analysis of experience to which phenomenology is devoted. Scheler's emphasis upon the emotional character of human life emphasized the passivity of the human subject and thereby reduced the active principle – that is to say, the will – to a mere epiphenomenon of the life of feeling within the totality of the ethical act.[219]

Wojtyla says of Scheler that he in fact 'fails to perceive a most elementary and basic truth, namely, that the only value that can be called ethical value is a value that has the acting person as its efficient cause'.[220] It is because he does not analyse this basic fact in his phenomenological description of experience that he ends up dealing with secondary elements that, in fact, become primary. Wojtyla believes this to be the 'error of Schelerian emotionalism, and both the will and reason, along with its theoretical and practical cognitive powers, fell victim to it'.[221]

Thus, when he comes to an analysis of the phenomenon of human love, he is unable to describe it adequately. He lacks the metaphysical framework to interpret what he describes phenomenologically. Love

---

[217] Jacques Maritain, *Existence and Existent* (Garden City, NY: Doubleday, 1957), p. 90.
[218] Wojtyla, *Love and Responsibility*, p. 126.
[219] Schmitz, *Center of the Human Drama*, p. 45.
[220] Wojtyla, *Person and Community*, p. 38.
[221] Ibid.

is not just a spontaneous human emotion; on the contrary, it is constitutive of my being as a person. Love refers to a realization of values, and in terms of the commandment of love, the value is of the 'other' as another *I* and this in turn expresses the causal efficacy of the human person.

Kupczak describes how

> Wojtyla concludes that an adequate theory of love has to describe the connection between obligation and value. Only a union of these two elements can grasp the essence of love. 'In love, these two elements of ethical experience do not eliminate but supplement each other. A deep experience of a value transforms an obligation into a firm and efficient act. On the other hand, a firm and efficient experience of obligation helps to create a profound realization of values in the human experience.'[222]

There are clear parallels between the Wojtylan perspective on the command of love as being the rule of being and von Balthasar's view that 'being is intelligible only as love'.[223] Wojtyla's and von Balthasar's insight is that a phenomenological analysis of love reveals 'what it means to act in the highest and deepest sense – and thereby what it means most fully *to be*'.[224] In other words, a metaphysics of love points to love as being the key 'to the order of being' and this, in fact, unfetters 'us from modernity's restriction of love to anthropology; from the modern assumption that love assists us, at best, in understanding only *human* being'.[225] This is why Wojtyla opens up the theme of the commandment of love as the rule of being and not just of human being.[226]

There is room for the development of this argument in Wojtyla's work. I have already mentioned in this chapter the dialogue between Clarke and Schindler on this matter. The reader would profit greatly in consulting the relevant material. The implications of a triadic rather than a dyadic structure in being, that is, being as '*from*' (*ab*), as '*in*' (*in*) and being as '*for*' or '*toward*' (*ad*) has to be further developed by philosophers.[227]

---

[222] Kupczak, *Destined for Liberty*, p. 21.
[223] Cf. David L. Schindler (ed.), *Hans Urs von Balthasar: His Life and Work* (San Francisco: Ignatius Press, 1991), p. 166.
[224] Schindler, *Heart of the World*, p. 294.
[225] Ibid.
[226] Wojtyla, *Acting Person*, p. 298.
[227] Schindler, *Heart of the World*, p. 296.

A commandment of love suggests that something is due, that there is an obligation to the 'Other'. Schindler suggests: 'the truth of the matter is rather that human *agere*, always and everywhere, is anteriorly a response to what is given, a response, radically, which always carries *within it* the prior initiative of the Other (and indeed, in some sense, of the other)'.[228]

So, essential features of the human person like 'self-determination', that is, taking the initiative, when open to the reality and context of the 'Other' suggest that the 'Other's' initiative is antecedent to that of the 'other's'. It's interesting to note that Levinas also begins to question the implications of the 'Other' for philosophy. Indeed, his whole philosophical career was 'dominated by one question: what does it mean to think of the Other as Other?'[229] The Other cannot be suppressed in the articulation of any adequate philosophy of the other.

The 'neighbour' in extremis

Without a doubt, it is a fact that human history is enlivened with examples of our need for each other. The Irish writer Brian Keenan, who went through the dehumanizing experience of captivity in Beirut, writes his cathartic account of the experience, in order to reveal, he says, man 'in extremis'.[230] Keenan believes that what he and the other hostages went through was in a sense 'far removed from normal human experience, yet one in which, paradoxically, so much more of what we are as human beings was revealed'.[231] In the extremes of his experience he does, I would contend, offer an insightful description of the question of the meaning of the 'I – Other' relation that we have been exploring, albeit on the personal level. The principal paradox of his account is 'how in the most inhuman circumstances men grow and deepen humanity. In the face of death but not because of it, they explode with passionate life.'[232] Throughout Keenan's experience of incarceration there surfaces the need for the '*other*'. He observes: 'Both of us [John McCarthy, Keenan's companion in captivity] had gone through experiences that opened up new definitions of what we are as

---

[228] Schindler, *Heart of the World*, p. 278.
[229] Colin Davis, *Levinas: An Introduction* (Notre Dame, IN: University of Notre Dame Press, 1996), p. 33.
[230] Brian Keenan, *An Evil Cradling* (London: Random House, 1992), p. xi.
[231] Ibid.
[232] Keenan, *Evil Cradling*, p. xiii.

human beings.'[233] Integral to this discovery was the fact that 'we were responsible for each other; no matter what happened we must not be separated. Our strength lay in one another.'[234] Shining through the prism of Keenan's suffering is the realization of

> what each of us all are. We are all made of many parts; no man is singular in the way he lives his life. He only lives it fully in relation to others . . . We cannot know ourselves or declare ourselves human unless we share in the humanity of another.[235]

Keenan and McCarthy were forced together into captivity but it is not merely this general aspect of 'togetherness' that Keenan alludes to, when he says that it gave rise to 'new definitions of what we are as human beings'.[236] Their experience and those of more dramatic cases like Maximilian Kolbe, Etty Hillesum and Edith Stein, confirm that the 'neighbour'

> establishes and confirms the universality of human existence, or the fact that, despite all particular differences that separate us from one another (historical, cultural, personal, and so forth), we all share in the one humanness and all achieve fulfilment through the same authentic dynamism of freedom and self-determination.[237]

The neighbour is, therefore, the paradigm of what it means to be a human person because if I alienate myself from my neighbour, I end up estranging myself 'from the terrain of [my] participation with the other – that humanity which is common to [me] and [my] neighbor'.[238] Wojtyla writes:

> Man's alienation from other men stems from a disregard for, or a neglect of, that depth of participation which is indicated in the term 'neighbor' and by the neglect of the interrelations and intersubordinations of men in their humanity expressed by this term, which indicates the most fundamental principle of any real community.[239]

In Aristotelian terms, alienation means that I cut myself off from my 'second self' but with the Wojtylan analysis we have a far more

[233] Keenan, *Evil Cradling*, p. 93.
[234] Keenan, *Evil Cradling*, p. 130.
[235] Keenan, *Evil Cradling*, pp. 277, 287.
[236] Keenan, *Evil Cradling*, p. 93.
[237] Simpson, *Karol Wojtyla*, p. 44.
[238] Buttiglione, *Karol Wojtyla*, p. 176.
[239] Wojtyla, *Acting Person*, p. 297.

philosophically differentiated notion of person and subsequently, of alienation. The category of the 'neighbour' as 'the fundamental system of reference'[240] in the *I – other* relationship preserves my own 'person-hood'. Any adequate philosophy of the human person will verify *how* the 'neighbour' is a paradigm of what it means to be a 'person'. Wojtyla maintains that his whole philosophical analysis of the 'neighbour' and the commandment of love can help us 'interpret such realities as friendship or a *communio personarum*'.[241] Communion can be distinguished from community because the former is: 'essentially an *I – other* relationship inwardly maturing into an interpersonal *I – thou* relationship'.[242]

Aristotle had already explained friendship to a considerable degree.[243] He observed among other things that 'it is maintained that the supremely happy, who are self-sufficient, have no need of friends ... therefore being self-sufficient they need nothing further; but a friend, who is "another self", supplies what a man cannot provide by his own efforts'.[244] He adjudges it to be 'surely paradoxical to represent the man of perfect happiness as a solitary; for nobody would choose to have all the good things in the world by himself, because man is a social creature and naturally constituted to live in company'.[245] Aristotle concludes, 'in company with others and in relation to others it is easier'.[246]

Wojtyla is in accord with Aristotle. But as we have seen in the analysis carried out, he complements Aristotle's perspective with the rich traditions of Thomism and phenomenology in order to unearth what is 'specific, unique and irreducible in the human person'.[247] Thus, he states:

> there can be no doubt that friendship is based upon the relationship of one human being as an *I* to another as an *I*. Friendship is simply an evolution of this relationship and an expression of its richness in proportion to the love that two people are capable of bringing to it.[248]

[240] Wojtyla, *Acting Person*, p. 295.
[241] Wojtyla, *Person and Community*, p. 204.
[242] Ibid.
[243] Ibid.
[244] Aristotle, *Nicomachean Ethics*, tr. J. A. K. Thomson (London: Penguin Books, 1976), p. 303 [1169a23–b11].
[245] Aristotle, *Nicomachean Ethics*, p. 304 [1169b11–35].
[246] Aristotle, *Nicomachean Ethics*, p. 305 [1169b35–1170a24].
[247] Kupczak, *Destined for Liberty*, p. 104.
[248] Wojtyla, *Person and Community*, p. 204.

Conclusion: a new ontological-ethical anthropology stemming from the 'as'

Wojtyla's exploration in terms of the anthropological significance of the commandment of love is as I have said sketchy in its initial stages. I find the genesis of Wojtyla's paper, entitled 'Participation or Alienation?'[249] informative in this regard. He includes in this essay the French translation of the last two sections from *The Acting Person*, that is, on 'Fellow member and Neighbor', and 'The Commandment of Love'.[250] Thus, the paper he submits to the Fourth International Phenomenology Conference is to be seen as 'a kind of commentary on the two sections of *Osoba I czyn* enclosed in translation'.[251] There is clear scope, therefore, for a creative retrieval of what Wojtyla alludes to initially in his exploration of the commandment of love in *The Acting Person*. In the first place, the commandment 'Thou shalt love',[252] Wojtyla observes, as I have already mentioned, 'entails the juxtaposition of my neighbor with my own ego'.[253] It means putting myself alongside another who is another *I*, seeing myself in terms of a similar system of reference. The words 'thy neighbor as thyself'[254] ('as yourself')[255], we can say, expand and develop the 'ontological-ethical' implications of that metaphysical reality. The neighbour is to be treated 'as yourself', that is, another *I*, hence, we can say that there is a new ontological-ethical anthropology stemming from the 'as'.

In writing specifically about the *I – Other* relationship, Wojtyla notes that:

> the actualization of the *I – other* relationship starts by my becoming aware of the fact of the humanity of a specific human being apart from myself, one of the others, but it takes place by my experiencing that other *I* as a person. Participation signifies a basic personalization of the relationship of one human being to another. I cannot experience another as I experience myself, because my own *I* as

[249] Wojtyla, *Person and Community*, pp. 197–207.
[250] Wojtyla, *Person and Community*, p. 207, n. 4.
[251] Wojtyla, *Person and Community*, p. 197.
[252] Wojtyla, *Acting Person*, p. 295.
[253] Ibid.
[254] Ibid.
[255] The reader will find the discussion by McEvoy on 'Loving Another As Oneself' in terms of Aristotle and Aquinas very helpful and interesting. Cf. McEvoy and Dunne (eds.), *Thomas Aquinas*, pp. 33–6.

such is non-transferable. When I experience another as a person, I come as close as I can to what determines the other's *I* as the unique and unrepeatable reality of that human being.[256]

In Wojtya's 'relational portrait of the person', he is always careful to point out that it 'presupposes the immanent (and indirectly 'substantial') portrait that unfolds before us'.[257] We can rightfully ask, why should we attach philosophical significance to the '*other as yourself*' in Wojtyla's analysis? The reason as we have already examined is because the 'other' is a 'person'. Wojtyla intimates this when he says, as we have just quoted: 'participation signifies a basic personalization of the relationship of one human being to another'.[258]

The importance of the commandment of love is that when I act according to it, 'I act' '*as*' a person-to-a-person. In so doing, I not only experience the 'other' but also actualize my own self-fulfilment. This is the 'personalization' or 'personalistic principle' Wojtyla speaks of. He explains that

> this principle is an attempt to translate the commandment of love into the language of philosophical ethics. *The person is a being for whom the only suitable dimension is love* ... Love for a person *excludes the possibility of treating him as an object of pleasure.* This is a principle of Kantian ethics and constitutes the so-called second imperative ... Nevertheless; Kant did not fully interpret the commandment of love. In fact, the commandment of love is not limited to excluding all behavior that reduces the person to a mere object of pleasure. It requires more; it requires *the affirmation of the person as a person.*[259]

Hence, that 'X is a person', it therefore follows, 'I should do X'. Wojtyla describes how in his actions 'the human person is eyewitness of the transition from the "is" to the "ought"'.[260] Dealing with the obligation the human person has to seek self-fulfilment, he observes:

> The fact that the assertion 'X is truly good' activates the conscience and thus sets off what is like an inner obligation or command to perform the action that leads to the realization of X is most strictly related with

[256] Wojtyla, *Person and Community*, p. 202.
[257] Wojtyla, *Person and Community*, p. 194.
[258] Wojtyla, *Person and Community*, p. 202.
[259] John Paul II, *Crossing the Threshold of Hope*, trs. Jenny and Martha McPhee (London: Jonathan Cape, 1994), pp. 200–1.
[260] Wojtyla, *Acting Person*, p. 162.

the specific dynamism of the fulfilment of the personal ego in and through the action.[261]

Place the commandment of love in this context, and we can understand more clearly the ontological-ethical importance stemming from the *'as yourself'*. Stated briefly, the 'other' is another *'I'*, a 'person' and there follows from this that I should 'Love my neighbour *as* myself', if I am going to be philosophically consistent. Put simply, to be a human person is to love your neighbour *as* yourself.[262]

[261] Wojtyla, *Acting Person*, p. 163.

[262] There is, as I have already stated, a whole area of correspondence between the Wojtylan analysis and the writings of Levinas. Levinas writes for example: 'I exist through the other and for the other, but without this being alienation: I am inspired. This inspiration is the psyche. The psyche can signify this alterity in the same without alienation in the form of incarnation, as being-in-one's-skin, having-the-other-in-one's-skin' (*Otherwise Than Being or Beyond Essence*, tr. Alphonso Lingis (Pittsburg: Duqesne University Press, 1999), pp. 114–15). Wojtyla himself notes: 'We are witness of a symptomatic return to metaphysics (the philosophy of being) through an integral anthropology . . . The philosophers of dialogue, such as Martin Buber and the aforementioned Levinas, have contributed to this experience . . . the path passes not so much through being and existence as through people and their meeting each other, through the "I" and the "Thou". This is a fundamental dimension of man's existence, which is always coexistence' (John Paul II, *Crossing the Threshold of Hope*, pp. 35–6).

3

The Enactment of the Drama
of the Human Person

From 'Wojtyla I' to 'Wojtyla II'

In this chapter I will explore how Karol Wojtyla's philosophical project
continues and develops when he finds himself 'called from a far
country' to become Pope John Paul II.[1] I have made the distinction
before between 'Wojtyla I' and 'Wojtyla II' in terms of his earlier and
later writings.[2] Wojtyla found himself in a new position: not just as
before, a bishop and a lecturer at the university of Lublin, but now as
leader acting on a world stage. It was Heidegger in his *Letter on
Humanism*[3] who characterized his later writings in terms of a 'turning'
or 'reversal' (*die Kehre*). This meant that commentators subsequently
spoke of 'Heidegger I' and 'Heidegger II' in terms of his writings.[4]
Moran describes *die Kehre*, in the case of Heidegger, as a rejection of
'the strait-jacket of transcendental philosophy [and the exploration
of] the meaning of Being through a meditative, if consciously wilful,
even idiosyncratic examination of poetry, art, architecture, and some
significant revelatory moments in the history of philosophy'.[5]

A survey of the 'Wojtyla II' writings, I suggest, will show that
they are characterized not so much by a 'turning' but by an 'opening-
up' (instead of *die Kehre* we could term it as *die Öffnung*) to new
horizons on the theme of the human person. The writings of the
'Wojtyla I' period were in a sense the first movement of the unfinished
symphony whose composition he had inaugurated. An attempt at its

---

[1] John Paul II, reflecting upon his election, introduced himself using these words to
the crowds gathered in St Peter's Square in 1978.
[2] Cf. Chapter 1.
[3] In a preface to William Richardson's *Heidegger: Through Phenomenology to
Thought* (The Hague: Martinus Nijhoff, 1963), Heidegger admits to making such a
reference to a 'turn' or 'reversal' in his *Letter on Humanism* (1947).
[4] Cf. Richardson, *Heidegger*, p. xxvi.
[5] Dermot Moran, *Introduction to Phenomenology* (London: Routledge, 2000),
pp. 198–9.

completion would now come in this second period. Underlying all his work is, in fact, an unceasing invocation to the human person.

The 'surface meets the depth'

Wojtyla can, I believe, be interpreted as describing the process involved in the growth and development of his own thought in the following verse, entitled: 'Thoughts on maturing':

> Maturity: a descent to a hidden core,
> layers fall from the imagination
> like leaves once locked in the trunk of their tree;
> the cells grow calm – though their sensitivity still stirs;
> the body in its own fullness
> reaches the shores of autumn.
> Maturity: the surface meets the depth;
> maturity: penetrating the depth,
> the soul more reconciled with the body,
> but more opposed to death,
> uneasy about the resurrection.
> Maturing towards difficult encounters.[6]

In his later writings (Wojtyla II) we can see the further 'opening-out' of what we have so far analysed in chapters 1 and 2 of this book, that is, *how* a human being is a 'person', and how the 'neighbour', the 'other', is a paradigm of personhood. The 'hidden core' Wojtyla understands as the irreducible kernel of the human person. This corpus of philosophical reflection will now reach its fullness in an articulation that will reconcile the concept of soul and body. He clearly foresees difficulties along the way but this will lead to maturity of thought. He reiterated many times that he had just touched the surface of the question in his earlier writings (Wojtyla I). In the essay, 'The Person: Subject and Community', he admits wanting to

> reexamine the connection that exists between the subjectivity of the human person and the structure of the community. This problem was already *outlined* [my emphasis] in *The Acting Person*, especially in the final section 'Participation'. Here I wish to develop that outline somewhat.[7]

---

6   Karol Wojtyla, *Collected Poems*, tr. Jerzy Peterkiewicz (London: Hutchinson, 1982), p. 158. This poem appears in a cycle of poems that appeared in 1975 under the pen name 'Gruda' which means 'a clod of earth'.

7   Karol Wojtyla, *Person and Community, Selected Essays*, tr. Theresa Sandok (New York: Peter Lang, 1993), p. 219.

The 'surface meets the depth'[8] in Wojtyla's later writings and penetrates more profoundly the question of the human 'person'. As a playwright, Wojtyla had already used different pseudonyms. For example, he often used the name A. Jawien, so that

> readers unfamiliar with the pseudonym would not have had any reason to suspect that the playwright was a priest. They would have recognized the author as a realist, not a sentimentalist, but a realist who found hope in love, which is always stronger than mere sentimentality.[9]

We could, I would suggest, in similar vein approach the study of Wojtyla's later writings, under the authorship of John Paul II. Wojtyla's philosophical fingerprints are to be clearly detected in his later work. Numerous commentators affirm such an interpretation of the later writings of Wojtyla. As to the question of actual authorship, Alasdair MacIntyre, referring to the publication of *Veritatis Splendor*, comments:

> I am well aware that generally several anonymous writers contribute to the drafting of encyclicals, and doubtless they did so on this occasion. But any reader of Karol Wojtyla's major philosophical writings, from his doctoral dissertation onward, will recognize, both in the style of arguments and the nuances with which particular arguments are developed, a single authorial presence in this text.[10]

John J. Conley writes:

> The phenomenological method of John Paul II is apparent in a number of his major texts. The method differs from the scholastic or rationalist methods of argumentation inasmuch as it does not seek truth by establishing a proposition, proving the proposition through schematic evidence and refuting counterpropositions. The phenomenological method tends to examine a problem by moving from less to more adequate insights as it describes the various dimensions of a particular question.[11]

---

[8] Wojtyla, *Collected Poems*, p. 158.
[9] George Weigel, *Witness to Hope: The Biography of John Paul II* (New York: HarperCollins, 1999), p. 116.
[10] J. A. DiNola and Romanus Cessario (eds.), *Veritatis Splendor and the Renewal of Moral Theology* (Princeton, NJ: Scepter Publishers, 1999), p. 73.
[11] 'The Philosophical Foundations of the Thought of John Paul II', cited in John M. McDermott (ed.), *The Thought of Pope John Paul II: A Collection of Essays and Studies* (Rome: Editrice Pontificia Università Gregoriana, 1993), p. 23.

The Jewish philosopher, Emmanuel Levinas, at a conference organized in Paris on 'The philosophical Thought of John Paul II', in 1980, observed that what he found most appealing in Wojtyla's thought was

> above all the utter fidelity to the norm of philosophical discourse: the persistence of analysis in a language that is rigorous in the light of day and which is suspicious, if one can say, of theological inspiration. I have to admit, although observing the same norm, I have always allowed myself in my modest writings, to return more often than not to what the Cardinal does, to the letter and to his hermeneutic.[12]

As to the development of the thematization of the human person in the later Wojtyla, experts on his writings like Jaroslaw Kupczak acknowledge that the period we would call 'Wojtyla I' was a clear foundation for 'John Paul II's teaching in such documents as *Centesimus Annus*,[13] *Veritatis Splendor*[14] and his *Letter to Families'*.[15]

Wojtyla's interest in a comprehensive philosophy of the human person could be described as initially being like a gushing spring that issues forth in a strong torrent of poetic and philosophical reflections. *Love and Responsibility*[16] and *The Acting Person*[17] are the fruits of those original inundations. When Wojtyla became Pope in 1979, we could say that this river of interest in human anthropology bursts its banks, so to speak, and bifurcates into a rich delta of philosophical-theological analysis. The philosophical anthropology he had sought to work upon is now further developed into far distant streams but the human person is still at the centre of his concerns.

In the series of poems written as 'Easter Vigil' in 1966, there is one poem entitled: 'Invocation to Man who became the body of history'. It speaks warmly of Wojtyla's fascination with the human person and

---

[12] Emmanuel Levinas, 'Note sul pensiero del Cardinale Wojtyla', *Communio*, 54 (1980), p. 99.

[13] This encyclical, written in 1991 in the aftermath of the 1989 revolutions, reflects on social doctrines in the light of the twenty-first century. All encyclicals and letters can be accessed on the web at this URL: www.vatican.va In quoting from such documents I will refer to the section numbers.

[14] An encyclical written by Wojtyla in 1993. It can be seen as a profound defence of human freedom as worked out by Wojtyla in earlier philosophical works.

[15] A letter written by Wojtyla in 1994, declared by the United Nations Organization as the 'International year of the Family'.

[16] Karol Wojtyla, *Love and Responsibility*, tr. H. T. Willets (London: Collins, 1981).

[17] Karol Wojtyla, *The Acting Person*, tr. Andrzej Potocki (Dordrecht and Boston: D. Reidel, 1979).

describes him/her as being 'an eternal seismograph of the invisible but real'. It merits quotation:

> I call you and I seek you, oh Man, in whom
> man's history finds its body.
> I go towards you and do not say 'come'
> but simply 'be'.
> Be where there is no record, yet where man was,
> was with his soul, his heart, desire, suffering and will,
> consumed by feeling, burnt by most holy shame.
> Be an eternal seismograph of the invisible real.
> Oh, Man, in whom our lowest depths meet our heights,
> for whom what is within is not a dark burden but the heart.
> Man in whom each man can find his deep design,
> and the roots of his deeds: the mirror of life and death
> eyeing the human flux.
> Through the shallows of history I always reach you
> walking towards each heart, walking towards each thought
> (history – the overcrowding of thoughts, death of hearts).
> I seek your body for all history,
> I seek your depth.[18]

Those words, 'I seek your depth', are like a philosophical depth charge Wojtyla seeks to lay beneath the rich dimensions of human existence. His later writings can be seen as such an invocation to man and the philosophical attempt to articulate comprehensively the enactment of the reality of the human person. Inherent to any ideology is a distinctive view of the human person. Philosophy to Wojtyla is the 'seismograph' that should measure the adequacy of any theory of the person. Whatever 'shallows of history' we go through, he is optimistic that although humanity can reach its 'lowest depths' it can find the 'deep design' and 'heights' of what it means to be a 'person'. In reading this verse composition my mind turns to the fact that we have often made reference to the depths reached by humanity in the death camps and Wojtyla's remark that yet 'in the concentration camps there were people who managed to relate to others as other *I*'s, as *neighbors* – often to a heroic degree'.[19]

Human history can simply be, as he says, 'the overcrowding of thoughts' and the 'death of [human] hearts' but the philosopher can

---

18 Wojtyla, *Collected Poems*, p. 135.
19 Wojtyla, *Person and Community*, p. 206.

take up the challenge of seeking the irreducible 'depth' of the person, the kernel 'for all history'. If the commandment of love as perceived by Wojtyla in *The Acting Person* is to be a task and a rule of being,[20] so also is the philosophical and human enactment of what it means to be a person in the different dimensions of human existence, that is, moral, philosophical, economic, social, political, artistic, and so on. And this is the task Wojtyla sets himself in his writings under the authorship of John Paul II.

Wojtyla's first encyclical, *Redemptor Hominis* [The Redeemer of Man] is the first ever devoted almost exclusively to Christian anthropology. In it Wojtyla begins to explore before a global audience the modern human condition. It is an analysis, as Weigel says, 'he had been refining for thirty years'.[21] According to Wojtyla, all progress must be x-rayed from the point of view of the question: is such progress for the advancement of the person or not? He argues that

> it is not a matter . . . merely of giving an abstract answer to the question:
> Who is Man? . . . It is a matter of the meaningfulness of the various
> initiatives of everyday life and also of the premises for many civilization
> programmes, political programmes, economic ones, social ones, state
> ones, and many others.[22]

Wojtylan anthropology applied

Hence, Wojtyla attempts to use philosophical personalism and apply it to different dimensions of human existence and this is 'not altogether unlike its use in what we now call applied or practical ethics, as in business ethics or medical ethics'.[23] Wojtyla always showed an openness to dialogue since 'all human beings desire to know', and he would argue strongly for philosophical pluralism, because, as he observes in *Fides et Ratio*:

> the truths of philosophy, it should be said, are not restricted only to the
> sometimes ephemeral teachings of professional philosophers. All men
> and women, as I have noted, are in some sense philosophers and have
> their own philosophical conceptions with which they direct their lives.
> In one way or other, they shape a comprehensive vision and an answer

---

[20]   Wojtyla, *Acting Person*, pp. 298–9.
[21]   Weigel, *Witness to Hope*, p. 288.
[22]   John Paul II, *Redemptor Hominis*, § 16.
[23]   Peter Simpson, *On Karol Wojtyla* (New York: Wadsworth Press, 2001), p. 70.

to the question of life's meaning; and in the light of this they interpret
their own life's course and regulate their behavior.[24]

Horizons of human existence

In the 'Wojtyla II' period we can detect, as I have said, an attempt at
the application of Wojtyla's theory of the human person to the different
aspects of human existence. He saw the need for a 'new discourse'
philosophically within the different horizons in which 'we-act-together-
with-others'. We cannot hope to survey in detail the vast expanse of
his written materials. It will suffice to take various examples from his
later writings in order to explore how he applies his analysis of the
acting person to that person's participation in the worlds of art,
economics and morality. Levinas comments that 'Wojtyla's philosophy
seeks in the freedom of the acting person the meaning of the human'.[25]
We likewise, will seek in Wojtyla's exploration of the various worlds
of human action his project at work in the articulation of an adequate
philosophy of the person. This is a phenomenological stance on the
part of Wojtyla, since it is a move to study the subject matter, that is,
the human person, through the manner in which he/she appears and
acts within different dimensions. The human person can be understood
as acting within the following horizons:

1. *homo ethicus-interpersonalis*
2. *homo aestheticus*
3. *homo oeconomicus*

The horizons outlined here are not exhaustive but just indications
of the broad stage upon which the drama of human existence is acted
and in the words of Wojtyla, 'this great drama can leave nobody
indifferent'.[26] I will now explore some of Wojtyla's writings that deal
with these different aspects.

Before I continue, a criticism could be made, however, that there is
a hiatus in Wojtyla's philosophy. His philosophical project perhaps
ends up 'stillborn' or truncated because of his pastoral commitments
in Kraków and his subsequent election as Pope John Paul II. No doubt
there is some truth in this. It is, nonetheless, not the whole story.

---

[24]   John Paul II, *Fides et Ratio* [Faith and Reason], § 30.
[25]   Levinas, 'Note sul pensiero' p. 99 [my translation].
[26]   John Paul II *Redemptor Hominis*, § 16.

Interestingly, biographers speak of how Wojtyla on a personal level was quite capable of doing several things at the same time. Students relate how he, and sometimes to their personal annoyance and amazement, could be listening to their presentation of a thesis and at the same time answering personal correspondence. Asked later, if he thought it was not insensitive or rude, he was amazed as to why it should have been considered as discourteous in the first place. At a seminar organized to discuss his own work in the University of Lublin, Wojtyla was seen to be actually reading a book during the deliberations. One of the participants in a rather annoyed fashion asked Wojtyla what he thought of the contributions just made. Wojtyla stood up and surprised one and all by being able to summarize exactly what had gone before and, indeed, make his own pertinent observations.[27] Thus, we can argue that Wojtyla's appointment as Pope John Paul II did not necessarily lead, as we will see, to a derailment of his fundamental philosophical project.

Homo ethicus-interpersonalis: ethical-phenomenological application to a new Galileo crisis

What I have just said is, of course, on the personal and perhaps anecdotal level, but it does show how it is in fact quite possible to argue that while Wojtyla had other important responsibilities on hand, he could still find time to embark upon the project of the further development and enactment of his anthropological principles. In fact, Wojtyla discovered with his new responsibilities an even greater need to work out and apply what he had been reflecting upon in the 'Wojtyla I' period. On becoming John Paul II he encountered what Weigel terms, in fact, as 'A New Galileo Crisis'.[28] The crisis concerned the encyclical *Humanae Vitae* issued in 1968. It was a communications disaster for the Church. Weigel says 'it was another Galileo case, this time involving not arcane cosmological speculations but the most intimate aspects of the lives of . . . people'.[29]

Wojtyla discovered that part of the reason for the disaster in terms of the communication of the teaching within the context of the contemporary world was the failure to articulate an adequate philosophy of the person. Furthermore, there was no understanding of the

[27] Weigel, *Witness to Hope*, p. 138.
[28] Weigel, *Witness to Hope*, pp. 334–6.
[29] Weigel, *Witness to Hope*, p. 335.

enactment of personhood within the human body. Wojtyla exhibited as ever his critical realism in an interview with Weigel, commenting: 'What did a humanity that expressed itself through maleness and femaleness tell us about the human condition in general, and about men and women in particular?'[30]

Wojtyla decided in August 1978 to set about answering the question by writing a book about this issue. By October 1978 he was elected John Paul II, but the question and the answers he had worked out were not left unforgotten. The material he had gathered for the book were subsequently used in talks he gave during 130 general audiences, stretching from 5 September 1979 to 2 April 1980. John S. Grabowski describes how 'John Paul II has continued to focus on the human person. In this context we can locate his weekly general audiences . . . these [talks] comprise a catechesis of the bodily dimension of human personhood'.[31]

The French phenomenologist, Merleau-Ponty had worked on a not unrelated theme in attempting to describe an adequate phenomenology of the body. According to him, 'we never start from zero. We must exist in a certain incarnation'.[32] Exploring the topic of the perception of our own bodies, he writes: 'it is precisely my body which perceives the other's body and finds there something like a miraculous pro-longation of our own intentions . . . Henceforth, just as the parts of my body jointly form a system, the other's body and mine are a single whole.'[33]

It would be interesting to explore further the relationship between Merleau-Ponty's concept of embodiment of the subject and Wojtyla's philosophy/theology of the human body. The reader would undoubt-edly recognize clear correlations between the two if they read, for example, chapter 4 of Merleau-Ponty's *Phenomenology of Perception*, entitled 'Other Selves and the Human World'. Suffice it to say that for Merleau-Ponty as for Wojtyla, the body is not 'an instrument loosely attached to me that I can use'.[34] The body can be understood as 'me

[30] Weigel, *Witness to Hope*, p. 336.
[31] John Paul II, *The Theology of the Body: Human Love in the Divine Plan* (Boston: Pauline Books, 1997), p. 16.
[32] Quoted in Herbert Spiegelberg, *The Phenomenological Movement: A Historical Introduction* (Dordrecht: Kluwer Academic Publishers, 1994), p. 568.
[33] M. Merleau-Ponty, *Phenomenology of Perception*, tr. Colin Smith (London: Routledge & Kegan Paul, 1962), p. 354.
[34] Eric Matthews, *The Philosophy of Merleau-Ponty* (Bucks: Acumen Publishing Ltd, 2002), p. 92.

myself as involved with the world and as expressing myself in its movements'.[35] Merleau-Ponty and Wojtyla would concur in the fact that we have not the luxury of retreating into the Cartesian asylum of the 'cloistered self', for we exist as embodied human persons acting-together-with-others.

Weekly addresses

Karol Wojtyla attempts through his talks[36] on the book of Genesis at the weekly general audiences to get back to original experiences of humanity that offer us basic anthropological truths about the embodied human person. He surveys three such original experiences: original solitude, original unity, and original nakedness. I do not intend to give a complete presentation of these weekly talks in this chapter since it falls outside the remit of my theme. Nevertheless, let me briefly summarize what Wojtyla says in some of his addresses because it gives an example of his explorations of these original experiences and the ethical application of his theory of the human person. Wojtyla would of course further develop this application in the encyclical *Veritatis Splendor*[37] and other writings. We will, however, begin with his explorations in the general addresses. John Grabowski comments on Wojtyla's analysis in these talks of the originary experience of solitude as follows:

> The first man depicted in Genesis, like all men and women, was aware of himself as a subject, an 'I'. Yet he also discovered the uniqueness of his existence because, unlike the animals whom he named (cf. Gen. 2:19), his body was capable of expressing his subjectivity and freedom. This solitude provided an opportunity to respond in gratitude . . . Yet it also created a profound longing for another being like himself (cf. Gen. 2:18). This longing is answered in the creation of woman – another person, equal in dignity, another 'I' revealed through the body. Yet this body was wonderfully different from that of the man, revealing a unique and 'original' way of being a person.[38]

The 'original solitude' described by Wojtyla is of 'man as such'; it is not just the solitude of man the male, caused by the lack of woman.

[35]   Ibid.
[36]   These talks were given, as I have already said, during the general audiences. The material was taken from a book Wojtyla had in preparation.
[37]   This encyclical was written in 1993.
[38]   In John Paul II, *Theology of the Body*, p. 17.

This condition of solitude displays certain characteristics, that is, 'subjectivity' and 'self-determination'. In naming others, that is, the other creatures, man becomes aware of his distinctiveness. Man is, therefore, in Aristotelian terms, a rational animal, differentiated from others. But it is this originary experience that further opens man up to another being who is to be a 'helper fit for him' (Gen. 2:18, 20) and to the experience of what Wojtyla terms 'original unity'.

In the general audience held on 14 November 1979, and indeed in many other addresses, we can, I would argue, observe the working out of the Wojtylan anthropological project into a new ethical-phenomenological application. This time his audience is not limited to Krac\'ow or Lublin but is addressed to the whole of humanity. A careful reading of the material from the 'Wojtyla I' period allows us to perceive the further enactment of the drama initiated in *The Acting Person* and other works and then elaborated in different contexts in the 'Wojtyla II' phase. Wojtyla is as always careful to begin with human experience. He writes:

> in his original solitude man acquires a personal consciousness in the process of distinction from all living beings (*animalia*). At the same time, in this solitude, he opens up to a being akin to himself . . . This opening is no less decisive for the person of man; in fact, it is perhaps even more decisive than the distinction itself.[39]

Wojtyla emphasizes that the 'openness' to the 'other' (the *inter-personalis* dimension) is in fact more fundamental for man than the first differentiation, that is, between animals and himself. Once again as in *The Acting Person* Wojtyla seeks in his elaborations during the general audiences to avoid a cosmological reductionism in the definition of the person in the attempt to achieve an adequate anthropology.[40] In fact, an analysis of the two creation accounts in the book of Genesis, he believes, actually affords us the opportunity of being able 'to find ourselves on the ground of an adequate anthropology, which tries to understand and interpret man in what is essentially human'.[41] Wojtyla points out that the originary experience of solitude manifests not only the discovery of the characteristic transcendence peculiar to the person but also 'the discovery of an

---

[39]   John Paul II, *Theology of the Body*, p. 45.
[40]   Karol Wojtyla, *Person and Community*, pp. 210–12.
[41]   John Paul II, *Theology of the Body*, p. 58.

adequate relationship "to" the person, and therefore as an opening and expectation of a "communion of persons"".[42]

Wojtyla had spoken previously in *The Acting Person* of how the commandment '"Thou shalt love" entails the *juxtaposition* [my emphasis] of my neighbor with my own ego: "thy neighbor as thyself".'[43] In the weekly audience to which I have been making special reference,[44] Wojtyla alludes again to the significance of the 'fact of existing as a person "beside" a person'.[45] He stresses that the term *communio* rather than community expresses with greater precision that 'help' which is derived from the juxtaposition of my neighbour with my ego. Beneath the axiological aspect of the fact that we live together with others lies the ontological aspect. The term 'community' is too generic for Wojtyla and does not express adequately the ontological underpinning essential to understanding acting-together-with-others.

In his earlier explorations (Wojtyla I), he dismissed the understanding of 'community' as an abstract artificial subject created out of individual subjects into a homogenized reality. The community is not of itself a real subject, as Simpson puts it: 'the only proper subjects are individual persons. Only they are real supposita and self-determining causes of action. The community is not a new person or suppositum alongside individual persons. It is not a hypostatized subject.'[46] Wojtyla in an examination of the term *communio* explains that:

> the concept of *communio* . . . does not refer just to something in common, to community as a certain effect or even expression of the being and acting of persons. It refers rather to the very mode of being and acting of those persons, which is *a mode of being and acting in mutual relation to one another* (not just 'in common' with one another) *such that through this being and acting they mutually confirm and affirm one another as persons.*[47]

If we take this into consideration, I think we can understand Wojtyla's development of his anthropology through his exploration of the

[42] John Paul II, *Theology of the Body*, p. 45.
[43] Wojtyla, *Acting Person*, p. 295.
[44] Cf. General Audience on 14 November 1979.
[45] John Paul II, *Theology of the Body*, p. 46.
[46] Simpson, *Karol Wojtyla*, p. 41.
[47] Wojtyla, *Person and Community*, p. 321.

'original unity' experience of Man and Woman during the general audiences. During the address of 14 November 1979, Wojtyla says:

> the communion of persons could be formed only on the basis of a 'double solitude' of man and woman, that is, as their meeting in distinction from the world of living beings (*animalia*), which gave them both the possibility of being and existing in a special reciprocity. The concept of 'help' also expresses this reciprocity in existence, which no other living being could have ensured. All that constituted the foundation of the solitude of each of them was indispensable for this reciprocity. Self-knowledge and self-determination, that is, subjectivity and consciousness of the meaning of one's own body, was also indispensable.[48]

An obvious parallel can be seen here between what Wojtyla terms the 'double solitude' of man and woman in that they both have full subjectivity and consciousness, and his earlier reflections on the 'I – other' relationship in which self-determination, self-consciousness and self-possession are fundamental.[49] Commentators have referred to the 'newer' philosophical understanding Wojtyla brings to the interpretation of the Genesis texts. The Wojtylan reading of the texts illustrate that 'to be human is not merely to be an individual, a human thing, a free nature, an isolated thinking and acting self, but it is to participate in a substance and in a union with someone else or with others in a reality that transcends the individual'.[50]

Earlier, on 24 October 1979, Wojtyla had already commented in an address entitled, 'Man's Awareness of being a Person': 'The concept of original solitude includes both self-consciousness and self-determination. The fact that man is "alone" conceals within it this ontological structure and at the same time indicates true comprehension.'[51] At the conclusion of another talk in October Wojtyla asserts that an analysis of the book of Genesis makes us witnesses to the fact of

> how man 'distinguishes himself' . . . from the whole world of living beings (*animalia*) with his first act of self-consciousness, and of how, therefore, he reveals himself to himself and at the same time asserts himself as a 'person' in the visible world.[52]

[48] John Paul II, *Theology of the Body*, p. 46.
[49] Wojtyla, *Person and Community*, pp. 198–9.
[50] Kenneth D. Whitehead (ed.), *John Paul II – Witness to Truth* (Indiana: St Augustine's Press, 2001), p. 102.
[51] John Paul II, *Theology of the Body*, p. 38.
[52] John Paul II, *Theology of the Body*, p. 37.

We can see unfolding through a careful phenomenological analysis of the Genesis event the Wojtylan anthropology. The philosophical exploration of the human experience of 'it is not good that the man should be alone' (Gen. 2:18), that is, 'original solitude' unearths the truth that 'there is no man, not as male, until there is a woman. There is no woman until there is man, and there is no real humanity until the human species exists'.[53] This is just one example of the intricate symbiosis of philosophical thought between what we have termed the writings of 'Wojtyla I' and those of 'Wojtyla II'. There is a rich cross-pollination between the two phases. Simpson writes that 'we find in Wojtyla's theological writings a noteworthy instance of philosophy aiding faith to express itself . . . Seeing how Wojtyla makes his philosophy do this is already a matter of no little philosophical interest.'[54]

This use of philosophy is not meant to reduce it but meaningfully to apply it. In his subsequent encyclical *Fides et Ratio* he writes:

> Theology in fact has always needed and still needs philosophy's contribution. As a work of critical reason in the light of faith, theology presupposes and requires in all its research a reason formed and educated to concept and argument. Moreover, theology needs philosophy as a partner in dialogue in order to confirm the intelligibility and universal truths of its claims.[55]

As I mentioned previously, when Wojtyla became John Paul II, he was faced with a situation in the case of *Humanae Vitae* where an adequate philosophy of the person was not used to communicate the teaching at the basis of the document. Wojtyla was critical of the displacement between philosophy and theology that had led to such a scenario. It is not my concern to enter into merits and defects surrounding this particular debate, but Wojtyla's response to the crisis in his addresses during the general audiences are in Simpson's words a 'noteworthy instance of philosophy aiding faith to express itself'.[56]

Veritatis Splendor

A whole chapter could be devoted to his encyclical *Veritatis Splendor*. We do not have time for such an analysis; however, it would be remiss

---

[53]   Whitehead (ed.), *John Paul II*, pp. 102–3.
[54]   Simpson, *Karol Wojtyla*, p. 70.
[55]   John Paul II, *Fides et Ratio*, § 77.
[56]   Simpson, *Karol Wojtyla*, p. 70.

of me if I do not make some brief observations about it. Morality for Wojtyla is not a case of a paste-on attachment to the acting person; rather, it is the application of what it means to advance and actualize the *good* of the human person. It is true that the human person's capacity to know the truth is at times eclipsed and the human will to seek the truth is sometimes weakened. Wojtyla and others of his generation were first-hand witnesses to this occurrence within the theatre of war and totalitarianism. Nevertheless, Wojtyla affirms, and here we can discern a philosophy of deep anthropological optimism:

> in the depths of [man's] heart there always remains a yearning for absolute truth and a thirst to attain full knowledge of it. This is eloquently proved by man's tireless search for knowledge in all fields. It is proved even more by his search for *the meaning of life*. The development of science and technology, this splendid testimony of the human capacity for understanding and for perseverance, does not free humanity from the obligation to ask the ultimate religious questions. Rather, it spurs us on to face the most painful and decisive of struggles, those of the heart and of the moral conscience.[57]

In other words, within the human condition there are the in-built deep-seated questions: 'What must I do? How do I distinguish good from evil?'[58] These questions emerge within the person and, thus, morality cannot be understood simply in terms of the application of an extrinsic legalism. Wojtyla stresses that it is always up to 'the acting subject [to personally assimilate] the truth contained in the law. He appropriates this truth of his being and makes it his own by his acts and the corresponding virtues'.[59]

If Wojtyla understood the necessity of working out an adequate philosophy of the person, he equally sees that there is a corresponding requirement to develop the theoretical-ethical underpinning to the moral dimension of personhood. He writes:

> certainly there is a need to seek out and to discover *the most adequate formulation* for universal and permanent norms in the light of different cultural contexts, a formulation most capable of ceaselessly expressing their historical relevance, of making them understood and of authentically interpreting their truth.[60]

[57]   John Paul II, *Veritatis Splendor*, § 1.
[58]   Ibid.
[59]   John Paul II, *Veritatis Splendor*, § 52.
[60]   John Paul II, *Veritatis Splendor*, §§ 53–4.

It is interesting to find within this context of giving foundation to a personalist ethic, a further reference to and use by Wojtyla of the commandment of love of neighbour. Writing in chapter 1 of the encyclical, Wojtyla remarks:

'You shall love your neighbour as yourself' (Matt. 19:19; cf. Mark 12:31). In this commandment we find a precise expression of *the singular dignity of the human person.* [The commandments] teach us man's true humanity. They shed light on the essential duties, and so indirectly on the fundamental rights, inherent in the nature of the human person.[61]

Safeguarded in the commandment of love of neighbour is the good of the person. That entails a freedom of human action informed by reason but ordered towards the truth 'and finds its fulfilment in the goodness – the *beatitude* – of human flourishing'[62] of oneself and the 'other'.

Wojtyla's analysis of the conversation between Jesus and the rich young man[63] is filled with the human drama of the question 'what must I do?' Here we can observe Wojtyla's clear personalist credentials. The rich young man is unnamed, thus in him

we can recognize every person . . . the *question* is not so much about rules to be followed [legalism], but *about the full meaning of life.* This is in fact the aspiration at the heart of every human decision and action, the quiet searching and interior prompting which sets freedom in motion. This question is ultimately an appeal to the absolute Good which attracts and beckons us.[64]

The rich young man's quest for eternal happiness is, therefore, everyone's search, and as Weigel states, the analysis in *Veritatis Splendor* very much 'reflects themes from the dramatic anthropology Karol Wojtyla had been unfolding since his days in the Rhapsodic Theatre'.[65]

Ethical questions as I outlined above are, thus, grafted into the nature of what it means to be a human person. It is in fact this reality, as Weigel puts it that

provides the 'grammar' [necessary] for serious moral conversation among people of different cultures and life experiences. This

---

[61] John Paul II, *Veritatis Splendor,* § 13.
[62] Weigel, *Witness to Hope,* p. 690.
[63] This conversation occurs in Matthew 19:16ff.
[64] John Paul II, *Veritatis Splendor,* § 7.
[65] Weigel, *Witness to Hope,* pp. 691–2.

understanding of the rootedness of the moral life in a universal nature is, the Pope further suggests, the foundation on which a new humanism capable of defending human dignity can be built.[66]

Wojtyla's analysis of the encounter between Jesus and the rich young man is in terms of philosophical methodology, phenomenological. As Conley says: 'the phenomenological method places great values on the attentive description of the various appearances of a question at each step of insight.'[67]

In the exploration Wojtyla gives a reflective description of the human search for answers to fundamental questions. He starts with the concrete question, and then he interprets what the question reveals about the seeker. Wojtyla says: 'we must carefully enquire into the meaning of the question asked by the rich young man.'[68] The rich young man articulates the question and gives his own answer in terms of how he has conformed to the Law. But the young man's question was: 'Teacher, what must I do to have eternal life?' (Matt. 19:16). The question is: Has the young man answered his own question adequately? Since he has posed the question in the first place, it would appear that the answer is in the negative because, in spite of saying 'I have kept all these [laws]',[69] he feels unfulfilled as a person. In other words, his own answer does not open up to the perspective of the infinite mystery of the human being and the realization and actualization of what it means to say that the human being is a *person*.

Wojtyla interprets the rich young man's question as ultimately leading towards the transcendent. He writes: 'To ask about the good, in fact, ultimately means to turn towards God, the fullness of goodness.'[70] The important point here is that the rich young man, that is, everyone, is actually in search of the 'fullness of goodness'. This Wojtyla sets out as the basis for dialogue with the whole of humanity in terms of the ethical nature of the human person. As MacIntyre observes, the rich young man 'must go beyond mere conformity with the law',[71] otherwise, he will not be a true moral agent

[66] Weigel, *Witness to Hope*, p. 689.
[67] Conley, 'Philosophical Foundations', p. 24.
[68] John Paul II, *Veritatis Splendor*, § 8.
[69] John Paul II, *Veritatis Splendor*, § 6.
[70] John Paul II, *Veritatis Splendor*, § 9.
[71] Alasdair MacIntyre, 'How Can We Learn What *Veritatis Splendor* Has to Teach', in DiNola and Cessario (eds.), *The Splendor of the Truth*, p. 89.

in the first place, that is, in the language of *The Acting Person* he must become an efficient cause of his own actions. Thus, MacIntyre writes, otherwise 'we will be unable to recognize the truth concerning our own nature and to realize its potentiality for an exercise of rational freedom through which we can perfect our individual and communal lives'.[72]

In conclusion, Wojtyla measures any moral theory in terms of its correspondence 'to the truth about man and his freedom'.[73] In *The Acting Person* Wojtyla had outlined the dangers of any reductionism in a philosophy of the human person. For example, he adverts to the risks inherent in the absolutization of consciousness. This approach understands the person solely from the perspective of the cognitive function. Wojtyla, in fact, seeks as we know to reverse 'the post-Cartesian attitude toward man'.[74] In *Veritatis Splendor*, he tries to apply his previous insights concerning the acting person to the ethical dimensions of the human person, and thus, strengthen the theoretical framework for the dialogue with the whole of humanity. He observes: 'The person, including the body, is completely entrusted to himself, and it is in the unity of body and soul that the person is the subject of his own moral acts.'[75]

Here Wojtyla outlines the importance of an integrated philosophy of the embodied person.[76] John F. Crosby points out how the embodied person is fundamental to Wojtyla's personalism. According to him, Wojtyla perceives in the modern world not only a materialism that reduces the person to the body but also 'a certain aversion to the body'.[77] Crosby writes that Wojtyla:

> speaks of a widespread 'neo-Manichean culture' – that conceives of persons as estranged from their bodies, as merely using their bodies in

---

[72] Ibid.
[73] John Paul II, *Veritatis Splendor*, § 48.
[74] Wojtyla, *Acting Person*, p. viii.
[75] John Paul II, *Veritatis Splendor*, § 48.
[76] There is an anticipation of the Wojtylan philosophy of the body in the philosopher Gabriel Marcel. As O'Malley states: 'embodiment, or incarnation is a recurrent and central theme of Marcel's philosophy' (cf. Paul Arthur Schlipp and Lewis Edwin Hahn (eds.), *The Philosophy of Gabriel Marcel* [Illinois: Open Court, 1991], p. 286). Marcel never developed the theme 'I am my body' in terms of human sexuality which in fact Wojtyla does (cf. Wojtyla, *Love and Responsibility*).
[77] John F. Crosby, 'John Paul's Vision of Sexuality and Marriage', in Geoffrey Gneuchs (ed.), *The Legacy of Pope John Paul II: His Contribution to Catholic Thought* (New York: Herder & Herder, 2000), p. 59.

an instrumental way . . . [Wojtyla] is distinguished . . . by the originality
with which he has unfolded the truth that our personhood is embodied,
and embodied as man and woman . . . [that the body] is a dimension of
the being of each person.[78]

He had already discussed this theme in his weekly addresses. It is
only in reference to the 'unified totality' of the human person that we
can grasp the meaning of the different dimensions of personhood. The
relevance of such a theme is understandable in the contemporary world
even in terms of the feminist critique of the advertising media's attitude
to the feminine body. 'Physicalism' reduces the person to an aspect of
themselves and not their totality. MacIntyre comments:

> Human bodies are more than physicochemical and biological structures,
> although they are both these things. This conception of the body [as
> outlined in *Veritatis Splendor*] as primarily a bearer of meanings links
> Aristotelian themes in the philosophy of mind and body with perspec-
> tives developed within Polish phenomenology by, among others, Karol
> Wojtyla, and also of course by a variety of followers of Husserl there
> and elsewhere, most notably by Merleau-Ponty but also, earlier and as
> strikingly by Edith Stein.[79]

The rich young man is invited in the encounter with Jesus to
participate in 'an act of moral and rational self-recognition'.[80] It would,
according to Wojtyla's approach, be an inauthentic human attitude
to just conform to an extrinsic legalism (as in the case of the young
man who says, 'I have kept all these' laws), because this means a
renunciation of true participation and ends up as a passive acceptance
of the law without understanding the need for the participation of the
human will. Wojtyla's exploration of the encounter in the encyclical
reveals the dynamic involved in acting so as to advance the moral
good of the person. The rich young man could not have remained
indifferent after he witnessed the response unfold to his question.
Similarly, the moral philosopher cannot remain unresponsive to
Wojtyla's fundamental argument that human freedom 'has a built-in
trajectory, a dynamism that produces in every human person an
aspiration to goodness and excellence'.[81]

---

[78]   Crosby, 'John Paul's Vision', pp. 59–60.
[79]   MacIntyre, 'How Can We Learn' p. 86.
[80]   MacIntyre, 'How Can We Learn', p. 77.
[81]   Weigel, *Witness to Hope*, p. 689.

Homo aestheticus: art as an attempt at recapturing the reality of the human person

Philosophers are not the only ones who can pose fundamental questions about the unfolding drama of human existence. Wojtyla was profoundly aware of this and herein lies his multidimensional approach to the question of the human person. The writings from the 'Wojtyla I' period display a type of 'philosophical pluralism', as I have commented on previously. Serretti speaks likewise of the 'multiform' nature of Wojtyla's thought, when he comments:

> This multifarious nature of thought, that is almost at this point in our cultural perspective unheard of, allows Wojtyla to approach the truth about man and about God from contrasting levels and perspectives that surprisingly finally come together. When there is unity in life and experience the consonance and convergence of its various expressions is not unexpected.[82]

The 'Wojtyla II' phase is equally characterized by a 'stereophonic use of different disciplines'[83] to illuminate the philosophical quest with respect to the truth about the human person. We can see that Wojtyla's 'literary training and theatrical experience were joined to a rigorous philosophical analysis to produce a picture of human life as inherently, "structurally" *dramatic*'.[84] Speaking about the specific contribution of writers and artists, he notes that they 'do not just teach, but they also please, by enticing minds and hearts to the truth'.[85]

Art capturing who we are

We can add that art does not just 'please' but it also provokes reactions within the reader or viewer. A pervasive category in modern art is that of the ugly. Ernst van Alphen tells us, for example, what an encounter with the art of Francis Bacon is like:

> Seeing a work by Francis Bacon hurts. It causes pain . . . I was literally speechless. I was touched so profoundly because the experience was one of total engagement, of being dragged along by the work. I was

---

[82] Cf. Introduction by Massimo Serretti in *Karol Wojtyla: Perché L'Uomo* (Vatican City: Libreria Editrice Vaticana, 1995), p. 11. This book is a collection in Italian of Wojtyla's essays most of which are also contained in *Person and Community*.

[83] Conley, 'Philosophical Foundations', p. 26.

[84] Weigel, *Witness to Hope*, p. 177.

[85] Weigel, *Witness to Hope*, p. 163.

perplexed about the level on which these paintings touched me: I could not even formulate what the paintings were about, still less what aspect of them hurt me so deeply.

As soon as I became aware of this incapacitation, however, I realized that it was not new, and that other works of literature and art also have this disabling effect on me.[86]

Indeed, Pasquale Foresi, in an article on the crisis of art, speaks about how contemporary art is characterized more by 'decompositions' than 'compositions'. He writes:

Contemporary art manages in some way to express the reality of who we are as human beings in the present day. It's still in a discordant style but really that's because it's man himself who as of yet experiences discord within and in his own relationships . . . If art articulates itself in decomposed forms, it means that we are already in an existence that is beyond and that has not yet found a formal perfection.[87]

Wojtyla was aware of the power of different forms of drama since he had himself translated Sophocles' *Oedipus* from the original Greek into Polish.[88] Thus, he was no stranger to the drama of Greek tragedy and its ability to 'illuminate a different aspect of the drama of humanity'.[89] It is no wonder that Wojtyla chose to translate this play for it 'remains a classic example of a gradual achievement of personal identity or integration in response to the test of existence'.[90] As a drama it unfolds as a remarkable attempt to recapture the reality of the human person and the struggle in achieving 'self-determination', 'self-governance' and 'self-possession'. All of which, according to Wojtyla, are fundamental stages in the full enactment of the human person.

The theologian Yves Congar relates an interesting facet of Wojtyla's attitude and openness to contemporary culture. Congar was on a drafting committee with Wojtyla during Vatican II for a document

---

[86]   Ernst van Alpen, *Francis Bacon and the Loss of Self* (Cambridge, MA: Harvard University Press, 1993), p. 9.

[87]   Pasquale Foresi, 'La crisi dell'arte', *Nuova Umanità* XXIII (May–August 2001) (Rome: Città Nuova), pp. 367, 369.

[88]   Karol Wojtyla, *The Collected Plays and Writings on Theater*, tr. Boleslaw Taborski (Berkeley: University of California Press, 1987), p. 4.

[89]   Brendan M. Purcell, *The Drama of Humanity: Towards a Philosophy of Humanity in History* (New York: Peter Lang, 1996), p. 75.

[90]   Purcell, *The Drama of Humanity*, p. 96.

concerning the Church and the modern world.[91] He kept a diary and in it he noted that Wojtyla had emphasized that

> the contemporary world also gives some answers to these questions [that is, the problems and questions that arise in the modern world about truth and meaning], and it is necessary for us to consider these answers as well . . . In the text that has been presented to us [that is, the draft text], there is no reference to the answers that the contemporary world is offering, and no discussion about the problems that are created because of these conflicting answers.[92]

Hence, we cannot but notice Wojtyla's 'dialogic' approach to the drama of human existence. He sees that modern art in all its forms also has the possibility of posing questions and proposing answers that lie at the heart of contemporary humanity. He would I am sure concur with Dostoevsky's admonition that 'the world would be saved by "beauty"'.[93] Indeed, in his letter written to artists in 1999, he acknowledges as much when he writes: 'Beauty is a key to the mystery and a call to transcendence. It is an invitation to savour life and to dream of the future.'[94]

Already in *The Acting Person* he had alluded to the fact of how artistic action can in itself serve 'the realization of truth, good, and beauty'.[95] He comments:

> [T]he notion of the 'transcendence of the person' may be broadened and examined in relation to all the traditionally distinguished transcendentalia: 'being', 'truth', 'good' and 'beauty'. Man has access to them through knowledge, and in the wake of knowledge, of the mind, through the will and through action . . . the transcendence of the person understood metaphysically is no abstract notion; the evidence of experience tells us that the spiritual life of man essentially refers to, and in its strivings vibrates around his experientially innermost attempts to reach truth, goodness, and beauty.[96]

---

[91] The document later became one of the central texts of Vatican II, entitled *Gaudium et Spes*.

[92] Weigel, *Witness to Hope*, p. 168.

[93] Fyodor Dostoevsky, *The Idiot*, tr. Alan Myers (Oxford: Oxford University Press, 1992), Part III, ch. 5, p. 402.

[94] John Paul II, *Letter of His Holiness Pope John Paul II to Artists*, § 16. Hereafter referred to as *Letter to Artists*.

[95] Wojtyla, *Acting Person*, p. 155.

[96] Wojtyla, *Acting Person*, pp. 155–6.

Wojtyla explores *how* this is possible through his own works of art,[97] commentaries[98] and finally in his addressing artists in his recent letter to them.[99] Wojtyla conceives of the artistic tools available to the artist as being both diagnostic and therapeutic in the task of recapturing the reality of the human person. The war and subsequent experiences of totalitarianism had shattered all confidence in the search for truth. There was a need for the redemption of man. Allied with this was the requirement for a proper diagnosis of what had gone wrong. Thus, the diagnosis is just as important as the therapeutic aspect. Wojtyla can be likened to one who seeks the recovery of the meaning of what it means to be a person in a world where 'the camp lights [of the prevailing ideology] drive away the stars';[100] a recovery which requires the injection of understanding and judgment, in order that 'winter twilight cannot be mistaken for the summer noonday sun'.[101]

Polish Romanticism as path to recovery

Wojtyla was very influenced during his earlier period by Polish Romanticism because he discovered in it a road to recovery on the individual and societal levels. Nineteenth-century Europe was full of revolutionary literature. For many theorists revolution meant a complete break with the past. This was not the case with Polish Romanticism. On the contrary, it

> considered revolution [in terms of] the recovery of a lost value that had been crucial in the nation's formation. The past was not to be overthrown but recovered as an instrument of national renewal . . . history had a spiritual core; the deterioration of its traditional national virtues had caused Poland's political collapse . . . In epic poems like *Pan Tadeuz*, in visionary poetic dramas like *Forefathers' Eve* (which had such an emotional impact on its audiences that czarist censors sometimes banned it), and in didactic works like *The Books of the Polish Nation and of the Polish Pilgrims* . . . history had a deep spiritual dimension in which suffering prepared the soul for glory. It was a familiar theme . . . redemptive suffering was also the discipline.[102]

[97] Wojtyla's plays and poems already used throughout this thesis.
[98] Wojtyla, *Collected Plays*.
[99] John Paul II, *Letter to Artists*.
[100] Alexander Solzhenitsyn, *One Day in the Life of Ivan Denisovich*, tr. Ralph Parker (London: Penguin Books, 1963), p. 18.
[101] Cf. Bernard Lonergan, *Insight: A Study of Human Understanding* (London: Longman, 1958), p. xix
[102] Weigel, *Witness to Hope*, pp. 33–4.

Cyprian Kamil Norwid (1821–83) is, for example, one of Wojtyla's favourite poets. His poetry was: 'an effort to probe the truth of things through art, and a deliberate rejection of "art for art's sake" '.[103]

Wojtyla, therefore, perceives art's therapeutic aspect as helping to recover the inner beauty of the human person. The positive aspect of the artist's work can be termed *anamnesis*, that is the task of restoring and complementing the reality of the human person on the historical, social and personal levels.

There is, I would argue, a close correlation between Wojtyla's interest in Polish Romanticism and the canons of the KUL philosophers we referred to in the opening chapter of this book. I stated then that

> the fourth canon for these philosophers was that the history of philo-
> sophy has insights relevant to the contemporary philosophical
> investigation of the human person ... In light of this, the reductive
> depersonalization experiences on the historical level can help us
> unravel anew a coherent philosophy of the person on the individual
> and social levels.

Art in a therapeutic sense is not just for its own sake but can be an experience of regaining and complementing our understanding of the truth about the human person. Stephen Dedalus in Joyce's *A Portrait of the Artist as a Young Man* attempts to describe to his friend Lynch how it 'would be a mistake to suppose that something beautiful is simply a means to some further glory rather than a glorious being in itself'.[104] Turning and walking towards Merrion Square in Dublin, Stephen and Lynch continue their discussion about beauty. Stephen points to a basket which a butcher's boy had put over his head, as he explains

> when you have apprehended that basket as one thing and have then
> analysed it according to its form and apprehended it as a thing you
> make the only synthesis which is logically and esthetically permissible.
> You see that it is that thing which it is and no other thing. The radiance
> of which he [Aquinas] speaks is the scholastic *quidditas*, the *whatness*
> of a thing. This supreme quality is felt by the artist when the esthetic
> image is first conceived in his imagination.[105]

---

[103] Weigel, *Witness to Hope*, p. 35.
[104] Oswald Hanfling (ed.), *Philosophical Aesthetics: an introduction* (Oxford: Blackwell, 1992), p. 123.
[105] James Joyce, *A Portrait of the Artist as a Young Man* (London: Paladin, 1988), p. 217.

Likewise, as we will see, Wojtyla perceives of similar qualities within the aesthetical in human experience. He clearly acknowledges the artist's role within the current context of philosophical *amnesia* as being restorative as to the truth and beauty of the human person.

Rhapsodic Theatre

Wojtyla is, as already evidenced in this study, an accomplished artist in his own right. His own acting career started in secondary school and continued right through the war years. At the age of 19 he wrote his first play, *David*, which was subsequently lost. In the summer of 1940 he wrote *Job* and *Jeremiah*. He subsequently wrote: *Our God's Brother* (c. 1949), *The Jeweller's Shop* (1960), and *Radiation of Fatherhood* (1964). During the German occupation of Poland Wojtyla collaborated with Mieczyslaw Kotlarczyk and others in the founding of the Rhapsodic Theatre (1941). This was 'a theater of the inner self'.[106] During the Stalinist period the theatre was closed down and Wojtyla consequently wrote several articles in its defence. They outline clearly how Wojtyla understood drama and the role of the actor. In them we can discern to some degree his *Weltanschauung* when it comes to an understanding of *homo aestheticus*.

He explains how this 'theatre of the word' was born out of the realities of everyday life:

> [O]f all the complex resources of theatrical art, there remained only the living word, spoken by people in extrascenic conditions, in a room with a piano. The unheard-of scarcity of the means of expression turned into a creative experiment. The company discovered, or rather confirmed an earlier belief, that the fundamental element of dramatic art is the living human word. It is also the nucleus of drama, a leaven through which human deeds pass, and from which they derive their proper dynamics.[107]

It is Wojtyla's contention that this new theatrical style in fact reaches

> beyond theater and into the philosophical concept of man and the world. The supremacy of word over gesture indirectly restores the supremacy of thought over movement and impulse in man. It turns out also that thought does not mean immobility; it has its own movement. It is this

---

[106] Mary Shivanandan, *Crossing the Threshold of Love: A New Vision of Marriage* (Washington, DC: Catholic University of America Press, 1999), p. 5.
[107] Karol Wojtyla, *Collected Plays*, p. 379.

movement of thought, this dynamics of thought that the living human word grasps and makes into a nucleus of action ... Man, actor and listener-spectator alike, frees himself from obtrusive exaggeration of gesture, from the activism that overwhelms his inner, spiritual nature instead of developing it. Thus freed, he grasps those propositions that he cannot reach and grasp in everyday life. Participation in a theatrical performance, almost in spite of him, becomes festive as it reconstructs in him the proportions between thought and gesture that man, at least subconsciously, sometimes longs for. In all this too is the catharsis, the psychological purification that the theater can bring out.[108]

What is interesting in terms of my analysis is the concept that emerges of the human person as 'actor'. Central is not so much the actor who 'acts' but the problem that 'acts' within him.[109] Wojtyla comments: 'The problem itself acts, rouses interest, disturbs, evokes the audience's participation, demands understanding and a solution.'[110]

The narrative is in fact peripheral to the problem. The actor is, according to Wojtyla, a rhapsodist, which does not mean that '[h]e simply "acts". Rather, he carries the problem ... The rhapsodic actor does not become a character but carries a problem; he is one of those who carry the problem of the whole performance.'[111] Wojtyla argues that this does not result in the rejection of realism in theatre but 'enables us to understand the inner base of human action, the very fulcrum of human movement'.[112] In *The Acting Person* Wojtyla makes the important distinction in regard to 'happening' in man, that is, between *agere* (man-acts) and *pati* (something-happens-in-man).[113] He writes:

> Man's experience culminates in the experience of his ego. It is the ego that is the agent of actions. When man acts, [*agere*] the ego has the experience of its own efficacy in action. When, on the other hand, there is something happening in man [*pati*], then the ego does not experience its own efficacy and is not the actor.[114]

[108] Karol Wojtyla, *Collected Plays*, p. 380.
[109] Wojtyla, *Collected Plays*, p. 373.
[110] Ibid.
[111] Wojtyla, *Collected Plays*, p. 374.
[112] Wojtyla, *Collected Plays*, p. 380.
[113] Cf. Chapter 2 of this book.
[114] Wojtyla, *Acting Person*, p. 80.

It is my contention that we can observe Wojtyla's philosophy of the acting person enacted in his theory of the theatre.[115] The actor does not just take on the character he is acting simply by gestures and special theatrical effects. It requires real 'participation', as Wojtyla says, a carrying of the problem. The actor is, therefore, not someone in whom something happens (*pati*), rather, he is someone who 'acts' (*agere*), he is efficacious in seeking a resolution to the problem. Wojtyla notes:

> This theater safeguards young actors against developing a destructive individualism . . . [because] he hardly ever has to be a given man, nor does he have to create a character; he has only to delineate it indirectly in the consciousness of the listeners-spectators.[116]

This is why it is called 'theatre of the inner self': its concern is with the 'realizing of man'.[117] Wojtyla and Kotlarczk took the masterpieces of the national Polish literature and used the Rhapsodic methods to present 'a "synthesis" of each literary work'.[118] Mickiewicz, Slowacki and Norwid were the great poets/dramatists of the Polish Romantic period that Wojtyla encountered and enjoyed. When Wojtyla and his colleagues put on these plays and developed the concept of the Rhapsodic Theatre it can be all understood in the light of an attempt at the anamnetic recovery of the lost value of the human person on the personal, social and historical levels.[119] Weigel reminds us that Kotlarczyk's 'theater of the inner word', 'would make present universal truths and universal moral values, [the truth about the human person] which stood in judgment on the here-and-now and offered the possibility of authentic transformation'.[120]

There is perhaps a parallel between the theory of the Rhapsodic Theatre and the Theatre of the Absurd. Martin Esslin coined the phrase 'theatre of the absurd' in 1961 to refer to a number of dramatists of the 1950s (for example Samuel Beckett and Eugène Ionesco) whose work evoke the absurd by abandoning logical form, character and so

---

[115] Taborski mentions how Wojtyla was influenced by lectures of the Polish phenomenologist philosopher Roman Ingarden 'who attributed particular importance to words spoken in a performance', in Karol Wojtyla, *Collected Plays*, p. 12.

[116] Wojtyla, *Collected Plays*, p. 386.

[117] Wojtyla, *Collected Plays*, pp. 386–7.

[118] Wojtyla, *Collected Plays*, p. 7.

[119] Wojtyla, *Collected Plays*, p. 380.

[120] Weigel, *Witness to Hope*, p. 37.

on. Harold Pinter and Václav Havel are other dramatists associated with the theatre of the absurd.

In speaking about the theatre of the absurd Esslin writes: 'The Theatre of the Absurd has renounced arguing *about* the absurdity of the human condition; it merely *presents* it in being.'[121] This is not unlike Wojtyla's observation on the role of the actor as not becoming a character but carrying the problem. Writing about the dramas of Harold Pinter, Esslin's comments about the starting point of Pinter's theatre are somewhat similar to that of the Rhapsodists. He notes that Pinter's theatre is 'a return to some basic elements of drama – the suspense created by the elementary ingredients of pure, preliterary theatre: a stage, two people, a door'.[122]

As we have seen, Wojtyla commented that the departure point for the Rhapsodic Theatre was 'the living word, spoken by people in extrascenic conditions, in a room with a piano. The unheard-of scarcity of the means of expression turned into a creative experiment.'

In an attempt to capture realism about the human condition Harold Pinter rejects the notion of a 'well-made play'. He rejects 'an over-defined motivation of characters in drama'.[123] This is to some extent comparable to Wojtyla's understanding that the narrative in Rhapsodic Theatre is secondary to the problem.[124] When Kenneth Tynan reproached Pinter in a radio interview for a lack of social realism in his plays, he replied that he was 'dealing with his characters "at the extreme edge of their living, where they are living pretty much alone", at a point, that is, when they are back in their rooms, confronted with the basic problem of being'.[125]

It is interesting to note it was in Poland that a number of very gifted artists turned also to the new type of play in the Theatre of the Absurd.[126] This is conceivably because, not unlike the Rhapsodists, they found in this kind of theatre 'an instrument for the communication of

---

[121] Martin Esslin, *The Theatre of the Absurd* (London: Penguin Books, 1983), p. 25.
[122] Esslin, *Theatre of the Absurd*, p. 235.
[123] Esslin, *Theatre of the Absurd*, pp. 242–3.
[124] Esslin, for example, comments: 'In turning their backs on the psychological or narrative theatre . . . the dramatists of the Theatre of the Absurd are . . . engaged in establishing a new dramatic convention'; *Theatre of the Absurd*, p. 265.
[125] Esslin, *Theatre of the Absurd*, p. 262.
[126] Esslin mentions Stanislaw Ignancy Witkiewicz (1885–1939) and Witold Gombrowicz (1904–1969) in this regard (cf. pp. 392–5).

human predicaments portrayed, not in their outward and accidental circumstances'[127] but in terms of the 'inner self'.

To all dedicated to the search for new 'epiphanies' of beauty

It is therefore, in my opinion, not at all surprising that in 1999 John Paul II should address a letter to artists.[128] This letter is an exploration of the role of the human person within the horizon of art. It bears the hallmark of the personalist dynamism of Wojtyla, which I will explore in due course, where the human person is above all characterized as a free human agent.[129] It can be understood in terms of the hermeneutic of the application of Wojtyla's theory of the human person to the context in which that person participates with others in the world of culture and art. As we have previously seen Wojtyla comes to this topic as an artist himself and as a theatrical practitioner. I have made reference to his earlier writings on theatre, which are contained in *The Collected Plays*. In the general audiences held as John Paul II, already referred to, he does make brief references to art. These particular addresses occurred in 1981 and in them he dealt with such themes as: 'The Human Body: Subject of Works of Art', 'Reflections on the Ethos of the Human Body in Works of Artistic Culture', 'Art Must Not Violate the Right to Privacy', and finally, 'Ethical Responsibilities in Art'.[130]

In these general addresses what we observe being elaborated is the implications of an adequate philosophy of the embodied person. The title of his first address indicates his fundamental starting point, that is, 'The Human Body: *Subject* [my emphasis] of Works of Art'.[131] Wojtyla observes that in

these reflections [the addresses given during the general audiences] we have systematically tried to show how the dimension of man's personal subjectivity is an indispensable element . . . which we must discover and presuppose at the basis of the problem of the human body . . . We cannot consider the body an objective reality outside the personal subjectivity of man, of human beings, of male and female. Nearly all of the problems of the ethos of the body are bound up at the same time with its ontological identification as the body of the person.

[127] Esslin, *Theatre of the Absurd*, p. 316.
[128] John Paul II, *Letter to Artists*, 1999.
[129] Wojtyla, *Acting Person*, p. 77.
[130] John Paul II, *Theology of the Body*, pp. 218–29.
[131] John Paul II, *Theology of the Body*, pp. 218–20.

They are also bound up with the content and quality of the subjective experience, that is, of the 'life' both of one's own body and its interpersonal relations.[132]

The human body of the person, within the Wojtylan perspective, is not just an object in works of art, but is also to be understood as subject. Wojtyla makes clear reference to 'the ontological identification' of the human body as person. Indeed, the use of the genitive case in the above quotation, that is, 'as the body *of* the person' is charged with philosophical significance if it is read in the light of the writings of the 'Wojtyla I' period I have already examined.[133]

The human person acts together with others in different concrete dimensions and this has implications in their attitudes and behaviour. In the language of Wojtyla, the 'other' is after all another 'I'. The works of art can actually facilitate the enactment of 'being an embodied person' and lead to an extension into the objective. In other words, culture in itself can allow the subjective consciousness and also the subjective experience of the body extend out into the objective dimension of the aesthetical. Wojtyla writes:

> Man meets the 'reality of the body' and 'experiences the body' even when it becomes a subject of creative activity, a work of art, a content of culture. Generally speaking, it must be recognized that this contact takes place on the plane of aesthetic experience. In this plane, it is a question of viewing the work of art (in Greek *aisthá nomai*: I look, I observe). Therefore, in the given case, it is a question of the objectivized body, outside its ontological identity, in a different way and according to criteria characteristic of artistic activity. Yet the man who is admitted to viewing in this way is a priori deeply bound up with the meaning of the prototype, or model. In this case the prototype is himself – the living man and the living body.[134]

Wojtyla's personalism is clearly evident here in this exploration of the embodied person as a subject of art. In a work of art (for example, a painting) I gaze upon the canvas and see the artist's depiction of an event or persons.[135] Nevertheless, we view the work of art as 'persons', and it speaks to us as 'persons'. We are, writes Wojtyla:

---

132 John Paul II, *Theology of the Body*, p. 218.
133 Cf. Wojtyla, *Acting Person*.
134 John Paul II, *Theology of the Body*, p. 218.
135 For example, take Caravaggio's 'The Calling of Matthew', in the Church of San Luigi delle Francesi, Rome.

too deeply bound up with it to be able to detach and separate completely
that act, substantially an aesthetic one, of the work in itself and of its
contemplation from those dynamisms or reactions of behavior and
from the evaluations which direct that first experience and that first
way of living.[136]

Hence, the horizon of art cannot be eclipsed from the reality of the
human person. Wojtyla in his subsequent addresses on this theme
explores how the human body has the meaning of a gift of the person
to the person (that is, the self-communicative nature of being in terms
of the person). Wojtyla writes that any

> objectivization of the human body in its male and female nakedness,
> in order to make it first of all a model and then the subject of the work
> of art, is always to a certain extent a going outside of this original and,
> for the body, its specific configuration of interpersonal donation.[137]

Within the horizon of culture and art, Wojtyla's anthropological
project seeks the avoidance of the situation where the human body
simply loses the subjective meaning of gift, which is ontologically
constitutive of what it means to be a human person.[138] This of course
leads Wojtyla on to the ethical applications of such anthropology.[139]
He would assert that any artist must take into account the full truth
about the human person and this must not be just in *abstracto* but
'must be transferred from the existential sphere of attitudes and ways
of behavior to the intentional sphere of creation or artistic repro-
duction'. It must naturally be transferred to the intentional sphere
because the artist as 'person' acts as an efficacious agent of his/her
own actions. This in fact concretizes the 'creative idea of the artist'.[140]
Wojtyla argues that this actually 'manifests [the artist's] interior world
of values, and so also his living the truth of his object'.[141] The artist
and the viewer are not to be understood solipsistically because,

> invited by the artist to look at his work, the viewer communicates not
> only with the concretizing, and so, in a sense, with a new 'materializing'
> of the model or of the material. But at the same time he communicates

---

[136] John Paul II, *Theology of the Body*, p. 218.
[137] John Paul II, *Theology of the Body*, p. 221.
[138] Ibid.
[139] Cf. 'Ethical Responsibilities in Art', *Theology of the Body*, pp. 226–9.
[140] John Paul II, 'Ethical Responsibilities in Art', *Theology of the Body*, p. 227.
[141] Ibid.

with the truth of the object which the author, in his artistic 'material-
izing', has succeeded in expressing with his own specific media.[142]

In his concluding remarks Wojtyla outlines how in the various
eras of art, Greek classical art being for him the greatest, it is
possible to contemplate 'the whole personal mystery of man'.[143] In
terms of the embodied person a truthful and responsible artistic
endeavour will attempt to overcome 'the anonymity of the human
body as an object "without choice"',[144] for the human person is the
efficient cause of his/her own actions, and therefore, possesses
'self-determination'.

The Letter to Artists

Wojtyla's letter to artists is a concise thirty-nine pages. It is in fact
addressed 'to all who are passionately dedicated to the search for new
"epiphanies" of beauty so that through their creative work as artists
they may offer these gifts to the world'.[145] His approach is clearly
reminiscent of his earlier philosophical openness; it is dialogic. He
writes:

> I feel closely linked [to you artists] by experiences reaching far back
> in time which have indelibly marked my life. In writing this letter I
> intend to follow the path of fruitful dialogue . . . this dialogue is not
> dictated merely by historical accident or practical need, but is rooted
> in the very essence of both religious experience and artistic creativity.[146]

The letter is dedicated 'to all', that is, to all those in search of what
he terms 'new "epiphanies" of beauty'[147] because artists are by nature
'alert to every "epiphany" of the inner beauty of things'.[148] The
philosopher Charles Taylor also speaks of 'an epiphanic art' and
articulates it in the sense of an epiphany which 'will free us from the
debased, mechanistic world [and bring] to light the spiritual reality
behind nature and uncorrupted human feeling'.[149]

---

[142] Ibid.
[143] Ibid.
[144] John Paul II, 'Ethical Responsibilities in Art', p. 229.
[145] John Paul II, *Letter to Artists*, opening dedication.
[146] John Paul II, *Letter to Artists*, § 1.
[147] John Paul II, *Letter to Artists*, opening dedication.
[148] John Paul II, *Letter to Artists*, § 6.
[149] Charles Taylor, *Sources of The Self: The Making of the Modern Identity* (Cambridge:
Cambridge University Press, 1989), p. 457.

Taylor comments that 'epiphanic art' became impossible due to the progress of industrial society and of a scientific, mechanistic world-view.[150] In an expansive discussion on the epiphanies of modernism that we will not delve into, Taylor concludes by saying:

> it is not that one can simply factor out the mythology or metaphysics or theology of Yeats, Mann, Lawrence, or Eliot and consider them just as an elaborate set of instruments to reorder their psyches. But some-thing has undoubtedly changed since the era of the great chain of being and the publicly established order of references. I have tried to express this by saying that the metaphysics or theology comes indexed to a personal vision, or refracted through a particular sensibility.[151]

Taylor proceeds to ask the question:

> [H]ow can I formulate the epiphany which opens through [Eliot's] *The Wasteland*? Going through the critical apparatus may facilitate the epiphany, but doesn't yield a formulation of it. Well, I can write another poem myself, index it to *my* personal vision. Otherwise, I can only indicate what it is by directing you to the poem itself. The beliefs remain embedded and interwoven in one person's vision and sensibility and even in his memory and biography, if we reflect how Pound and Eliot's works often gain clarity and force when we understand some of the personal allusions in the fragments that make them up.
>
>   That is why the centre of gravity is displaced onto words in so much modern poetry. The roots of poetry go deep into the invocative uses of language; those whereby we bring something about or make something present by what we say. These have played a big part in religious life from the earliest days up to the reciting of the Quran or the saying of Mass. But they also exist in secular life, in performances or on the most banal forms, such as when we open a conversation.[152]

In a similar vein, Wojtyla seeks to set out and recapture the meta-physical reality, the 'order of reference' in which the artist works. One of the fundamental canons for the KUL philosophers was of a realist metaphysics, of a need for a clear 'tether to reality'.[153] Wojtyla, as ever the student of philology,[154] sets this up not by making meta-physical pronouncements but by referring to the normal human

---

[150] Ibid.
[151] Taylor, *Sources of the Self*, p. 491.
[152] Taylor, *Sources of the Self*, pp. 492–3.
[153] Cf. Chapter 1 of this book.
[154] Weigel, *Witness to Hope*, p. 40.

experience of language and here he refers to his own native Polish. He observes that there is in the Polish language a lexical link between 'the words *stowórca* (creator) and *twórca* (craftsman)'.[155] He comments: 'the *one who creates* bestows being itself, he brings something out of nothing – *ex nihilo sui et subiecti*, as the Latin puts it . . . The *craftsman*, by contrast, uses something that already exists, to which he gives form and meaning.'[156] This is, according to Wojtyla, the mode of operation peculiar to the human person. The human person in the artistic dimension participates with 'others' and with the 'Other'. Another way that the artist can become aware of this reality is through the notion of 'gift'. Wojtyla notes that:

> the more conscious [artists] are of their 'gift', [they] are led all the more to see themselves and the whole of creation with eyes able to contemplate and give thanks, and to raise to God a hymn of praise. This is the only way for them to come to a full understanding of themselves, their vocation and their mission.[157]

The artist possesses 'artistic creativity' as a 'gift' and his awareness of this fact opens up his/her horizons to the reality of, to use a neologism, the 'Gifter'. The opening section of the letter is entitled: 'The artist, image of God the Creator.' In *The Acting Person* Wojtyla starts with the acting person; thus, in his *Letter to Artists*, he commences with addressing the 'acting' artist, writing:

> none can sense more deeply than you artists, *ingenious creators of beauty* [my emphasis] that you are, something of the *pathos* with which God at the dawn of creation looked upon the work of his hands. A glimmer of that feeling has shone so often in your eyes when – like artists of every age – captivated by the hidden power of sounds and words, colours and shapes, you have admired the work of your inspiration, sensing in it some echo of the mystery of creation with which God, the sole creator of all things, has wished in some way to associate you.[158]

The task of the artist

Hence, contained in the opening sections of Wojtyla's *Letter to Artists* are the beginnings of a phenomenological description of the artistic

---

[155] John Paul II, *Letter to Artists*, § 1.
[156] Ibid.
[157] Ibid.
[158] Ibid.

experience coupled with the important interpretation in terms of the metaphysical reality of the dimensions of the *Lebenswelt* of that particular dimension of human existence. In section 2 of the document Wojtyla moves on to consider the special duty of the artist. For the artist, art is not just an experience but also a task.[159] Wojtyla comments 'not all are called to be artists in the special sense of the term'.[160]

In a very poetic manner Wojtyla speaks of the important role of 'self-determination' in the human drama of the person. He describes how 'all men and women are entrusted with the task of *crafting their own life*: in a certain sense, they are to make of it a work of art, a masterpiece . . . [They are] to be the authors of their own acts'.[161]

There is a very close parallel between this and what Wojtyla had previously described in *The Acting Person*. In it he had given an analysis of human efficacy in the light of the human dynamism of 'I act'. He observes that

> every ego is a human being and every human being is this, that, or any other ego. Hence, when it is 'you', 'he', or 'anybody else' who acts, their acting can be understood on the ground of experiencing our own acting, in 'I act'. The experience of the acting is subjective in the sense that it keeps us within the limits of the concrete subjectivity of the acting human ego, without however obscuring the intersubjectivity [participation] that is needed for the understanding and interpretation of human acting.[162]

Therefore, in the *Letter to Artists* he makes reference to this principle in the general discussion of human activity but he then adverts to the special action of the artist. An artist is someone who is the efficient cause of his/her own action but he/she also 'respond[s] to the *demands of art* and faithfully accept art's specific dictates'.[163] This is important because the artist is to be understood as an *efficient* cause and this means that he/she is 'capable of producing *objects*'[164] just as the human person is capable of 'self-fulfilment'.

To summarize: according to Wojtyla human beings are authors of their own acts. They act in harmony with the criterion of moral good

---

[159] Cf. Chapter 2, in section on 'The Commandment of Love as a Task'.
[160] John Paul II, *Letter to Artists*, § 2.
[161] Ibid.
[162] Wojtyla, *Acting Person*, p. 60.
[163] John Paul II, *Letter to Artists*, § 2.
[164] Ibid.

and evil, since this is constitutive of being a person. Consequently, the artist, as a person, acts also according to the demands of art, that is, the right criterion of production.[165] The *homo oeconomicus* will equally act according to the proper demands of economics. In artistic creativity we are not speaking of 'self-creation' but of 'actualizing one's productive capacity'[166] as a person.

Wojtyla observes that there is a difference between the moral and the aesthetic aspect concerning the human person. But the connection between them is also of fundamental importance because 'each conditions the other in a profound way'.[167] He notes that

> in producing a work, artists express themselves to the point where their work becomes a unique disclosure of their own being, of *what* they are and *how* they are what they are. And there are endless examples of this in history.[168]

In *The Acting Person* he had started by positing the question:

> in reality, does man reveal himself in *thinking* or, rather, in the actual *enacting* of his existence? – in observing, interpreting, speculating, or reasoning . . . or in the confrontation itself when he has to take an active stand upon issues requiring vital decisions and having vital consequences and repercussions? In fact, it is in reversing the post-Cartesian attitude toward man that we undertake our study: by approaching him through action.[169]

Wojtyla, thus, perceives *homo aestheticus* to be an important actor in the *dramatis personae* of participating in the enacting of his own existence. As Rocco Buttiglione has commented:

> *The Acting Person* is neither an attempt to demonstrate that man is a person nor an attempt to classify human acts from the point of view of their personalistic value. It is a question, rather, of understanding *how* [my emphasis] a human being is a person, in which way *the person reveals himself in action*, and how the action can serve to interpret the person who manifests himself only in his acting.[170]

[165] Ibid.
[166] John Paul II, *Letter to Artists*, § 2.
[167] Ibid.
[168] Ibid.
[169] Wojtyla, *Acting Person*, pp. vii–viii.
[170] Rocco Buttiglione, *Karol Wojtyla: The Thought of the Man Who Became Pope John Paul II,* tr. Paola Guietti and Francesca Murphy (Grand Rapids: Eerdmans, 1997), p. 125.

Similarly, through artistic activity we can catch a glimpse of the irreducible in the human person, in the words of Wojtyla 'of *what* they [artists as human persons] are and *how* they are what they are'.[171] If what Wojtyla says is true, that is, 'action *reveals* the person, and we look at the person through his action . . . action constitutes the specific moment whereby the inherent essence of the person is revealed',[172] then artistic activity can in itself be especially revelatory in the unfolding human drama of the person.

This has, Wojtyla believes, implications for the history of art. It is because:

> through his works, the artist *speaks to others and communicates with them*. The history of art, therefore, is not only a story of works produced but also a story of men and women. Works of art speak of their authors; they enable us to know their inner life, and they reveal the original contribution which artists offer to the history of culture.[173]

There is a possible correlation between this understanding of the history of art and Eric Voegelin's reflections on his attempt at a *History of Political Ideas*. Voegelin explains that he discovered that 'there were no [political] ideas unless there were symbols of immediate *experiences*'.[174] He noted, in fact, that the effort to document a 'history of political ideas was a senseless undertaking . . . [when in fact] ideas turned out to be a secondary conceptual development [that are] liable to deform the truth of the experiences and their symbolization'.[175]

In similar fashion Wojtyla would assert that any adequate history of art should take into account that art speaks of its originators and their efforts in enacting their personal human existence as persons[176] and not just the mere chronological cataloguing of works.

Call to beauty

Wojtyla quotes the Polish poet, Cyprian Norwid, when he writes: 'beauty is to enthuse us to work, / and work is to raise us up'.[177] Norwid (1821–83) was a Polish Romantic poet and as I have remarked earlier,

---

[171] John Paul II, *Letter to Artists*, § 2.
[172] Wojtyla, *Acting Person*, p. 11.
[173] John Paul II, *Letter to Artists*, § 2.
[174] Eric Voegelin, *Autobiographical Reflections*, ed. Ellis Sandoz (Baton Rouge: Louisiana State University Press, 1989), p. 62.
[175] Voegelin, *Autobiographical Reflections*, p. 78.
[176] John Paul II, *Letter to Artists*, § 2.
[177] John Paul II, *Letter to Artists*, § 3.

the Romantics looked upon the past not as something to be overthrown but as a means to the recovery of values that had been lost.[178] Norwid's poetical work was 'an effort to probe the truth of things through art, and a deliberate rejection of the notion of "art for art's sake"'.[179]

Wojtyla, like Norwid, understands art as not just for its own sake but also as being at the service of beauty. Beauty is in itself 'the *visible form of the good*, just as the good is *the metaphysical condition of beauty*.[180] Human actions are not blind and the human person as such longs after the truth of the way things are. Wojtyla comments that the facts of human experience attest to the strivings 'to reach truth, goodness, and beauty'.[181] The Greeks understood this well when

> by fusing the two concepts [that is, the good and beautiful, they], coined a term which embraces both: *kalokagathía*, or *beauty – goodness*. On this point Plato writes: 'The power of the Good has taken refuge in the nature of the Beautiful.'[182]

It is above all in human action that the human person 'establishes [a] relationship with being, with the truth and with the good'.[183] The artist can be said to have a vocation in the service of beauty because that is the particular dimension in which the task arises for him/her to realize themselves as persons. If there is a gift to the artistic vocation of being a poet, writer, sculptor, architect, musician, actor and so on, Wojtyla sees this as entailing a corresponding obligation not to waste a talent but 'to develop it, in order to put it at the service of neighbour and of humanity as a whole'.[184] This obligation pertains to artistic activity because as in any human action properly understood, the duty moves the human will of the artist and makes him/her the efficacious agent of his/her own actions.

Art is, therefore, not just mere luxury, froth and bubble within the stream of history but is one of the human dimensions in which the drama of the human person can be enacted. Wojtyla argues:

> society needs artists, just as it needs scientists, workers, professional people, witnesses of the faith, teachers, fathers and mothers, who ensure

---

[178] Cf. present chapter, section on Polish Romanticism.
[179] Weigel, *Witness to Hope*, p. 35.
[180] John Paul II, *Letter to Artists*, § 3.
[181] Wojtyla, *Acting Person*, pp. 155–6.
[182] John Paul II, *Letter to Artists*, § 3.
[183] Ibid.
[184] Ibid.

the growth of the person and the development of the community by means of that supreme art form which is 'the art of education'.[185]

Wojtyla continues in his *Letter* to trace the historical origins of art right through the Middle Ages, the Renaissance and then on the need in our own day for a renewed dialogue. In this he sees art as remaining

> a kind of bridge to religious experience. In so far as it seeks the beautiful, fruit of an imagination which arises above the everyday, art is by its nature a kind of appeal to mystery. Even when they explore the darkest depths of the soul or the most unsettling aspects of evil, artists give voice in a way to the universal desire for redemption.[186]

Wojtyla had argued previously in the 'Wojtyla I' period about the reality and value of 'negative verifications' with respect to 'participation'. In the essay 'Participation or Alienation?', he wrote: 'in addition to these *positive* verifications of participation, we should also consider its *negative* verifications. They may, in fact, speak even more plainly of the kind of reality of participation in the humanity of another human being is'.[187] The feelings or attitudes such as hatred, aggression and jealousy show 'at least that I am not indifferent to the human being as another I'.[188]

So too in art, the category of the ugly and the negative feelings or attitudes they bring into relief can provoke within me the question of the significance or otherwise of the 'other'.[189] I already mentioned

---

[185] John Paul II, *Letter to Artists*, § 4.
[186] John Paul II, *Letter to Artists*, § 10.
[187] Wojtyla, *Person and Community*, pp. 204–5.
[188] Wojtyla, *Person and Community*, p. 205.
[189] Examples of such negative verification can be seen in the work of the artists like Francis Bacon and Mark Gertler. Gertler painted a canvas entitled the 'Merry-Go-Round' in 1916. In it he turns a harmless Hampstead carousel into a metaphor for the military machine that transforms everyone caught up in its diabolic motion. He had regarded the fun-fair as a place of happiness and liberation but he records: 'lately the whole horror of the war [the First World War] has come freshly upon me' (cf. Noel Carrington (ed.), *Mark Gertler Selected Letters* (London: 1965), p. III). Richard Cork, commenting upon this work of art housed in the Tate Gallery, London, writes that in this macabre canvas Gertler gives vent to a civilian's view of a world enmeshed in the insanity of a conflict with no foreseeable resolution. Although the soldiers on the roundabout are presumably savouring their leave from active service, Gertler insists that there can be no escape. Seated so stiffly on the wooden horses, both they and their companions remain robbed of their individual humanity. All the riders have become infected by the standardized rigidity of the mounts they straddle . . . Gertler's rasping moral allegory expresses the despair of an artist who now saw the entire population caught up in the inexorable momentum

Francis Bacon in relation to this category of the 'ugly' within art. But
the novels of Dostoevsky could equally be mentioned in this context.
William Hubben describes Dostoevsky's texts as illustrative of an
'astounding confusion between beauty and viciousness in man's
interior world'.[190] Through the development of the polyphonic novel[191]
Dostoevsky, the artist, leaves his readers 'unsettled and confused, yet
strangely moved'.[192] The beauty that emerges is of a higher order
because it opens up the human soul to new dimensions. Those who,
for example, encounter the main character, Prince Myshkin, in
Dostoevsky's *The Idiot* see him depicted as an outsider in an ugly
environment. The ugliness of the other characters and their surround-
ings open up the realization that the 'inward centre' of order is not to
be found within themselves or 'in their society but is part of the
Divine'.[193]

Here I must conclude my reflections on *Homo aestheticus* in the
light of Wojtyla's writings. I have explored briefly how he sought to
develop further and enact his anthropological principles in the horizon
of art and culture. Wojtyla's acting person is concrete and not abstract
and therefore participates with others in the world of art. At the core
of any adequate analysis of the artist and viewer as acting persons is
the understanding that artistic creativity should not negate the actualization of each person's own self-determination but should on the contrary
enrich it. It is for such a reason that 'Humanity in every age, and
even today, looks to works of art to shed light upon its path and its
destiny'.[194]

of a process over which no one had any control. His painting's garish vitality revealed
the horrible attraction exerted by the war, for the riders are captivated by the
carousel as well as imprisoned within its coils (cf. Richard Cork, *A Bitter Truth:
Avant-Garde Art and The Great War* (New Haven: Yale University Press, 1983),
p. 137). Gertler's painting can be understood as an artistic exploration of the
philosophical theme of depersonalization. A copy of this painting is included in the
appendix to this book.

[190] William Hubben, *Dostoevsky, Kierkegaard, Nietzsche & Kafka* (New York: Simon
& Schuster, 1997), p. 62.
[191] Mikhail Bakhtin describes how 'a plurality of independent and unmerged voices
and consciousnesses, a genuine polyphony of fully valid voices is in fact the chief
characteristic of Dostoevsky's novels'. Cf. Bakhtin, *Problems of Dostoevsky's
Poetics*, tr. Caryl Emerson (Minneapolis: University of Minnesota Press, 1984),
p. 6.
[192] Bakhtin, *Problems of Dostoevsky's Poetics*, p. 65.
[193] Bakhtin, *Problems of Dostoevsky's Poetics*, p. 67.
[194] John Paul II, *Letter to Artists*, § 14.

Homo oeconomicus

Wojtylan 'personmeter'

In the encyclicals *Laborem Exercens*[195] [On Human Work] and *Centesimus Annus*[196] [The Hundredth Year] we can explore how Wojtyla applies his philosophical anthropology to that horizon of human existence that involves the human person in the world of work and of economic activity, that is, the human person as *homo oeconomicus*. Maciej Zieba speaks of how, based upon Wojtyla's personalism, one could speak of using a 'personometer' and apply it to given systems in order to ascertain if they measure positively in terms of an adequate philosophy of the person.[197] In this section I will attempt such an application to the concepts of work and economic activity. The encyclical *Laborem Exercens*[198] contains some thirty-one pages excluding footnotes. It is divided into twenty-seven sections, which are further divided into subsections. I will explore very briefly those parts of the encyclical in which we can usefully apply the 'personometer' so as to illustrate the application and growth of Wojtyla's personalism. *Centesimus Annus*[199] is slightly longer and runs to some thirty-seven pages exclusive of footnotes. The text is divided into sixty-two sections. I will, because of the limits of space, make very brief reference to those parts of this encyclical that are relevant to the present theme.

Laborem Exercens: A dialogue of 'listening'

If Marx and Engels were responsible for the publication of the *Communist Manifesto*, I deem Karol Wojtyla to be accountable for what I would term a corresponding *Manifesto of the Human Person*. There is no doubt that Wojtyla took Marxism seriously. It is interesting to note that 'the publication of Wojtyla's habilitation thesis in 1959 went almost unnoticed by the Polish press'.[200] A few reviews were written of it, but it was a Marxist philosopher, Jozef Keller, who attacked it vehemently, although, according to Kupczak, 'he failed to

---

[195] John Paul II, 14 September 1981.
[196] John Paul II, 1 May 1991.
[197] Maciej Zieba, *The Surprising Pope: Understanding the Thought of John Paul II*, tr. Karolina Weening (New York: Lexington Books, 2000), p. 113.
[198] Cited hereafter as *LE*.
[199] Cited hereafter as *CA*.
[200] Jaroslaw Kupczak, *Destined for Liberty*, p. 24.

give even one philosophical reason for his criticism'.[201] Wojtyla himself recounts how when he wrote the book *The Acting Person*, 'the first to take notice of it, obviously in order to attack it, were the Marxists'.[202]

George Huntston Williams probably accurately identifies the final part of *The Acting Person*, that is, chapter 7, entitled: 'Intersubjectivity By Participation', as being directed against what he terms, Wojtyla's 'social opponents'.[203] He writes: 'Living and writing in Cracow from the perspective of a Communist society, where he could not openly attack Marxism in print . . . the author presents to philosophers . . . the basis of so understanding the person that participation or intersubjectivity is possible.'[204]

As I have remarked before, etched into the fabric of Wojtyla's philosophical approach is 'dialogue' with the prevailing culture. Writing about this he comments:

> dialogue can draw out what is worthwhile and correct and throw into relief what are purely subjective positions or approaches . . . The principle of dialogue is not to pull back from the tensions, conflicts and struggles which characterize life in the various forms of human communities, but to take them up, retrieving from them that which is just and correct, that which can be a wellspring of good for human beings.[205]

There is, I would propose, a Levinasian methodology in this debate, because Wojtyla also gives primacy to 'listening'. Writing about the priority of 'listening' in the philosophy of Levinas, Battista Borsato notes how he 'gives primacy to the dimension of listening. If "others" are "other", the only approach is to allow others to visit me. And the condition for this visitation is listening, which Levinas encapsulates in the word "passivity"'.[206]

Likewise Wojtyla argues that in order to understand Communism we must listen and understand its history.[207] There are parallels between

[201] Ibid.
[202] John Paul II, *Crossing the Threshold of Hope*, tr. Jenny and Martha McPhee (London: Jonathan Cape, 1994), p. 199.
[203] George Huntston Williams, *The Mind of John Paul II: Origins of His Thought and Action* (New York: Seabury Press, 1981), p. 204.
[204] Ibid.
[205] Quoted in Zieba, *Surprising Pope*, p. 74.
[206] Battista Borsato, *L'Alterità come Etica: Una lettura di Emmanuel Levinas* (Bologna: EDB, 1995), p. 124.
[207] Weigel gives an example of Wojtyla's insistence on 'dialogue'. During a papal conclave he was spotted reading a Marxist philosophical journal. He was asked by one of the other participants if this was not somewhat scandalous. Wojtyla simply smiled and said that his conscience was clear (cf. Wiegel, *Witness to Hope*, p. 252).

Wojtyla's attitude to Marxism and that of the French philosopher, Jacques Maritain.[208] Guarding against over simplistic readings of Marx, Maritain remarks that

> [he] saw more deeply into things, and just as we may speak of a first 'spiritual' impulse in him (his indignation at the conditions imposed on man oppressed by things born of himself and his work, and himself made a thing), so we must say that in spite of certain formulas he always believed in a reciprocal action between economic and other factors, economics taken alone was not in his view the one and only source of history.[209]

The Marxist history is one 'of protest in the face of injustice, as [Wojtyla] recalled in the encyclical *Laborem Exercens* – a protest on the part of the great world of workers, which then became an ideology'.[210] Thus, it is important to understand the historical-philosophical background to *Laborem Exercens*. Benjamin Fiore comments how among Polish philosophers there had been a 'longstanding disdain of Marxism as unworthy of serious study when it appeared earlier in the century'.[211] Hence, Wojtyla's writing of *Laborem Exercens* is both of historic and philosophical significance in its undertaking to study seriously the problems various ideologies seek to answer.

The historical philosophical background

It is important to set the historical and philosophical context behind the writing of *Laborem Exercens*. Wojtyla wrote the encyclical while recovering from an assassination attempt against him.[212] The debate

---

208 Numerous commentators make reference to the influence of Maritain's writings upon Wojtyla. Weigel, for example, notes that 'Wojtyla had his first serious encounter [at the University of Lublin] ... with Jacques Maritain's modern Thomistic reading of Catholic social ethics, including Maritain's moral defense of democracy as the modern method of government most reflective of human dignity. It was Swiezawski [a professor at the University of Lublin], for example, who introduced Wojtyla to Maritain's *Integral Humanism*' (Weigel, *Witness to Hope*, p. 139).

209 Jacques Maritain, 'The Roots of Soviet Atheism', in Joseph W. Evans and Leo R. Ward (eds.), *The Social and Political Philosophy of Jacques Maritain: Selected Readings* (New York: Image Books, 1965), p. 252.

210 John Paul II, *Crossing the Threshold of Hope*, pp. 130–1.

211 Benjamin Fiore, 'Laborem Exercens', in McDermott (ed.), *Thought of Pope John Paul II*, p. 231.

212 Weigel, *Witness to Hope*, p. 419.

over why and under whose orders did Mehmet Ali Agca shoot the
Pope is still open. Weigel argues that the reason can be found when
we can answer the question 'Who benefited? [And this in turn] will
keep alive the intuition that the Soviet Union was not innocent in
this business.'[213] There is no causal link between the shooting and the
writing of the encyclical. Nevertheless, it is a very personal account
of the moral meaning of human work. In it he brings his own experience
as a manual worker[214] and also the experiences of the two regimes
under which he worked, that is, National Socialism and Communism.
His reflections, therefore, do not take place within a vacuum but
concern the concrete human person in the dimension of work.

Battle of the Vistula

Buttiglione is careful to point out that the version of Marxism Wojtyla
debates with is of the Western variety. The Wojtylan analysis cannot
just be dismissed as the critique of Marxism of the Eastern bureaucratic
type. There are philosophical and political roots to Marxism both of
which are important. The 'battle of the Vistula', August 1920, is of
decisive historical significance. The Red Army sought to advance
westwards and join up in helping the German revolutionaries. General
Józef Pilsudski of the Polish army stopped them at Warsaw. As
Buttiglione observes: 'just outside the Russian border, the Soviet
revolution came up against the national idea and was not able to defeat
it'.[215]

Thus, the significance of the event does not just go down to
Pilsudski's daring action in withdrawing some of Poland's best fighting
divisions from the front line and redeploying them to take advantage
of a gap between two groups of Trotsky's army.[216] In the battle 'the
West refused to be conquered by Russia out of the conviction of its
own irrenounceable cultural superiority'.[217] In other words the national
idea is cultural and it is within this context that a philosophy of human
action, of praxis that might have been thought particular to Marxism
emerges. Marxist philosophy finds itself refining its analysis in order

---

[213] Weigel, *Witness to Hope*, p. 424.
[214] John Paul II, *LE*, § 9. He observes: 'it is quite possible to use work in various ways
against man . . . it is possible to punish man with the system of forced labour in
concentration camps'.
[215] Buttiglione, *Karol Wojtyla*, p. 294.
[216] Weigel, *Witness to Hope*, p. 17.
[217] Weigel, *Witness to Hope*, p. 294.

to understand culture because it is only by means of a cultural domination that world revolution will be secured. Fundamental to culture is the agency of human action. The Wojtylan dialogue with Marxism begins, therefore, at the level of its theory of alienation and human praxis. Wojtyla is not interested in entering into polemics, for example, as to the inefficiency or otherwise of one system in comparison to another, in terms of economics: that should be left to economists. This would be to miss the opportunity for proper philosophical discourse. He believes that far more substantial in terms of philosophy would be 'the ability to deal in a convincing way with the question of what human beings are'.[218]

How you define human praxis is dependent in the first place upon *how* you define the human person. A fundamental question, since we are concerned with the dimension of human work (praxis), is how can I act together with others and at the same time not alienate my own *I* or the *other* in the process? Wojtyla would query whether Marx is asking the same question in his study and treatment of human alienation.

The experience of alienation

Marx had, as Voegelin describes it,

> laid his finger on the sore spot of modern industrial society . . . that is the growth of economic institutions into a power of such overwhelming influence on the life of every single man, that in the face of such power all talk about human freedom becomes futile.[219]

Wojtyla agrees that there is a need within the contemporary world for the continuous retrieval of the freedom of the human person. The question he poses can be put like this: Is the Marxist analysis and subsequent resolution adequate enough to such a task, in terms of a comprehensive philosophy of the human person? Writing on Marx, Wojtyla says that alienation occurs

> according to Marx's philosophy, [because] human beings are alienated by their products: their economic and political systems, their property, and their work. Marx also included religion in this category. Such a formulation of the problem leads, of course, to the conclusion that all

---

[218] Weigel, *Witness to Hope*, p. 292.
[219] Eric Voegelin, *From Enlightenment to Revolution*, ed. John H. Hallowell (Durham, NC: Duke University Press, 1975), p. 299.

we have to do is transform the world of products, change the economic and political systems, and rally against religion – [through human praxis] and then the age of alienation will come to an end and a 'reign of freedom' will ensue, bringing with it complete self-actualization for one and all.[220]

Thus, according to the Marxian perspective, the human praxis of transforming material conditions is what is required, in order to transform reality. But Wojtyla contends that the theory of praxis underlying this analysis is insufficient. In reality, the concept of alienation inherent in this Marxian analysis actually transfers the problem beyond the human person to 'what could be called the social structures of our social existence'.[221] It is Wojtyla's contention that this is an application of the concept of alienation in which the human person becomes displaced. Hence, we could argue that there lies hidden beneath the Marxian account a 'depersonalized' notion of alienation. Wojtyla comments that, of course,

> the concept of alienation, when properly applied, can aid in the analysis of human reality – not primarily on the plane of external influences from the extra-human world, [as in the case of Marxism] but mainly in the realm of specifically human and interhuman relationships – and, therefore, in the analysis of the *I – other* relationship.[222]

Wojtyla is of the view that Marx rightfully adopted the nineteenth-century philosophical term 'alienation' to apply to the prevailing conditions of human existence. Maritain speaks similarly, of what he terms Marx's profound intuition:

> an intuition we believe to be the great flash of truth running through his work – of the conditions of heteronomy and estrangement engendered in the 'capitalist' world of slave-labour, and the dehumanization with which the owners and the proletariat are thereby simultaneously stricken.[223]

Nonetheless, the Marxist solution of changing the material circumstances does not seem to go to the heart of what is essential in the resolution of the human predicament. The core of the problem,

---

[220] Wojtyla, 'Participation or Alienation?' in *Person and Community*, p. 205.
[221] Wojtyla, 'Participation or Alienation?', p. 206.
[222] Wojtyla, 'Participation or Alienation?', p. 205.
[223] Maritain, 'Roots of Soviet Atheism', p. 252.

according to Wojtyla, is rather how we relate to one another, even somehow despite the circumstances. We know, for example, that in the most abject of human conditions there are people who manage to relate to others as other *I*'s, as *neighbours* – often to a daring magnitude.[224]

Once again, Maritain concurs with the Wojtylan analysis, when he judges Marx to have gone astray in the initial intuition because 'he immediately conceptualized this intuition in an anthropocentric monist metaphysics, in which work is hypostasized into the very essence of man'.[225] Wojtyla's comments about how history throws up examples of individuals who gallantly relate to others as other *I*'s recalls afresh Adorno's question about the possibility of doing philosophy after Auschwitz and reveals perhaps that what is really crucial in any proper analysis of the human condition, is that a philosophy of the person emerges that allows us the 'ability to experience another human being as another *I*',[226] almost in spite of the external circumstances. I would argue, in fact, that Wojtyla radicalizes and personalizes the notion of human alienation, when he writes: 'alienation basically means the negation of participation, for it renders participation difficult or even impossible. It devastates the *I – other* relationship . . . and inhibits the possibility of friendship and the spontaneous powers of community (*communio personarum*).'[227] For this reason, any given political or economic system, adjudges Wojtyla

> must be evaluated in the light of this basic criterion: Do [the structures] create the conditions – for this is their only real function – for the development of participation? Do they enable and help us to experience other human beings as other *I*'s? Or do they do just the opposite? Do they obstruct participation and ravage and destroy this basic fabric of human existence and activity, which must always be realized in common with others? The central problem of humanity in our times, perhaps in all times, is this: *participation or alienation*?[228]

---

[224] Wojtyla, 'Participation or Alienation?', p. 206. I have made reference earlier to Maximilian Kolbe's actions. An adequate account of human action must seek to include an explanation of the significance of such heroic action despite the circumstances. For the sake of philosophical integrity any account must be inclusive rather than exclusive of such human action.

[225] Maritain, 'Roots of Soviet Atheism', p. 252.

[226] Wojtyla, 'Participation or Alienation?' p. 206.

[227] Ibid.

[228] Ibid.

Wojtyla would accept that Marx was correct in targeting 'alienation' as a fundamental human experience to be dealt with philosophically. Allied with this, Marx develops his own particular theory of human praxis that will, he believes, lead to a resolution of the estrangement. The difficulty is that his theory of praxis can be interpreted solely in terms of his analysis of alienation,[229] and we have seen how Wojtyla questions this understanding.

Towards an adequate theory of praxis

The central claim of Marxism is that man creates himself through his own work. That task is frustrated by the master–slave dialectic conditioning human work. Overcome the dialectic and salvation will be in man's own hands. As Buttiglione puts it:

> this idea of the self-creation of man through praxis constitutes the authentic core of Marx's thought and permits him to be presented as one who has both inherited and actualized the Promethean dream dormant within the whole of modern thought.[230]

Wojtyla's *The Acting Person* can be understood in itself as a re-statement of a philosophy of praxis.[231] Just as he has an alternative view on alienation, so too, he has on the theory of human action. Integral to the Wojtylan philosophy is the understanding of the human subject as the efficient cause of his/her own actions. He perceives Marxian theory of human praxis, rather than overcoming the master–slave dialectic, as ending up by dissolving '*the subjectivity of the concrete man into praxis*'.[232] This is because of a certain *Vergesslichkeit* of the metaphysical subjectivity, the *suppositum* of the person. There appears to be a certain hypostatization of one aspect of human action in the Marxian account. Human praxis so conceived is what remains of human action if you eclipse out of it, its ethical and personalistic meanings. Hence, 'just as in traditional philosophy of consciousness the subject is lost in thought, so in the philosophy of praxis the concrete human subject is lost in social work'.[233]

In a paper presented at the University of Milan in 1977, just two years before he became Pope, Wojtyla highlighted the fact that his

---

[229] Buttiglione, *Karol Wojtyla*, p. 302.
[230] Buttiglione, *Karol Wojtyla*, p. 293.
[231] Ibid.
[232] Buttiglione, *Karol Wojtyla*, p. 295.
[233] Buttiglione, *Karol Wojtyla*, p. 297.

own reflections on human praxis were 'intimately linked to an understanding of the human being as a person: a self-determining subject'.[234]
In this significant essay he defines culture as 'basically oriented not so
much toward the creation of human *products* as toward the creation of
the human *self*, and then radiated out into the world of products'.[235]
He then proceeds to present the Thomistic view of human action as
being

> simultaneously *transitive* and *intransitive*. It is transitive as it tends
> *beyond the subject*, seeks an expression and effect in the external
> world, and is objectified in some product. It is intransitive, on the other
> hand, insofar as it *remains in the subject*, determines the subjects
> essentially human *fieri*. In acting, we not only perform actions, but we
> also become ourselves through those actions – we fulfil ourselves in
> them.[236]

This 'transitive' and 'intransitive' distinction within human action
is one that is occluded within the Marxian interpretation. That analysis
lays emphasis upon the 'transitive' aspect to the neglect of the 'intransitive'. It is all-important for Wojtyla to stress that human action has
an effect 'within' the person,[237] as well as 'externally'. This Wojtylan
use of terminology might be negative in itself; nonetheless, he seeks
to give an adequate phenomenological description of human work and
then to interpret it in terms of metaphysical reality.[238] Lonergan speaks
of meaning as being cognitive, efficient, constitutive and
communicative.[239] We could similarly apply this notion to human work
and realize that when Wojtyla uses the word 'intransitive' he infers
that work is, in fact, self-constitutive of the human subject. Buttiglione
asserts that it is because Marx 'eliminated the metaphysical aspect of
the subject (*suppositum humanum*), [that he] does not have a sufficient
grip upon this fundamental effect of action'.[240]

---

[234]   Karol Wojtyla, 'The Problem of the Constitution of Culture Through Human Praxis',
     in *Person and Community*, p. 265.
[235]   Ibid.
[236]   Wojtyla, 'Constitution of Culture', pp. 265–6.
[237]   I referred in an earlier part of book how Wojtyla makes the distinction between
     agere and *pati*, that is, 'man-acts' and 'something happens in man'.
[238]   Cf. chapter 1 of this book where reference is made to the KUL canons in which the
     primacy of realistic metaphysics is emphasized.
[239]   Bernard Lonergan, *Method in Theology* (London: Darton, Longman & Todd, 1972),
     pp. 76–81.
[240]   Buttiglione, *Karol Wojtyla*, p. 300.

Application in Laborem Exercens

I have devoted some space to exploring the historical and philosophical background behind the encyclical *Laborem Exercens*. I have made reference to the theory of alienation in Marx and Wojtyla and to an adequate theory of praxis. This is useful, I would suggest, because it is in this encyclical that Wojtyla begins for the first time to apply his personalistic theories of human action in terms of a new social theory. It is important to say that Wojtyla's dialogue is not only bilateral, that is, between the Church and Marxism but also trilateral, in that he includes capitalism in his analysis. Michael J. Walsh comments that in *Laborem Exercens* Wojtyla 'insists on a criticism that is every bit as severe on Capitalism as it is on Marxism'.[241] I would be more cautious in the use of the word 'criticism' because it can suggest condemnation. In my opinion, this does not properly convey the philosophical task Wojtyla sets himself, which is to apply to different economic and social systems the litmus test of the possibility of true human participation by the individual human person. Does the given system, whatever its name, allow me to experience myself as a self-determining *I*, and does it help me experience the *other* as another *I*? This is the application of Zieba's 'personmeter' I made reference to earlier and is the relevant question to have in mind when reading the writings of the 'Wojtyla II' period.[242]

Phenomenological description

In *Laborem Exercens* Wojtyla begins with a phenomenological description of work and in it he discerns some irreducible elements. He is careful in his analysis not to give a reductive understanding of labour. Thus, he says:

[241] Michael J. Walsh, in an introduction to Michael Walsh and Brian Davies *Proclaiming Justice and Peace: Documents from John XXIII to John Paul II* (London: Collins, 1984), p. xviii.

[242] The publication of *Laborem Exercens* and *Centesimus Annus* has led to a significant debate among intellectuals and political philosophers. David L. Schindler argues that 'at the heart of any discussion of economics lies the question of human creativity, in its character as image of God'. But he contends that the 'neo–conservatives' such as Michael Novak, Richard John Neuhaus and George Weigel make the assertion that John Paul II's proposals are compatible with their own on behalf of an Anglo-American version of liberal capitalism. It is such an assertion that Schindler disputes in a fine exposition on the Pope's primitive concept of 'creativity' as being inclusive of a primordial 'receptivity'. Cf. David L. Schindler, *Heart of the World, Center of the Church: Communio Ecclesiology, Liberalism*, and *Liberation* (Grand Rapids, Eerdmans: 1996), pp. 114–42.

work means any activity by man, whether manual or intellectual, whatever its nature or circumstances; it means any human activity that can and must be recognized as work, in the midst of all the many activities of which man is capable and to which he is predisposed by his very nature, by virtue of humanity itself.[243]

The human person is not reduced to 'work' nor is 'work' itself reduced to one specific human activity, since Wojtyla describes it as meaning 'any activity by man'. This is clearly a phenomenological starting point, since he 'does not so much define work as describe it in its various manifestations'.[244] This in itself is new even in terms of the traditional understanding of human work by the Church, which viewed it simply as concerning the mastery of nature. Such a phenomenological account allows Wojtyla to observe that work is something peculiar to human beings. He writes: 'work is one of the characteristics that distinguish man from the rest of creatures, whose activity for sustaining their lives cannot be called work.'[245] A concept of work conceived as an activity directed towards the mere sustenance of life would be a diminishing of the personalistic value of work. Wojtyla's style is as ever somewhat convoluted when he affirms: 'only man is capable of work, and only man works.'[246] He means by this, that the capacity within the human person for manual and intellectual action exhibits in itself how specific work is to man, and in turn how in terms of that dynamism we can subsequently say that man alone works. Wojtyla also notes the intersubjective nature of work, writing: 'work bears a particular mark of man and of humanity, the mark of a person operating within a community of persons.'[247] Wojtyla adds that this feature, that is, the intersubjective nature of work, 'decides its interior characteristics; in a sense it constitutes its very nature'.[248]

There is a correlation between this description of work and the manner in which, in chapter 7 of *The Acting Person*, Wojtyla saw the need for an investigation into the human person's acting 'together with others'. There Wojtyla wrote: '[W]e cannot conclude our investigation of the acting person without considering, even if only

---

[243] John Paul II, *LE*, opening paragraph.
[244] Cited in *Proclaiming Justice and Peace*, p. xviii.
[245] John Paul II, *LE*, opening paragraph. § 1.
[246] Ibid.
[247] Ibid.
[248] Ibid.

in a cursory way, the issue of intersubjectivity.'[249] Thus, we can say that the 'other' is an important paradigm for understanding human personhood even within the horizon of work.

Laborem Exercens: *the application of the Wojtylan theory of human praxis*

We could read the encyclical line for line in order to trace the Wojtylan personalistic fingerprints but this would in itself be a separate project. Given that Wojtyla's earlier work can be considered as a fundamental reflection on human action, it is appropriate to focus on how he has developed and applied this particular aspect in *Laborem Exercens*.

Wojtyla mentions how the various sciences, such as 'anthropology, palaeontology, history, sociology, psychology and so on [all point to the fact] . . . that work is a fundamental dimension of man's existence'.[250] In *The Acting Person*, in his study of the personal structure of self-determination and the analysis of the human will, he makes similar use of the contributions of contemporary scientists and in particular of psychologists.[251] Kupczak confirms this in relationship to the work of the 'Wojtyla I' phase, when he writes:

> Wojtyla points out that twentieth-century experimental psychology [e.g. Narziss Ach] falsifies Scheler's claim that the human person does not experience himself as the cause of his own actions. Some of the representatives of this school emphasize that there is a distinct psychic element that cannot be reduced to anything else and that can be experienced by the human subject as 'I will', 'I should', or 'I must'.[252]

Thus, Wojtyla's whole approach to the question of human work is multi-disciplinary. He uses 'the whole heritage of the many human sciences devoted to man'[253] and the insights drawn from an analysis of the Book of Genesis that 'makes us aware that they express – sometimes in an archaic way of manifesting thought – the fundamental truths about man, in the context of the mystery of creation itself'.[254]

I wish to stress that Wojtyla's argument is philosophically reasonable if we keep in mind the significance he attaches in his methodology

[249] Wojtyla, *Acting Person*, p. 261.
[250] John Paul II, *LE*, § 4.
[251] Wojtyla, *Acting Person*, p. 126.
[252] Kupczak, *Destined for Liberty*, p. 29.
[253] John Paul II, *LE*, § 4.
[254] Ibid.

not to give a phenomenological description alone but also the need for the application of an adequate interpretation of reality. A comprehensive understanding of human work entails a corresponding necessity to appreciate the metaphysical stage upon which the drama of human work unfolds.

In *Laborem Exercens* Wojtyla uses the phrase 'work as a transitive activity'.[255] It was, as we have seen, in his earlier paper sent to Milan University that he had used the distinction between 'transitive' and 'intransitive' human action.[256] He now clearly applies and develops these same thoughts about human praxis in the document. Considering man as a real protagonist and not just a mere spectator within human history, Wojtyla acknowledges that 'work understood as a "transitive" activity, that is to say an activity beginning in the human subject and directed towards an external object, presupposes a specific dominion by man over the "earth"'.[257]

Of course, along with dominion of the earth there would be a corresponding requirement for self-dominion or in Wojtylan language, a need for self-possession. As he previously commented in *The Acting Person*:

[T]o fulfill oneself means to actualize, and in a way to bring to the proper fullness, that structure in man which is characteristic for him because of his personality and also because of his being somebody and not merely something: it is the structure of *self-governance* and *self-possession*.[258]

One of the many biblical texts analysed by Wojtyla in *Laborem Exercens*, for example, is 'subdue the earth' (Gen. 1:28), and he perceives within it the important understanding of the transitive nature of human action. In fact, the concept itself embraces

equally the past ages of civilization and economy, as also the whole of modern reality and future phases of development, which are perhaps already to some extent beginning to take shape, though for the most part they are still almost unknown to man and hidden from him.[259]

The transitive nature of action is, according to Wojtyla, universal, in that it 'embraces all human beings, every generation, every phase of

---

[255] Ibid.
[256] Wojtyla, 'Constitution of Culture', pp. 265–6.
[257] John Paul II, *LE*, § 4.
[258] Wojtyla, *Acting Person*, p. 151.
[259] John Paul II, *LE*, § 4.

economic and cultural development'.[260] He concludes paragraph four of the encyclical by asserting that it is furthermore 'a process that takes place *within* each human being, in each conscious subject'.[261] In other words, human action is constitutive of the person; it is also, as Wojtyla would say, intransitive in nature.

Work in the objective and subjective sense

Wojtyla now proceeds to apply the earlier 'transitive' and 'intransitive' distinction he made in terms of human praxis to the concept of human work in the encyclical.[262] This is an attempt at an application of his earlier analysis of a philosophy of human action to *homo oeconomicus*. In the application, he wants to employ a theory of praxis that has sufficient amplitude for a comprehensive philosophy of the person. The crux of the problem is stated as follows by Buttiglione:

> [H]ow can one think about praxis without renouncing the fundamental principle of the existence of a subject (*subiectum*) or metaphysical substratum (*hypokeimenon*) of man, which underline any historical change, dictates, with its specific conformation, the fundamental lines of possible modification, and furnishes the criterion upon which one can make an ethical judgment on them?[263]

In answer to this problematic that arises uniformly in all social economic systems, Wojtyla examines in the encyclical the meaning of work in what he terms both the 'objective' and 'subjective' senses. It is, I believe, vital to appreciate the question he seeks to address. At the heart of his project is the concern to present a theory of human praxis that not alone preserves 'the existence of the subject', the *I* but also of the 'other' *I*. These concerns are, indeed, very relevant to contemporary philosophical debate. Steven Hendley writes, for example, that

> the recent revival of communitarian lines of thought, directed against the shortcomings of liberal political theory, has stressed the importance of a sense of community, in anchoring a sense of justice in the lives of those who would be subject to it . . . [through this they] can come to

---

[260] Ibid.
[261] Ibid.
[262] John Paul II, *LE*, § 5–6.
[263] Buttiglione, *Karol Wojtyla*, p. 299.

realize their mutual importance to one another and, consequently, see the point of being just to one another.[264]

We cannot, therefore, fail to x-ray systems 'from this point of view. What is in question is the advancement of persons, not just the multiplying of things that people can use'.[265] Wojtyla's, Levinas's and others' own memories were already flooded with examples of 'inhumanities witnessed this century . . . of a "crisis" of modern humanism, an apparent inability to foster and sustain a sense of responsibility for the other'.[266]

In his *Letter to Families* Wojtyla spoke similarly when he asked, 'who can deny that our age is one marked by a great crisis, which appears above all as a *profound "crisis of truth"*?'[267] Hence, within this context it is critical for Wojtyla to give an account of the meaning of work seeking to explain the inherent dynamism within human action that respects the truth of the *I* and the *other*.

To this end Wojtyla gives a brief historical survey of 'the meaning of work in the objective sense'.[268] From the domesticating of animals, the extraction of natural resources of the earth, land cultivation, the development of agriculture, the transformation of products, to subsequent industrialization, man can understand how through his work he 'subdues the earth'. Technology can be seen as man's ally in human work. Nonetheless, Wojtyla points out that

> in some instances, technology can cease to be man's ally and become almost his enemy, as when the mechanization of work 'supplants' him, taking away all personal satisfaction and the incentive to creativity and responsibility, when it deprives many workers of their previous employment, or when, through exalting the machine, it reduces man to the status of its slave.[269]

Nevertheless, modern history shows technology to be 'a basic coefficient of economic progress'.[270] Wojtyla would, what is more,

---

[264] Steven Hendley, *From Communicative Action to the Face of the Other: Levinas and Habermas on Language, Obligation, and Community* (New York: Lexington Books, 2000), p. 101.

[265] John Paul II, *Redemptor Hominis*, § 16.

[266] Hendley, *Communicative Action*, p. 117.

[267] John Paul II, *Letter to Families*, 1994, § 13.

[268] John Paul II, *LE*, § 5.

[269] Ibid.

[270] Ibid.

see technology as a coefficient of human progress, so long as it is always 'accompanied by the raising of essential questions concerning human work in relation to its subject, which is man'.[271]

In terms of the horizon of human work Wojtyla sees these questions as of central significance. He would be of the opinion that Marx's analysis of praxis failed in one way because it did not address such personalist questions. Marx reduces the essence of man to its socio-economic dimension rather than appreciating its unique metaphysical reality. Thus, when the means of production alienate the worker, according to the Marxian analysis, if you change the conditions of social ownership, that is, the outward objective conditions then, in effect, you remove the source of the alienation.

But if you take this step, you actually move away from philosophy and shift onto the plane of economics and sociology.[272] This is where, I would contend, Wojtyla radicalizes the notion of human work and seeks a return to the metaphysical subject. It is in this regard that he speaks in *Laborem Exercens* of 'Work in the Subjective Sense: Man as the Subject of Work'.[273] Wojtyla observes:

> Man . . . is a person, that is to say, a subjective being capable of acting in a planned and rational way, capable of deciding about himself, and with a tendency to self-realization. As a person, man is therefore the subject of work. As a person he works, he performs various actions belonging to the work process; independently of their objective content, these actions must all serve to realize his humanity, to fulfil the calling to be a person that is his by reason of his very humanity.[274]

We can clearly recognize that the analysis of the human person applied here is that taken directly from *The Acting Person* and subsequent writings. The human person is described as 'capable of deciding about himself'. This in itself suggests 'self-determination', and then 'self-realization', and so on.

Wojtyla emphasizes in the encyclical that the 'dominion', or 'governance' that is spoken of in terms of human work 'refers not only to the objective dimension of work but at the same time introduces us to an understanding of its subjective dimension'.[275] Actually, the

[271] Ibid.
[272] Buttiglione, *Karol Wojtyla*, p. 296.
[273] John Paul II, *LE*, § 6.
[274] Ibid.
[275] Ibid.

objective meaning of work (transitive) only makes sense in terms of the subjective significance (intransitive). The objective and subjective elements are, in a sense, two coefficient factors in terms of the realization of the human person. Governance, or dominion in the objective sense 'whereby man and the human race subdues the earth' can be understood to be so 'only when throughout the process man manifests himself and confirms himself as the one who "dominates"'.[276]

Wojtyla goes so far as to say that the dominion spoken of with regard to work 'refers to the subjective dimension even more than to the objective one: this dimension conditions the very ethical nature of work'.[277] This implies the priority of the human person as the essential subject of human action (*operari sequitur esse*). The ancient world introduced a 'differentiation of people into classes according to the type of work done'.[278] Hence, manual work was seen as 'unworthy of free men'.[279] It was Christianity, in fact, which 'brought about a fundamental change of ideas in this field'.[280] The ancients also lacked an adequate concept of person although this was to be one of Christianity's unique contributions to philosophy. So, historically with the advent of Christianity we have the fundamental insight

> that the basis for determining the values of human work is not primarily the kind of work being done but the fact that the one who is doing it is a person. The sources of the dignity of work are to be sought primarily in the subjective dimension, not in the objective one.[281]

In his paper presented at Milan, Wojtyla had already explored how the priority of the person with regard to praxis should be understood. It is evident that he applies this analysis to the discussion found in *Laborem Exercens*. In the essay, he wrote:

> work, or human praxis, is possible to the extent that the human being already exists: *operari sequitur esse*. The priority of the human being as the subject of essentially human activity – a priority in the metaphysical sense – belongs to the concept of praxis for the simple reason that the human being determines praxis. It would be absurd to understand the matter the other way around and accept some sort of subjectively indeterminate praxis, which would then define or determine

---

[276] Ibid.
[277] John Paul II, *LE*, § 6.
[278] Ibid.
[279] Ibid.
[280] Ibid.
[281] Ibid.

its subject. It is not possible to think of praxis in an *a priori* manner, as though this 'quasi-absolute' category would give rise – by way of evolution – to particular forms of activity that define their agent. If we accept such a basic premise that activity (praxis) most fully allows us to understand the agent, that action most fully reveals the human being as a person, then such an epistemological stance entails the conviction and certainty that the human being, or subject, has priority in relation to activity, or praxis, which in turn, allows us most fully to understand the subject.[282]

As mentioned previously Wojtyla attaches the same metaphysical priority to the human person acting as *homo oeconomicus*. This is obvious in the encyclical where we can read that

> the *primary basis of the value of work is man himself*, who is the subject . . . [and that] in the first place work is 'for man' and not man 'for work'. Through this conclusion one rightly comes to recognize the pre-eminence of the subjective meaning of work over the objective one.[283]

Praxiological priority

The criticism could be made that there is nothing very original in Wojtyla's philosophical approach to human work. It can be seen as the straightforward application of the Thomistic perspective on human action. In the encyclical Wojtyla does, after all, indicate that he will explore '*new meanings of human work*'.[284] A critic could rightfully ask: where in this document is any new meaning of human work disclosed? This is a plausible criticism, but I believe that a closer study of *Laborem Exercens* leads us in a somewhat new direction in respect of the traditional conception of human work.

As I have already underlined, Wojtyla gives an innovative meaning to human work. This is apparent in his writings, as when he describes that

> as a person works, he performs various actions belonging to the work process; independently of their objective content, these actions must all *serve to realize his humanity* [my emphasis], to fulfill the calling to be a person that is his by reason of his very humanity.[285]

---

[282] Wojtyla, 'Constitution of Culture', p. 266.
[283] John Paul II, *LE*, § 6.
[284] John Paul II, *LE*, § 2.
[285] John Paul II, *LE*, § 6.

The traditional approach had been to give precedence to the objective aspect of work; neglected was the meaning that work had for the realization of the human person himself or herself. Wojtyla emphasizes this repeatedly in *Laborem Exercens*, when he argues that work is a good thing in itself for man.[286] He stresses that

> it is not only good in the sense that it is useful or something to enjoy; it is also good as being something worthy, that is to say, something that corresponds to man's dignity, that expresses this dignity and increases it. If one wishes to define more clearly the ethical meaning of work, it is this truth that one must particularly keep in mind. Work is a good thing for man – a good thing for his humanity – because through work man *not only transforms nature*, [the objective sense] adapting it to his own needs, but he also achieves *fulfillment* as a human being [the subjective sense] and indeed, in a sense, becomes 'more a human being'.[287]

In the Milan paper Wojtyla had written that in accentuating the 'intransitive' dimension of human action he wanted to give priority to the human subject, not alone 'in the metaphysical sense but also [to give] priority in what might be called the praxiological sense. This is where the distinction between the transitive (*transitens*) and the intransitive (*intransitens*) in human action has key significance'.[288] I would be the first to agree that the term 'praxiological sense' is not what one would call user friendly. He does not use the term in *Laborem Exercens* but he does clearly apply such a priority to his understanding of human work. According to Wojtyla, work is not just accidental to human nature; more exactly it is 'constitutive' of it, a[...] would suggest, that his personalism, when applied[...] human work, becomes radicalized. The Milan[...] hermeneutic in the philosophical exploratio[...] Wojtyla explains

> whatever we make in our own action, wha[...] bring about in it, we always simultaneou[...] well (if I may be permitted to put it thus[...] some way shape ourselves, we in a ce[...] acting, we actualize ourselves, we[...]

---

[286] John Paul II, *LE*, § 9.
[287] Ibid.
[288] Wojtyla, 'Constitution of Culture', p. 266

certain – albeit partial – fulfillment (*actus*) both what and who we are potentially (*in potentia*). From the perspective of experience and phenomenological insight, this is the meaning of the term action in the category of *actus*: *actus humanus*.[289]

Wojtyla affirms that without understanding the 'praxiological sense' of work it would be, for example, 'impossible to understand the meaning of the virtue of industriousness'.[290]

It is possible, of course, to use work against the human person, contrary to its praxiological meaning, and Wojtyla alludes to this in *Laborem Exercens* when he asserts that work can be used

> to punish man with the system of forced labour in concentration camps ... [but] all this pleads in favour of the moral obligation to link industriousness, as a virtue with the *social order of work*, which will enable man to become, in work, 'more a human being' and not be degraded by it not only because of the wearing out of his physical strength (which, at least up to a certain point, is inevitable), but especially through damage to the dignity and subjectivity that are proper to him.[291]

New categories

Wojtyla contends that the investigation undertaken into the truth of the meaning of the human person[292] actually creates the basis for 'a new way of thinking, judging and acting'[293] and this is not just within the horizon of *homo oeconomicus* but also within the other dimen-sions.[294] In the Wojtylan analysis, not even the Thomistic perspective

[...] ubject is left unchallenged. The understanding of the [...] the point of view of this tradition tends, as we [...] in favour of substance. This is, of course, [...] at some of the methods of phenomenology [...] istic tradition. Wojtyla can go along with [...] an ontologically pre-exists his action'.[295] [...] action is what phenomenology can aid [...] opriates himself as subject precisely as

[...] p. 266, 267.

[...] *o aestheticus* and so on.

person-in-action,[296] that is, he can actually realize himself as subject in praxis. It is when this is applied in *Laborem Exercens* to human action as in work, that we can begin to discern the novelty of the philosophical development that Wojtyla is attempting to construct. There is ample opportunity for growth and development of these ideas. I presume that Wojtyla perceives *Laborem Exercens* philosophically that is, not as a terminus *ad quem* but as terminus *a quo* for philosophers, economists, and political theorists to discuss.

There are naturally always threats to the new ways of thinking, judging and acting, and these are inherent in any social or economic system. These must be opposed. Wojtyla mentions specifically 'the various trends of *materialistic* and *economistic* thought'[297] that have to be resisted in which '*man is treated as an instrument of production*'[298] and in which he is not, in fact, treated as the efficacious subject of his own actions. Indeed, the 'worker question', or the 'proletariat question' and the call to worker solidarity, in the late nineteenth century were in fact a 'reaction *against the degradation of man as the subject of work*'.[299] There will always be the need to study the subject of work, thus, Wojtyla perceives that in order to avoid the threats against, for example, the praxiological meaning of work as he has outlined 'there is a need for ever new *movements* of solidarity of the workers and with *the workers*'.[300] Buttiglione develops this point further and applies it, when he affirms that

> if we fully wish to grasp the richness of human praxis, we must consider not only the way in which the objective effect of the praxis (a domesticated nature and transformed environment) reacts upon [the human person] by changing him, but also the way in which praxis directly changes the man who brings it into being, either by making him more authentically human or by causing him to lose his humanity. This new way of looking at the matter strongly affects the way in which we look at economic and political praxis. In the case of economic practice there is a glimmering within many phenomena (found most of all in mature capitalist countries) which shows a growing demand for *quality of work* and *self-realization through work*.[301]

---

[296] Cf. Bernard Lonergan, 'The Future of Thomism', in W. Ryan and B. Tyrrell (eds.), *A Second Collection* (Philadelphia: Westminster, 1974), p. 51.
[297] Ibid.
[298] John Paul II, *LE*, § 7.
[299] Ibid.
[300] John Paul II, *LE*, §. 8.
[301] Buttiglione, *Karol Wojtyla*, p. 301.

Lonergan, writing about praxis, describes that it acknowledges what he terms

> the end of the age of innocence. It starts from the assumption that authenticity cannot be taken for granted. Its understanding, accordingly, will follow a hermeneutic of suspicion as well as a hermeneutic of recovery. Its judgment will discern between products of human authenticity and products of unauthenticity. But the basic assumption, the twofold hermeneutic, the discernment between the authentic and the unauthentic set up a distinct method.[302]

Indeed, I would argue that *Laborem Exercens* can be understood in this sense of setting up a twofold hermeneutic: on the one hand, critical suspicion as to various theories of praxis (including of the Marxian and Capitalist versions); on the other, active retrieval and recovery of what it means to participate authentically as a human person together with others in the horizon of human work.

Centesimus Annus

I can only make very brief reference to the encyclical entitled: *Centesimus Annus* [The Hundredth Year].[303] It was written in 1991 to mark the centenary of Leo XIII's *Rerum Novarum* [New Things]. The historical backdrop to it was the collapse of Communism and the revolution of 1989.[304] In 1990 a group of economists were invited to a workshop at the Vatican. Similar to John Paul's other gatherings of intellectuals, this meeting was held in order to assist in the drafting of a new encyclical on contemporary economics. The different contributions were drafted into a synthesis.[305] Wojtyla consulted other experts and studied the synthesis of the scholars. What emerged was the view that the new encyclical should, in fact,

---

[302] Bernard Lonergan, in Frederick Crowe (ed.), *A Third Collection: Papers by Bernard J. F. Lonergan* (New York: Paulist Press, 1985), pp. 159–61.

[303] Hereafter cited as *CA*.

[304] 'The chronological reference, central to *Centesimus Annus*, which is the fall of the Berlin Wall in 1989, confirmed the necessity of an updating of social doctrine', cited in *Centesimus Annus: Assessment and Perspectives for the Future of Catholic Doctrine* (Vatican City: Libreria Editrice Vaticana, 1998), p. 6.

[305] Weigel explains the background to the encyclical in *Witness to Hope*, pp. 612–13. The seminar was entitled *Social and Ethical Aspects of Economics: A Colloquium in the Vatican*, subsequently published by the Pontifical Council for Justice and Peace.

make more use of the personalism central to [Wojtyla's] philosophical studies . . . the result was an encyclical that did not deal with economics from the top down, in terms of macro-aggregates, but from the bottom up. It would attempt a description of 'the economic person' as one dimension of 'the acting person'.[306]

I think it important to stress here, that although the encyclical can certainly be understood in terms of a contribution to modern socio-economic principles, it is nevertheless much more than this. Indeed, to give it a solely economic interpretation would introduce a reductive economic determinism into its understanding of the human person. This is, of course, what Wojtyla criticizes in the Marxian analysis and naturally he does not want to repeat the failure.

Homo politicus: The Acting Person *written large*

We can arguably present *The Acting Person* of the 'Wojtyla I' phase as analysing the basic structure of personal human action, and *Laborem Exercens* of the new 'Wojtyla II' period as exploring the experience of work on the personal level. *Centesimus Annus* is the application of the investigation to social, economic and political structures. Zieba writes:

> It is sufficient to apply the personometer to first the one [e.g. socialist] and then the other [e.g. capitalist] system and observe the results. John Paul II carries this experiment out to great effect in *Centesimus Annus*. There he analyses the kind of person promoted by socialism and the kind promoted by capitalism.[307]

We could, therefore, read this encyclical in the light of *The Acting Person* seen as Wojtyla's attempt at an employment of its philosophy as 'written large' and applied to society. The application of Wojtyla's theory of the acting person has implications on the different horizons of human existence. I have tried to analyse some of these dimensions in this chapter. I would maintain that there also emerges in *Centesimus Annus* a unique perspective on the person as *homo politicus*. Wojtyla writing in this encyclical affirms that

> it is in interrelationships on many levels that a person lives, and that society becomes 'personalized'. The individual today is often suffocated

---

[306] Weigel, *Witness to Hope*, p. 613.
[307] Maciej Zieba, *Surprising Pope*, p. 118.

between two poles represented by the State and the marketplace. At times it seems as though he exists only as a producer and consumer of goods, or as an object of State administration. People lose sight of the fact that life in society has neither the market nor the State as its final purpose, since life itself has a unique value which the State and the market must serve. Man remains above all a being who seeks the truth and strives to live in that truth, deepening his understanding of it through a dialogue which involves past and future generations.[308]

Hence, the issues raised throughout the encyclical are relevant to political philosophers and theorists alike. There is much debate today about European integration and upon what political and philosophical principles it should be based. Václav Havel, a few years ago on a visit to Ireland, spoke about how Europe needed a soul, a heart. He commented that if the only thing that united Europe was a common price for tomatoes, then the soil, in which the plant of unity was growing, was very shallow indeed.[309] There has been a lot of debate since Havel made these comments. More recently, he has remarked that there is evidence of a deeper questioning as to the paradigm upon which European unity is built. Pasquale Ferrara in an essay on the political principles of the European Union notes that:

> [I]n reflections on European integration, Václav Havel has observed, a new emphasis being placed on the spiritual dimension and on the values that underlie it. In effect, up to now European unification and its meaning for history and society has been eclipsed behind technological, economic, financial and administrative questions.[310]

A social theory: the paradigm of the person/neighbour applied

Romano Prodi, president of the European parliament, has spoken of the need for a 'humanistic perspective' in regard to the European project. In an address given at the European parliament, he commented that the economic and social system should, day after day, be systematically stimulated so as to recognize the primacy of human dignity.[311] The paradigm Wojtyla offers philosophers, as a framework

---

[308] John Paul II, *CA*, § 49.
[309] Havel visited Trinity College, Dublin, in June 1996.
[310] Pasquale Ferrara, 'I Principi Politici Dell'Unione Europea: Tracce, Direzioni, Percorsi', *Nuova Umanità* (Rome: Città Nuova, 2001), XXIII, p. 470.
[311] His address was given in Strasbourg, 15 February 2000. Cited in Ferrara, 'I Principe Politici', p. 472.

for an adequate social theory is richly personalist in tone. He does this since it affords a conception of society that entails

> the possibility, and indeed the necessity, of participating with others, 'as neighbours' [other *I*'s] and 'helpers' in addressing the problems and needs of the whole of humanity, in an attempt to realize the universal common good.[312]

Writing about socialism Wojtyla claims that 'the fundamental error of socialism is anthropological in nature'.[313] In light of this he perceives that the pivotal question to ask of any social theory is: what paradigm does it hold of the human person? Discussing the socialist theory, he speaks of how it

> considers the individual person as an element, a molecule within the social organism, so that the good of the individual is completely subordinated to the functioning of the socio-economic mechanism . . . man is thus reduced to a series of social relationships, and the concept of the person as the autonomous subject of moral decision disappears, the very subject whose decisions build the social order.[314]

The theory of the human person he adumbrates here in *Centesimus Annus* is, of course, the one that he had set out earlier in *The Acting Person*. There necessarily follows from an adequate concept of the person a corresponding social framework and man acts within that dimension also as *homo politicus*.[315]

Wojtyla argues vehemently in regard to the relation of the person and the State that

> the social nature of man is not fulfilled in the State, but is realized in various intermediary groups, beginning with the family and including economic, social, political and cultural groups which stem from human nature itself and have their own autonomy, always with a view to the common good. This is what I have called the 'subjectivity' of society which, together with the subjectivity of the individual, was cancelled by 'Real Socialism'.[316]

---

[312] Kevin Doran, *Solidarity: A Synthesis of Personalism and Communalism in the Thought of Karol Wojtyla/Pope John Paul II* (New York: Peter Lang, 1996), p. 241.

[313] John Paul II, *CA*, § 13.

[314] Ibid.

[315] John Paul II, *CA*.

[316] Ibid.

Wojtyla refers to the subjectivity of society in terms of 'the creation of structures of participation and shared responsibility'.[317] Donald Gallagher tells us how Maritain too anticipated Wojtyla's claim of the necessity for new structures[318] in calling for 'a reformation of the structures and the spirit of the economic order'.[319] When these structures are not preserved and protected, then the common good(s) constituted by free, collaborative agents is eclipsed out of the system and that can turn, no matter what the system is, 'into open or thinly disguised totalitarianism'.[320] The concept contained in *Centesimus Annus* – that 'society' as well as the individual, has a 'subjectivity' – is novel and merits further development.[321] It is a direct application of the Wojtylan theory of the subjectivity of the human person to those persons who act 'together-with-others' in society for the sake of the common good.

The Wojtylan application of 'subjectivity' to society opens up and extends the whole understanding of the human person as political participant. Referring to the consequences of the approach of applying the aspects of subjectivity and of consciousness found in *The Acting Person* to social and political philosophy, Buttiglione writes:

> in order for an action performed together with others to be just, it is
> not sufficient for it to protect and to accomplish the objective good of
> all the participants. Beyond this, it is necessary that the participants
> take part in it in a fully human way, engaging their intelligence and
> will in it. A social action without participation cannot be just even if,

[317] John Paul II, *CA*, § 46.
[318] Schindler expands the debate considerably in his reaction to the neo-conservatives post-*Centesimus Annus* writings. He asserts that they (particularly Neuhaus and Novak) are unable 'to grasp the pope's critique of *consumerism as a "structure of sin"*' and hence the need for 'new structures'. The neo-conservatives understand the Pope's critique as being of the excesses of the market system but not of the market itself. It is true that behind a sinful structure you have the person or persons who concretely actualize it. But structures too within themselves can be depersonalizing. Karol Wojtyla's challenge to contemporary philosophers is to apply the 'personmeter' to all the structures of society so as to measure their adequacy with respect to the nature of the human person. It is not within the scope of this book to enter into the Schindler–Neo-conservatives debate, suffice it is to say that the reality of the discussion in itself is clear evidence of the Wojtylan dialogical methodology employed in *Centesimus Annus*. Cf. Schindler, *Heart of the World*, pp. 114–42.
[319] Donald Arthur Gallagher, Introduction, tr. Doris C. Anson, in Jacques Maritain, *Christianity and Democracy and The Rights of Man And Natural Law* (San Francisco: Ignatius Press, 1986), p. xxxvii.
[320] John Paul II, *CA*, § 46.
[321] Weigel, *Witness to Hope*, p. 616.

hypothetically, it would realize the objective good of a particular group.[322]

The concept 'subjectivity of society', I would argue, further radicalizes the contemporary notion of democracy in which the acting person cannot remain a mere bystander. It opens up the whole notion of participatory democracy to critical evaluation. Thus, neither the State nor governments should see fit to usurp the 'subjectivity' of society, for in so doing they remove the basis for such governance in the first place.

In an essay on the contribution of John Paul II's contribution to social thought, Russell Hittinger remarks that in *Centesimus Annus* he 'treats the modern state as a potentially dangerous concentration of coercive power that uproots the "subjectivity of society" and makes itself coincident with the common good'.[323] I do not agree with Hittinger's interpretation of Wojtyla's attitude to the state. It suggests that the Wojtylan outlook is largely pessimistic. I would argue strongly that his views in relation to the acting person's participation in society and the consequent attitude to the state are positive, expansive and creative. It is true that the application of his personalist philosophy of the person to the whole dimension of *homo politicus* needs greater development and clarification. Are there, for example, possible correlations between the Wojtylan analysis and the contributions of political theorists who propose the communitarian paradigm in the critique of modern liberal theory?[324] These are questions and points of clarification that we will have to leave for another time, as they still remain part of the unfinished Wojtylan philosophical symphony.

---

[322] Buttiglione, *Karol Wojtyla*, pp. 368–9.
[323] Russell Hittinger, 'Making Sense of the Civilization of Love', in Gneuchs (ed.), *The Legacy of Pope John Paul II*, p. 84.
[324] Cf. Amitai Etzioni, *The New Golden Rule: Community and Morality in a Democratic Society* (New York: HarperCollins, 1996). For example, a comment from the front dust jacket reads: '*The New Golden Rule* takes its title from the familiar adage to "do unto others as you would have them do to you".' But when taken to a society-level, the Golden Rule's admonition expands, taking the formulation 'respect and uphold society's moral order as you would have society respect and uphold your autonomy to live a full life'.

4

Footbridge Towards the Other:
Conclusions

Joseph Ratzinger writing about John Paul II's encyclical *Fides et Ratio*[1] sees it in terms of an appeal for the restoration to humanity of the courage to seek the truth.[2] I believe that any investigation into the notion of the human person in the writings of Karol Wojtyla will unearth in them a similar attempt at recapturing the truth of the human person. I have endeavoured in this book to survey Wojtyla's extensive writings in order to convey the beauty of the truth of what it means to be a person within the Wojtylan perspective.

In this analysis there are some things old and some things new. In chapter 1 I sought to get to the heart of the drama of the acting person. Rather than setting out on the investigation with an abstract theory of the person, Wojtyla prefers to start with concrete human experience. Action is the prism through which we can discover what is irreducible in the human person. Even this step is fraught with difficulties, for we must not reduce experience to one particular aspect of it, instead, we should attempt to understand it in terms of the fullness of reality.

Wojtyla quarries away at human experience using the tools of phenomenology as an aid in the philosophical articulation *how* it is that we are human persons. At the heart of his analysis is the discovery that the modern methods of phenomenology can actually lead towards a dynamic retrieval and renewal in our understanding of the original traditional Thomistic perspective on the person. Wojtyla seems to say to phenomenologists and Thomists alike: 'Be not afraid!' Phenomenology and Thomism actually complement each other in their understanding of the mystery of the human person. Pure description (phenomenology) alone is not enough but neither is the purely metaphysical approach of Thomism. Phenomenology allows us pause at the irreducible in human experience but metaphysics helps us understand the contents of the experience in terms of the whole

[1] Encyclical on 'Faith and Reason' written in 1998.
[2] Cardinal Ratzinger, 'Culture and Truth: Reflection on the Encyclical', in *Origins*: *CNS documentary service*, Vol. 28, No. 36 (25 February 1999), p. 627.

of reality. As Buttiglione describes, it is not a matter of showing phenomenologically that man is a person, but applying phenomenology to see '*in which way man is a person*'.[3] Wojtyla maintains that if the philosopher x-rays lived human experience, then the human person as *suppositum* will be revealed; in fact, it is given directly 'in our experience of ourselves, it is taken up into that experience and becomes part of it'.[4]

With such an approach Wojtyla was not without opponents. Kupczak writes:

> his methodology is one of the most debated and criticized areas of his philosophy. Because he attempted to create a synthesis between phenomenology and metaphysics, Wojtyla became vulnerable to criticism and misunderstanding from both sides. Thus, phenomenologists often hold that he does not pursue the phenomenological investigation far enough; neo-Thomists criticize him for his use of the phenomenological method, as well as for his limited application of metaphysics.[5]

At the same time, however, Wojtyla is not without proponents of his approach and many of them are mentioned in this study. I have in mind those who have undertaken studies into his thought such as Buttiglione, Crosby, Schmitz and others. Norris Clarke, for example, accepts Wojtyla's criticism of Thomistic philosophy's failure adequately to articulate a comprehensive analysis of the person that would include its inherent relationality.[6]

In chapter I I spoke of how Wojtyla's poetic and dramatic writings are a kind of 'phenomenological manifesto', in that they seek to reach and communicate the truth of what it means to be a person. They clearly portray a continuity of thought with regard to the person in the writings of Wojtyla. A brief outline of Wojtyla's *The Acting Person* was also presented in order to situate the theme of the book. Of particular interest

---

[3] Rocco Buttiglione, *Karol Wojtyla: The Thought of the Man who Became Pope John Paul II*, tr. Paola Guietti and Francesca Murphy (Grand Rapids: Eerdmans, 1997), p. 356.

[4] Karol Wojtyla, *Person and Community, Selected Essays*, tr. Theresa Sandok (New York: Peter Lang, 1993), p. 16.

[5] Jaroslaw Kupczak, *Destined for Liberty: The Human Person in the Philosophy of Karol Wojtyla/John Paul II* (Washington, DC: Catholic University of America Press, 2000), p. 149.

[6] W. Norris Clarke, *The Aquinas Lecture: Person and Being* (Milwaukee: Marquette University Press, 1993), p. 2.

here was the treatment given by Wojtyla to the transcendence of the person in action. In his analysis of the personal structure of self-determination, Wojtyla shows how the human person can be considered to be the efficient cause of his/her own action. Hence, action is revelatory of the human person and in an analysis of it there is revealed the characteristics of self-determination, self-governance and self-possession. These elements in themselves disclose the irreducible within the human person. Man is somebody instead of something exactly because of these fundamental characteristics.[7]

Wojtyla's contribution can be seen as developing a type of 'low-ascending' anthropology, although in so doing, he keeps in mind the importance of the canons of the KUL philosophers. He argues that in constructing an adequate theory of the person we must keep ourselves 'tethered to reality' and that entails employing a realistic ontology. Our philosophical examination of human experience must be exhaustive in order to be realistic. Wojtyla argues that he wants to 'allow *experience to speak for itself as best it can right to the* end'.[8] Here he recognizes the central role of philosophical anthropology in such an enquiry. The traditional approach was to start with a general theory of the universe (cosmology) and then situate man in that context. However, the cosmological perspective analyses man or woman as being a particular human being, that is, as an individual of a certain species. This does not arrive at man or woman as a personal subject, and consequently, does not adequately account for the human experiences that stem from that reality and indeed often occur in the most abject of human conditions.[9] I would argue that this is where Wojtyla is philosophically novel and courageous because he contends that by carrying out a thoroughgoing analysis of human experience we can get to the truth of things-in-themselves. Applying this to the human person we can reach the irreducible contents of personhood.

Another important element in the investigation is to have a relational approach to philosophy so as to avoid a collapse into idealism; this is evidenced in his treatment of consciousness as an aspect of the human person but not as his or her totality. Finally, the Wojtylan perspective

---

[7] Karol Wojtyla, *The Acting Person*, tr. Andrzej Potocki (Dordrecht and Boston: Reidel, 1979), p. 151.

[8] Wojtyla, *Acting Person*, p. 133.

[9] Wojtyla writes that in the concentration camps there were prisoners who 'managed to relate to others as other *I*'s, as *neighbors* – often to a heroic degree'. Cf. *Person and Community*, p. 206.

is open to the insights accumulated within the history of philosophy and in other cultures. There are seeds of the truth[10] sown in all philosophical traditions and it is up to the philosopher to seize the opportunity they afford for the whole of humanity. There is no room in Wojtylan eyes for intellectual snobbery or philosophical tribalism in the search for the truth. The philosophical tenets I have just mentioned are employed by Wojtyla throughout his career and can be clearly seen in my study of his writings on the human person. We see this in his openness to the philosophy of phenomenology, to the various human sciences, the dialogue with Marxism and his reflections upon art. He is, I would argue, a philosophical optimist. There is the awareness that we belong to a worldwide civilization of reason, which may have lost direction. But there is also the challenge and opportunity of rediscovering our path 'if we can find the way to re-awaken the common humanity we feel we share with people of every other background, culture and religion or moral conviction'.[11] Wojtyla writes:

> In both East and West, we may trace a journey which has led humanity down the centuries to meet and engage truth more and more deeply. It is a journey which has unfolded – as it must – within the horizon of personal self-consciousness: the more human beings know reality and the world, the more they know themselves in their uniqueness, with the question of the meaning of things and of their existence ever more pressing . . . The admonition Know Yourself was carved on the temple portal at Delphi, as testimony to a basic truth to be adopted as a minimal norm by those who seek to set themselves apart from the rest of creation as 'human beings', that is as those who 'know themselves'.[12]

This study makes special reference to the paradigm of the 'neighbour' in the writings of Wojtyla. Chapter 2 of the book is entitled: 'The Paradigm of the Neighbour: Towards an adequate Philosophy of the Person'. This title itself suggests the uniqueness of Wojtyla's insight into the nature of 'participation'. It is only in terms of the 'other' (the gospel term is the 'neighbour') that we can achieve a comprehensive

---

[10]   In an interview with *La Stampa* newspaper, Wojtyla surprised the interviewer by speaking about the 'seeds of truth' present within communism. Cited in Luigi Accattoli, *Karol Wojtyla: L'uomo di fine millennio* (Milan: San Paolo, 1998), p. 241.

[11]   Brendan Purcell, 'Fides et Ratio: Charter for the Third Millennium', in *The Challenge of Truth: Reflections on Fides et Ratio*, ed. James McEvoy (Dublin: Veritas, 2002), p. 240.

[12]   John Paul II, *Fides et Ratio*, § 1.

philosophy of the person. A theory of the person based upon the fullness of human experience must account for the reality of participation. This is not for Wojtyla a primarily epistemological problem. It was therefore, a new element that he considered needed further elaboration and development. In his book *The Acting Person* he had not given it due attention. In his poetic and dramatic works we can trace clearly the significance Wojtyla attaches to the category of the 'neighbour'. The main focus in the analysis in *The Acting Person* had been upon the 'I act'. Nonetheless, the reality is 'I act' together-with-others. This leads to the question of 'participation' and it is dealt with in summary fashion in the final part of *The Acting Person*. An analysis of this common human experience solely on the level of a societal explanation is, Wojtyla suggests, wholly unsatisfactory. The question of the 'other' must also be dealt with on the ontological level. This is vital and Wojtyla's treatment of the question is fundamental in his critique of the extreme forms of Marxism and capitalism to which I referred in chapter 3 of the book. The main problem with Marxism is not merely a question of the inefficiency of a social system; it is something far more deep-seated. He sees the core difficulty as anthropological.

The question posed in terms of participation is: how can I act together-with-others and at the same time avoid the alienation of the 'I'? Acting together with others should not negate the actualization of the person's own self-determination; rather, it should lead to its fulfilment. In short, Wojtyla attempts to work out the ontological under-pinning attached to the common human experience of 'participation'. A purely phenomenological description of the reality cannot interpret the philosophical significance of acting together-with-others for the personal 'I'.

It is in dealing with this problematic that Wojtyla introduces the term the 'neighbour'. This is an innovative way to deal with the question. I have made reference in my study to the philosophy of Emmanuel Levinas and the possible correlation between his thought and the Wojtylan project. There is obviously room for further research into these connections. There are clear parallels too with the work of the Scottish philosopher John Macmurray.[13] Wojtyla argues that the 'other' we act with is the 'neighbour'. He affirms, in fact, that the neighbour is revelatory of the full significance of participation. To the

---

[13] John Macmurray (1891–1976). Cf. *The Self as Agent* (London: Faber & Faber, 1969) and *Persons in Relation* (London: Faber & Faber, 1970).

question: who is the neighbour? Wojtyla would respond by saying: the neighbour is another 'I', and he or she cannot be reduced to the reality of mere 'interhuman relations'. The neighbour is another 'person', one like oneself.

In numerous essays, Wojtyla further clarifies and develops what he means by the introduction of the category of the neighbour into the problematic of participation or 'intersubjectivity' as it is more often called. It is, as I have said, a novel approach to the problem, and obviously not unlike his methodology, one that is open to criticism. He summarizes his thought as follows:

> 'the *other*' does not just signify that the being existing next to me or even acting in common with me in some system of activities is the same kind of being as I am. Within the context of this real situation, 'the *other*' also signifies my no less real – though primarily subjective – participation in that being's humanity, a participation arising from my awareness that this being is another *I*, which means 'also an *I*'.[14]

Thus, any realistic theory of the human person must take into account the fact that 'I act' together-with-others and that these 'others' are 'persons'. The 'neighbour' is another 'I' who seeks to carry out his/her actions according to the requirements of self-determination. There is, therefore, a reciprocity between the 'I' and the 'neighbour'. Wojtyla argues that there are onto-ethical implications attached to this philosophical insight. In answer to the question: *How* can I become a fully realized person and participate with others? Wojtyla introduces the 'evangelical commandment of love',[15] that is, 'Love your neighbour as yourself'.

In chapter 2 of the book I began to discuss the ethical expansion of participation contained in the commandment of love. When I act according to the commandment of love, 'I act' *as* a person-to-a-person. In doing this, I not only 'experience' the 'other' as 'other' but I also actualize my own self-fulfilment. Wojtyla puts it succinctly in *Love and Responsibility*:

> Strictly speaking the commandment says: 'Love persons', and the personalistic norm says: 'A person is an entity of a sort to which the proper and adequate way to relate is love.' The personalistic norm does, as we have seen, provide a justification for the New Testament

---

[14] Wojtyla, *Person and Community*, p. 200.
[15] Wojtyla, *Acting Person*, p. 295.

commandment. And so, if we take the commandment together with its justification, we can say that it is the same as the personalistic norm.[16]

As we already mentioned, the book *Love and Responsibility* is chronologically prior in Wojtyla's writings but would, in fact, merit reading after an examination of his work *The Acting Person*. The former is an exploration of participation in terms of marriage in which the well-being, self-determination and self-realization of each person is mutually important to each other. It is an interesting contribution to the philosophical articulation of participation in terms of interpersonal relationships.

I concluded chapter 2 with my own suggestion as to possible areas for further growth in the Wojtylan reflections. If the neighbour is to be treated (loved) 'as yourself', that is, as another 'person', can we perhaps build a new ontological-ethical anthropology developing from the '*as*' in the commandment of love? The term '*as*' contains in itself the whole concept of the basic personalization of relationships that Wojtyla goes on to develop in what I described as the 'Wojtyla II' period of his career. This is when the application of Wojtyla's theory of the human person now moves on from the personal level to the various horizons of human existence.

These dimensions of human existence are outlined in chapter 3 in terms of: *homo ethicus-interpersonalis*, *homo aestheticus* and *homo oeconomicus*. This part of the enquiry is an investigation into the literature of the 'Wojtyla II' phase in the light of an application of the original Wojtylan anthropology. This is, one may say, the public face of Wojtylan philosophy. Very few people will have read *The Acting Person*, but having found himself placed on the world stage in becoming John Paul II, something of what he said about 'morality', 'art' and 'human work' will have been read by many more. In virtue of this fact alone he must easily be the most widely read philosopher in the contemporary world.

My suggestion is that there is a maturation in the philosophical thought of Wojtyla in this later stage of his career. I characterized it in terms of *die Öffnung*, an opening-up to new horizons on the theme of the human person. In this part of the exploration, just as we come across terms like 'applied mathematics' or 'applied physics' we can

---

[16] Wojtyla, *Love and Responsibility*, tr. H. T. Willets (London: Collins, 1981), p. 41.

say that the study in chapter 3 is of Wojtyla's 'applied anthropology'. He saw the need for a 'new philosophical discourse' within the different horizons in which we act together-with-others.

The approach is, once again, decidedly phenomenological. He sets out to study the human person through the manner in which he or she appears and acts within different realities. The first area we study is the ethical. There is an examination of his weekly addresses at the general audiences and then a few brief observations on the encyclical *Veritatis Splendor*. An important point here is that morality is not a paste-on attachment for Wojtyla. It is essentially about the working out of the onto-ethical implications of an adequate theory of the human person. It concerns the application of what it means to advance the *good* of the human person.

In *Veritatis Splendor* I studied Wojtyla's phenomenological description of the encounter between Jesus and the rich young man. The young man, who is everyone because he remains unnamed, asks: 'What must I do?' A response that adequately accounts for the reality of the human person cannot just collapse into the application of an extrinsic legalism. This is where Wojtyla's personalism is seen to be radical and thoroughgoing. He argues that, at all times, personal assimilation of the truths of morality is up to 'the acting subject . . . He appropriates this truth of his being and makes it his own by his acts and corresponding virtues.'[17] In this perspective the ethical questions are grafted into the nature of what it actually means to be a human person. The commandment of love appears again in the Wojtylan writings as the way in which the good of the human person is protected. Wojtyla writes:

> in this commandment we find a precise expression of the *singular dignity of the human person*. [The commandments] teach us man's true humanity. They shed light on the essential duties, and so indirectly on the fundamental rights, inherent in the nature of the human person.[18]

The world of art is another dimension in which the human person acts. Art, in fact, can be understood in terms of a remarkable attempt to recapture the reality of the human person and the struggle involved in achieving 'self-determination', 'self-governance', and 'self-possession'. All these are in the Wojtylan perspective, fundamental

---

[17] John Paul II, *Veritatis Splendor*, § 52.
[18] John Paul II, *Veritatis Splendor*, § 13.

stages in the full enactment of the human person. Attached as an appendix to this book is a copy of the canvas by Mark Gertler entitled the 'Merry-Go-Round'. It is an artistic exploration of the philosophical theme of depersonalization or alienation. The investigation of such themes is not left to philosophers alone; artists too can pose fundamental questions about the unfolding drama of human existence and the person's role therein.

When we come to examine Wojtyla's anthropology in terms of *homo aestheticus* we discover another horizon of human existence ripe for development. Wojtyla sees the artistic tools available to artists as being both diagnostic and therapeutic in the task of recapturing the reality of the human person. Art can phenomenologically describe the human experience. But that is not all it is. In other words, it is not just art for art's sake. Wojtyla in his own life as an artist turned to Polish Romanticism because in it he discovered art's therapeutic aspect. We can restore damaged paintings but art too can help us recover the inner beauty of the person. In this book I referred to this as art's anamnetic nature, that is, it can lead towards the restoration of the truth of the human person on the personal, social and historical levels.

Brief mention is also made of Wojtyla's theory of the theatre. We can, I would claim, see Wojtyla's philosophy of the acting person enacted in his theory of drama. It is the theatre of the 'inner self'. The actor does not just take on the character he/she is acting, merely by outward gestures and special theatrical effects. It requires real 'participation' by the actor, a carrying of the problem. The actor, according to this perspective, is someone who 'acts' (*agere*); he/she is the efficacious agent (acting person) who seeks a resolution to the dramatic dilemma. I also observed parallels between this theory and that of the Theatre of the Absurd.

In light of the material examined in terms of Wojtyla's writings on *homo aestheticus* it is therefore not surprising that he addresses a *Letter to Artists*. Our study of this letter also reveals the application of the Wojtylan anthropology. Wojtyla gives a phenomenological description of the artistic experience and then he proceeds to outline an important interpretation of the experience in terms of the metaphysical reality of the *Lebenswelt* of that particular dimension of human existence. The important role of 'self-determination' also emerges. Wojtyla describes it like this: 'all men and women are entrusted with the task of *crafting their own life*: in a certain sense they are to make of it a work of art, a masterpiece . . . [They are] to be authors of their own acts.'[19]

In *The Acting Person* Wojtyla had given an analysis of human efficacy in the light of the human dynamism of 'I act'. In the *Letter to Artists* there is an application of this to the 'I act' of the artist. The understanding that unfolds is that the artist is someone who is the efficient cause of his or her own action. Nonetheless, what is specific to the artist is that they also 'respond to the *demands of art* and faithfully accept art's specific dictates'.[20] The demands of art are the right criterion of production,[21] just as, the demands of acting together-with-others is to 'love persons' because the personalistic norm reveals that a person is an entity of a type to which the only proper way to relate is love.

Wojtyla affirms that through artistic activity we can catch a glimpse of the beauty of the irreducible in the human person. It is not one-way – both artist and observer can participate in the enactment of the drama of the human person. In *The Acting Person* Wojtyla investigated how 'action reveals the person'.[22] I have argued in this book that Wojtyla conceives that, so too, artistic activity can be a prism through which we can see reflected the meaning of the human person.

Finally, we come to the application of the Wojtylan anthropology to the human person as *homo oeconomicus*. Maciej Zieba[23] uses the analogy of applying a 'personmeter' found in Wojtyla's writings to contemporary social theory. It can be applied to given social systems to see if they measure up positively in terms of an adequate philosophy of the person. The litmus test for any social theory is: does the system allow for true human participation by the individual human person? Does the given system, whatever its name, allow me to experience myself as a self-determining *I*, does it help me experience the *other* as another *I*?

Chapter 3 proceeds then to study Wojtyla's encyclicals *Laborem Exercens* and *Centesimus Annus* using *The Acting Person* and other writings from the 'Wojtyla I' period as a philosophical-hermeneutical key. *The Acting Person* is in itself a presentation of a philosophy of praxis. Wojtyla further develops his understanding of human action

[19] John Paul II, *Letter to Artists*, § 2.
[20] Ibid.
[21] Ibid.
[22] Wojtyla, *Acting Person*, p. 11.
[23] Maciej Zieba, *The Surprising Pope: Understanding the Thought of John Paul II*, tr. Karolina Weening (New York: Lexington Books, 2000), p. 113.

in the encyclical on human work. In fact, I maintain that he radicalizes the notion of human action. We can see this particularly in the distinction he makes between the objective and subjective senses of work. The traditional view on human work had always emphasized the objective meaning. Wojtyla stresses the need for a balance in the philosophical analysis of human work. In *Laborem Exercens* he writes:

> Work is a good thing for man – a good thing for his humanity – because through work man *not only transforms nature*, [the objective sense] adapting it to his own needs, but he also achieves *fulfillment* as a human being [the subjective sense] and indeed, in a sense, becomes 'more a human being'.[24]

Thus, in the Wojtylan perspective work is not just accidental to human nature. A purely sociological analysis of human work is not sufficient, since as an investigation it will not arrive at an understanding of work-in-itself. Work is, according to Wojtyla, constitutive of who we are as human persons.

It is in light of this that I have spoken in chapter 3 of the twofold hermeneutic at work in *Laborem Exercens*. There is, on the one hand, the critique of various theories of praxis (Capitalist and Marxian varieties), and on the other, there is the attempt actively to recover what it actually means to participate authentically as a human person together-with-others in the horizon of human work.

Centesimus Annus is, I suggest, *The Acting Person* written large, that is, applied to the human person's participation in social, economic and political structures. This is why I spoke of *die Öffnung* in terms of this whole phase in Wojtyla's life, because we see here what I term the enactment of the drama of the human person within the different worlds of morality, art and economics. There are implications for social theory in terms of the paradigm of the human person that Wojtyla advances. Kevin Doran sums it up well when he acknowledges that Wojtyla's paradigm of the human person affords a conception of society that entails 'the possibility, and indeed the necessity, of participating with others, "as neighbours" [other *I*s] and "helpers" in addressing the problems and needs of the whole of humanity, in an attempt to realize the universal common good'.[25]

[24] John Paul II, *Laborem Exercens*, § 6.
[25] Kevin Doran, *Solidarity: A Synthesis of Personalism and Communalism in the Thought of Karol Wojtyla/Pope John Paul II* (New York: Peter Lang, 1996), p. 241.

There is a case for more analysis and debate in Wojtyla's novel application of his theory of the subjectivity of the human person to 'society'. There is much room here for discussion, as the notion of the 'subjectivity of society' radicalizes the whole concept of democracy in which the acting person emerges as a *homo politicus*, as a 'participant' and not a mere spectator in the unfolding drama of the human person within the dimension of politics. I have mentioned the approach of the neo-conservatives in embracing liberal democracy as the best system to safeguard the dignity of the human person. This opens up a whole area of discussion but we have no time now to enter into it. Robert P. Kraynak's book *Christian Faith and Modern Democracy*[26] is a timely contribution to the debate. He actually defends the view that liberalism is unable to justify the human dignity on which liberal human rights are based. He describes modern liberalism as being 'essentially neo-Kantian in grounding human rights in the dignity of persons as rational and moral agents and in viewing democracy as the sole legitimate form of government'.[27] Kraynak draws heavily upon Solzhenitsyn's writings to articulate his argument. He asserts that Solzhenitsyn's support for democracy is in light of the fact 'that we are choosing it as a means, not an end in itself'.[28] Solzhneitsyn maintains that 'the structure of the state is secondary to the spirit of human relations. Given human integrity, any honest system is acceptable, but given human rancour and selfishness, even the most sweeping of democracies would become unbearable.[29]

Solzhenitsyn would hold a similar view with respect to the human person acting within the dimension as *homo oeconomicus*. He observes that 'neither a market economy nor even general abundance constitutes the crowning achievement of human life'.[30] This debate is for another time and place. My particular study attempts to set out the notion of the human person contained in Wojtyla's writings. Integral to such a philosophy is the concept of the 'neighbour'. I have indicated in these conclusions, areas for further debate and development. In terms of the 'neighbour' there are, as I have mentioned, parallels with the work of

[26] *Christian Faith and Modern Democracy: God and Politics in the Fallen World* (Notre Dame, IN: University of Notre Dame Press, 2001).
[27] Cf. 'First Things', February 2002, No. 120, p. 8.
[28] Alexander Solzhenitsyn, *Rebuilding Russia: Reflections and Tentative Proposals* (New York: Farrar, Straus & Giroux, 1990), pp. 62–3.
[29] Solzhenitsyn, *Rebuilding Russia*, p. 49.
[30] Ibid.

some of the philosophers of the 'Other'. I have made reference to the philosophy of Emmanuel Levinas. There is scope for a comparison between the Wojtylan and Levinasian concepts of the person. I also spoke of how the paradigm of the person/neighbour when applied to social theory opens up a debate for social and political theorists. The American sociologist, Amitai Etzioni, for example, writes about how the philosophy of communitarianism aspires to promote 'the re-invigorated community, the neighbourhood: those "social webs of people who know one another . . . and have a moral voice, who can draw on interpersonal bonds to encourage members to abide by shared values"'.[31] There are obvious correlations here between this perspective and the whole Wojtylan project.

I used the phrase 'footbridge toward the other' in the opening page of this book. Solzhenitsyn gives the admonition that all we have to do is not to lie.[32] Within the Wojtylan perspective this would read: all we have to do is not to lie about the 'Other'. I hope this study has been of service in unfolding the truth about the human person. I would like to conclude by quoting a poem written by Wojtyla. It sums up for me the experience of this investigation.

Thoughts about a footbridge

I take my first steps on a footbridge.
My heart – is it a footbridge throbbing in each joist?
Is thought a footbridge?
(My thoughts only trace what my heart is tracking. Feelings, perceptions – but which fill me more?)
This footbridge is all.
And yet I grow differently,
feel the wind differently, differently sway.
Both strong and weak speak to me
and strength is the contrast:
the world leans differently
on strength and on weakness.

Is the bridge just an image of somebody crossing?
Over the deep, groping for the shore, he throbs
at the merging of currents.

[31] Cited in *The Personal World: John Macmurray on Self and Society*, selected and introduced by Philip Conford (Edinburgh: Floris Books, 1996), p. 24.
[32] Alexander Solzhenitsyn, *From Under the Rubble*, tr. Michael Scammell (London: Collins & Harvill Press, 1975), p. 276.

In himself man feels no weight of hours:
they hang overhead, and they vanish below.

And yet I stand,
a profile cut from the wave
which withdraws and leaves me behind.
My motion is different:
there a shape is enclosed in transparent brackets,
here the truth is confirmed
in my own life.

Wait. Have patience, I will draw You
from all riverbeds, streams, springs of light,
from the roots of trees and the plains of the sun.
When all this is in me,
when I contain the dual weight of terror and hope
and reach depths translucent as sky
then no one will say
that I simplify.[33]

---

[33]   Karol Wojtyla, *Collected Poems*, tr. Jerzy Peterkiewicz (London: Hutchinson, 1982), pp. 110–11.

Bibliography

Works by Karol Wojtyla

Collected Poems. Tr. Jerzy Peterkiewicz. London: Hutchinson, 1982.

The Collected Plays and Writings on the Theatre. Tr. Boleslaw Tabroski. Berkeley: University of California Press, 1987.

Easter Vigil and Other Poems. Tr. Jerzy Peterkiewicz. London: Hutchinson, 1979.

Love and Responsibility. Tr. H. T. Willets. London: Collins, 1981.

The Acting Person. Tr. Andrzej Potocki. Ed. A. Tymieniecka. Dordrecht and Boston: Reidel, 1979.

Person and Community, Selected Essays. Tr. Theresa Sandok. Ed. A. N. Woznicki. New York: Peter Lang, 1993.

Perché L'Uomo: Scritti inediti di Anthropologia e Filosofia. Vatican City: Libreria Editrice Vaticana, 1995.

'The Task of Christian Philosophy Today', in *Proceedings of the ACPA*, 52, 1979.

Sources of Renewal. Tr. P. S. Falla. New York: Collins, 1980.

Persona e Atto. Trs. Giuseppe and Patrycja Mikulska. Romagna: Rusconi Libri, 1999.

Person und Tat. Freiburg: Herder, 1981.

JOHN PAUL II, *Crossing the Threshold of Hope.* Tr. Jenny and Martha McPhee. London: Jonathan Cape, 1994.

JOHN PAUL II, *The Theology of the Body: Human Love in the Divine Plan.* Boston: Pauline Books, 1997.

The following Encyclicals and Apostolic Letters of John Paul II can be accessed at www.vatican.va

> *Laborem Exercens*, 1981.
> *Redemptor Hominis*, 1987.
> *Centesimus Annus*, 1991.
> *Veritatis Splendor*, 1993.
> *Letter to Families*, 1994.
> *Fides et Ratio*, 1998.
> *Letter to Artists*, 1999.

Works on Karol Wojtyla

ACCATTOLI, LUIGI, *Man of the Millennium: John Paul II*. Tr. Jordan Aumann O.P. Boston, MA: Pauline Books, 2000.

BEIGEL, GERARD, *Faith and Social Justice in the Teaching of Pope John Paul II*. New York: American University Studies, 2000.

BUTTIGLIONE, ROCCO, *Karol Wojtyla, The Thought of the Man Who Became Pope John Paul II*. Tr. Paolo Guietti and Francesca Murphy. Grand Rapids: Eerdmans, 1997.

BUTTIGLIONE, ROCCO, *La Filosofia di Karol Wojtyla: Atti del Seminario di studi dell'Università di Bari*. Bologna: CSEO, 1983.

DINOLA, J. A. and CESSARIO, R., *Veritatis Splendor and the Renewal of Moral Theology*. New Jersey: Scepter Publishers, 1999.

DORAN, KEVIN, *Solidarity: A Synthesis of Personalism and Communalism in the Thought of Karol Wojtyla/Pope John Paul II*. New York: Peter Lang, 1996.

GNEUCHS, GEOFFREY (ed.), *The Legacy of Pope John Paul II: His Contribution to Catholic Thought*. New York: Herder & Herder, 2000.

GREGG, SAMUEL, *Challenging the Modern World: Karol Wojtyla/John Paul II and the Development of Catholic Social Teaching*. Maryland: Lexington Books, 1999.

KUPCZAK, JAROSLAW, *Destined for Liberty: The Human Person in the Philosophy of Karol Wojtyla/John Paul II*. Washington, DC: Catholic University of America Press, 2000.

McDERMOTT, JOHN (ed.), *The Thought of Pope John Paul: A Collection of Essays and Studies*. Rome: Editrice Pontificia Università Gregoriana, 1993.

PHAM, JOHN-PETER, *Centesimus Annus: Assessment and Perspectives for the Future of Catholic Social Doctrine*. Vatican City: Libreria Editrice Vaticana, 1998.

SCHMITZ, KENNETH L., *At the Center of the Human Drama: The Philosophical Anthropology of Karol Wojtyla/Pope John Paul II*. Washington, DC: Catholic University of America Press, 1993.

SHIVANANDAN, MARY, *Crossing the Threshold of Love: A New Vision of Marriage in the Light of John Paul II's Anthropology*. Washington, DC: Catholic University of America Press, 1999.

SIMPSON, PETER, *On Karol Wojtyla*. New York: Wadsworth Press, 2001.

WEIGEL, GEORGE, *Witness of Hope: The Biography of John Paul II*. New York: HarperCollins, 1999.

WEIGEL, GEORGE, *Soul of the World: Notes on the Future of Public Catholicism*. Washington, DC: Ethics and Public Policy Center, 1996.

WHITEHEAD, KENNETH D., *John Paul II: Witness to Truth*. Indiana: St Augustine Press, 2001.

WILLIAMS, GEORGE HUNTSTON, *The Mind of John Paul II: Origins of His Thought and Action*. New York: Seabury Press, 1981.

ZIEBA, MACIEJ, *The Surprising Pope: Understanding the Thought of John Paul II*. Tr. Karolina Weening. New York: Lexington Books, 2000.

General Bibliography

ADLAM, CAROL et al. (eds.), *Face-to-Face: Bakhtin in Russia and the West*. Eds. Carol Adlam, Rachel Falconer, Vitalii Makhlin and Alastair Renfrew. Sheffield: Sheffield Academic Press, 1997.

ARISTOTLE, *The Politics of Aristotle*. Harmondsworth: Penguin Books, 1992.

ARISTOTLE, *The Works of Aristotle Translated into English*: Vol. IX. *Ethica Nicomachea, Magna Moralia, Ethica Eudemia*. Ed. David Ross. Oxford: Oxford University Press, 1966.

BAKHTIN, M. M., *Towards a Philosophy of the Act*. Tr. Vadim Liapunov. Ed. Michael Holquist and Vadim Liapunov. Austin: University of Texas Press, 1993.

BORSATO, BATTISTA, *L' Alterità come Etica: Una Lettura di Emmanuel Levinas*. Bologna: EDB, 1995.

BRUCE, SUSAN (ed.), *Icon Critical Guides: King Lear*. Cambridge: Icon Books, 1997.

CICCHESE, GENNARO, *I Percorsi dell'Altro: Anthropologia e Storia*. Rome: Città Nuova, 1999.

CLARKE, W. NORRIS, *The Aquinas Lecture: Person and Being*. Milwaukee: Marquette University Press, 1993.

CLARKE, W. NORRIS, *Explorations in Metaphysics: Being – God – Person*. Notre Dame, IN: University of Notre Dame Press, 1994.

CORK, RICHARD, *A Bitter Truth: Avant-Garde Art and The Great War*. New Haven: Yale University Press, 1983.

CONFORD, PHILLIP, *The Personal World: John Macmurray on Self and Society*. Edinburgh: Floris Books, 1996.

CROSBY, JOHN F., *The Selfhood of the Human Person*. Washington, DC: Catholic University of America Press, 1996.

DOSTOEVSKY, FYODOR, *The Brothers Karamazov*. Tr. Andrew R. MacAndrew. New York: Bantam, 1981.

DOSTOEVSKY, FYODOR, *The Idiot*. New York: Bantam, 1963.

ERICSON, EDWARD E., *Solzhenitsyn and the Modern World*. Washington, DC: Regnery Gateway, 1993.

ESSLIN, MARTIN, *The Theatre of the Absurd*. London: Penguin Books, 1983.

ETZIONI, AMITAI, *The Golden Rule: Community and Morality in a Democratic Society*. New York: HarperCollins, 1996.

FEUERBACH, LUDWIG, *Principle of the Philosophy of the Future*. Tr. Manfred H. Vogel. Indiana: Hackett Publishing Company, 1986.

FRANKL, VIKTOR, *Man's Search for Meaning: An Introduction to Logotherapy*. Tr. Ilse Lasch. New York: Simon & Schuster, 1962.

FROSSARD, ANDRE, *Forget Not to Love: The Passion of Maximilian Kolbe*. San Francisco: Ignatius Press, 1991.

HAMMOND, MICHAEL et al., *Understanding Phenomenology*. Oxford: Blackwell, 1991.

HENDLEY, STEVEN, *From Communicative Action To the Face of the Other: Levinas and Habermas on Language, Obligation and Community*. New York: Lexington Books, 2000.

HUDSON, DEAL W. and MORAN, DENNIS WM. (eds.), *The Future of Thomism*. Notre Dame, IN: University of Notre Dame Press, 1992.

KEENAN, BRIAN, *An Evil Cradling*. London: Random House, 1992.

KRAYNAK, ROBERT P., *Christian faith and Modern Democracy: God and Politics in the Fallen World*. Notre Dame, IN: University of Notre Dame Press, 2001.

LEVINAS, EMMANUEL, *Otherwise than Being or Beyond Essence*. Tr. Alphonso Lingis. Pittsburg: Duquesne University Press, 1999.

LEVINAS, EMMANUEL, *Outside the Subject*. Tr. Michael B. Smith. Eds. Werner Hamacher and David E. Wellbery. Stanford: Stanford University Press, 1993.

LONERGAN, BERNARD, *Insight: A Study of Human Understanding*. London: Longman, 1958.

LONERGAN, BERNARD, *Method in Theology*. London: Darton, Longman & Todd, 1972.

LONERGAN, BERNARD, *A Second Collection*. Eds. W. Ryan and B. Tyrrell. Westminster: Philadelphia, 1974.

LONERGAN, BERNARD, *A Third Collection: Papers by Bernard J. F. Lonergan*. Ed. Frederick Crowe. New York: Paulist Press, 1985.

MACMURRAY, JOHN, *The Self as Agent*. London: Faber & Faber, 1969.

MACMURRAY, JOHN, *Persons in Relation*. London: Faber & Faber, 1970.

MAHONEY, DANIEL J., *Aleksandr Solzhenitsyn: The Ascent from Ideology*. New York: Rowman & Littlefield, 2001.

MARITAIN, JACQUES, *Existence and Existent*. Garden City, NY: Doubleday, 1957.

MARITAIN, JACQUES, *Christianity and Democracy and The Rights of Man and Natural Law*. San Francisco: Ignatius Press, 1986.

MARITAIN, JACQUES, *The Social and Political Philosophy of Jacques Maritain: Selected Readings*. Eds. Joseph W. Evans and Leo R. Ward. New York: Image Books, 1965.

MATTHEWS, ERIC, *Twentieth-Century French Philosophy*. Oxford: Oxford University Press, 1996.

MATTHEWS, ERIC, *The Philosophy of Merleau-Ponty*. Chesham, Bucks: Acumen Publishing, 2002.

MCLELLAN, DAVID, *Karl Marx: Selected Writings*. Oxford: Oxford University Press, 1977.

MORAN, DERMOT, *Introduction to Phenomenology*. London: Routledge, 2000.

MUTAJWAHA, STANISLAUS, 'Some Recent Insights in the Philosophy of the Other'. Rome (doctoral dissertation, Urban University), 1992.

O'CONNOR, BRIAN (ed.), *The Adorno Reader*. Oxford: Blackwell, 2000.

PEPERZAK, ADRIAAN, *To the Other: An Introduction to the Philosophy of Emmanuel Levinas*. Indiana: Purdue University Press, 1993.

PEPERZAK, ADRIAAN, CRITCHLEY, SIMON and BERNASCONI, ROBERT (eds.), *Emmanuel Levinas: Basic Philosophical Writings*. Indianapolis: Indiana University Press, 1996.

PURCELL, BRENDAN M., *The Drama of Humanity: Towards a Philosophy of Humanity in History*. New York: Peter Lang, 1996.

RICHARDSON, WILLIAM, *Heidegger: Through Phenomenology to Thought*. The Hague: Martinus Nijhoff, 1963.

RICOEUR, PAUL, *The Philosophy of Paul Ricoeur: The Library of Living Philosophers*. Vol. XXII. Ed. Lewis Edwin Hahn. Chicago: Open Court, 1995.

SCHELER, MAX, *Formalism in Ethics and Non-Formal Ethics of Values: A New Attempt toward the Foundation of an Ethical Personalism*. Trs. Manfred Frings and Roger L. Funk. Evanston: Northwestern University Press, 1973.

SCHELER, MAX, *Person and Self-Value: Three Essays*. The Hague: Martinus Nijhoff, 1987.

SCHINDLER, DAVID L., *Heart of the World, Center of the Church: Communio Ecclesiology, Liberalism, and Liberation*. Grand Rapids: Eerdmans, 1996.

SOLZHENITSYN, ALEKSANDR, *August 1914*. Tr. H. T. Willets. New York: Farrar & Giroux, 1989.

SOLZHENITSYN, ALEKSANDR, *One Day in the Life of Ivan Denisovich*. Tr. Ralph Parker. London: Penguin, 1963.

SOLZHENITSYN, ALEKSANDR, *The Gulag Archipelago* [2]. Tr. Thomas P. Whitney. London: CollinsHarvill, 1975.

SPIEGELBERG, HERBERT, *The Phenomenological Movement: A Historical Introduction.* 3rd edn, Dordrecht: Kluwer, 1994.

TAYLOR, CHARLES, *Sources of the Self: The Making of the Modern Identity.* Cambridge: Cambridge University Press, 1989.

VAN ALPEN, ERNST, *Francis Bacon: and the Loss of Self.* Cambridge, MA.: Harvard University Press, 1993.

VOEGELIN, ERIC, *The Collected Works of Eric Voegelin: Published Essays 1966–1985.* Vol. 12. Ed. Ellis Sandoz. Baton Rouge: Louisiana State University Press, 1990.

VOEGELIN, ERIC, *The New Science of Politics.* Chicago: Chicago University Press, 1952.

VOEGELIN, ERIC, *Order and History* Vol. 3 *Plato and Aristotle.* Baton Rouge: Louisiana State University Press, 1985.

VOEGELIN, ERIC, *From Enlightenment to Revolution.* Ed. John H. Hallowell. Durham, NC: Duke University Press, 1975.

VOEGELIN, ERIC, *Autobiographical Reflections.* Ed. Ellis Sandoz. Baton Rouge: Louisiana State University Press, 1989.

WALSH, DAVID, *After Ideology: Recovering the Spiritual Foundations of Freedom.* Washington, DC: Catholic University of America Press, 1995.

Appendix

See overleaf for a copy of Mark Gertlers' painting entitled,
'Merry-Go-Round', 1916

Courtesy of The Tate Gallery, London

'Merry-Go-Round.' Mark Gertler
Courtesy of The Tate Gallery, London

Index

Purcell, Brendan; *The Drama of
  Humanity: Towards a Philosophy
  of Humanity in History* 40

Ratzinger, Joseph 149
reductionism 13, 19, 20, 91, 98
revolution 103
Rhapsodic Theatre 105, 106, 107
Ricoeur, Paul 22

Sartre, Jean-Paul 15
Scheler, Max 15, 16, 20, 36–7, 47, 66–7,
  73
Schindler, David L. 75
Schmitz 24, 33, 51–2, 150
science 132, 152
Second Vatican Council 6, 101
Second World War 9–10, 21, 22, 63
self-awareness 41–2, 50–2, 64
self-determination 25, 36–41, 51, 75, 76,
  79–80, 90, 93, 112, 151, 154, 155,
  156, 157
self-fulfilment 25, 79–80
self-governance 25, 51, 38, 133, 151, 156
self-possession 25, 38, 49, 133, 151, 156
self-realization 136, 138, 139–40, 141,
  155
Serretti, Massimo 100
Shakespeare; *King Lear* 57–8
Simpson, Peter 29, 41, 56–7, 69, 76, 94
social class 137, 141
social theory 141, 143–4, 145, 146, 158,
  159, 160
socialism 145
solitude 90–1, 91–2, 93
Solzhenitsyn, Aleksandr 22, 38–40, 160
  August 1914 38–40
  One Day in the Life of Ivan Denisovich
  21
Sophocles; *Oedipus* 101
soul 82
Spiegelberg, Herbert 15
Stalin 63
State 144, 145
Swiezawski, Stefan 9–10

Taylor, Charles 112–13
technology 135–6
theatre 100, 101, 105–9, 157
  Rhapsodic Theatre 105, 106, 107
  and Wojtyla's concept of the person
  105–7

Theatre of the Absurd 106–8, 157
'theatre of the word' 105–6
theology in need of philosophy 94
Thomism 11–12, 16, 20, 45, 49, 77, 138,
  140, 149
thought and action 105–7
Tischner, Józef 32
Tynan, Kenneth 10

uniqueness of persons 3, 7, 19, 31, 46,
  90

Voegelin, Eric 125; *History of Political
  Ideas* 117

Walsh, Michael J. 130
weekly addresses 89, 90–3, 99, 109–10,
  156
Weigel, George 27, 96–7, 124
Whitehead, Alfred North 14
Williams, George Hunston 11–12, 26, 27,
  52–3, 122
Wojtyla, Karol (Pope John Paul II)
  characteristics of later writings 81–6,
  155–6
  life 9–10, 20–1, 44, 60, 81, 122
  assassination attempt 123–4
  personality 87–8, 101
  philosophy reflected in poetry and
  plays 4–8, 31–3, 41, 150
  see also plays of Karol Wojtyla;
  poems of Karol Wojtyla; Pope
  John Paul II; weekly addresses
  work 87, 116, 121–43, 155, 158–9
  and degradation 141
  and Genesis 132, 133
  and Marxism 122–30, 136
  as mastery of nature 131, 133, 135,
  136–7
  multidisciplinary approach 132
  objective (transitive) and subjective
  (intransitive) sense 129, 134–9,
  159
  as realization of human person
  138–40
  specific to Man 131
  and technology 135–6
  value of 137, 138

Zieba, Maciej 121, 130, 143, 158